PROTEST!
SHAPING AOTEAROA
MANDY HAGER

OneTree HOUSE

Published by OneTree House Ltd, New Zealand, 2021

© Mandy Hager, 2021
978-0-9951176-9-3

All rights reserved. No part of this publication may be reproduced, stored in a retrieval system or transmitted in any form or by any means, electronic, mechanical, photocopying, recording or otherwise, without the prior permission of the publisher.
Printed by Your Books
10 9 8 7 6 5 4 3 2 1   1 2 3 4 5 6 7 8 / 2
Editor: Anna Golden
Designed by: Vasanti Unka

CONTENTS

INTRODUCTION — 4

1. LAND PROTESTS
Hōne Heke — 8
Parihaka — 11
Māori Land Hikoi 1975 — 14
Bastion Point 1977-78 — 17
Ngā Tamatoa — 20
Raglan Golf Course 1978 — 21
Pakaitore (Moutoa Gardens) 1995 — 21
Foreshore and Seabed 2004 — 21
Waitangi Day protests — 24
Ihumātao — 24

2. EMPLOYMENT — STRIKING FOR A BETTER LIFE
The Great Strike 1912-13 — 25
The Waihī Strike 1912 — 26
The Wharves Strike 1913: war on the wharves — 27
The Waterfront Dispute 1951 — 28

3. SHAKING UP THE SYSTEM: GENDER AND DISABILITY RIGHTS
Women's Suffrage: fighting for the right to vote — 31
MMP: fairer representation for all — 34
Abortion rights — 36
Women Reclaim the Night — 37
Slutwalk rallies: 'Yes means yes and no means no' — 38
#MeToo — 39
Rainbow Romances: gay rights — 40
Access for all: rights for the disabled — 42

4. THE PEACEMAKERS
World War One: the war to end all wars — 44
Archibald Baxter and "The fourteen" — 45
Te Puea Hērangi and the Māori anti-war resistance — 47
World War Two: hard labour — 48
Vietnam — 49
Iraq War 2003: The "Coalition of the Willing" — 52
Ploughshares Protest: the Waihopai three — 54
Ban the Bomb: anti-nuclear protests — 55

5. CALLING OUT RACISM — AT HOME AND ABROAD
The Springbok Rugby Tour 1981: the great divide — 63
The Dawn Raids: racism never sleeps — 69

6. PEOPLE NOT PROFIT — WE ARE THE 99%
The Occupy Movement — 74
People Not Profit: Anti-TPP(A) Protests — 77

7. PROTECTING THE ENVIRONMENT:
Part one: Lakes, forests, wetlands and rivers
Damn the Dam: the 'Save Manapouri' campaign — 80
The Clyde Dam — 86
The fight to save our forests – beech forests — 87
The Fight for Ōkārito — 89
Pureora and the Rise of the Tree Dwellers — 91
Native Forest Action and the Timberlands Dispute — 93
Rivers and Fresh Water — 96
Save Aramoana Campaign — 97
Part two: GE, Mining and Oceans
Frankenfish & toad potatoes: the anti-GE protests — 100
Mining: digging in to protect our land and oceans — 106
Save Happy Valley Coalition: fighting "an unfortunate experiment" — 111
Mining for oil and gas — 117
Other Ocean-related Campaigns: Anti-whaling — 127
Trawling the seabed — 128
Protecting our unique dolphins — 131

8. THE BIGGEST ISSUE OF ALL: CLIMATE CHANGE ACTION
School Strike 4 Climate — 133

9. OUR PACIFIC NEIGHBOURS — PAST AND FUTURE PROTESTS
Samoa: the Mau Movement — 138
Solomon Islands: Maasina Ruru Independence Movement — 144
Tonga: The Ma'a Tonga Kautahi: Tonga for Tongans — 146
Kiribati: We are not drowning we are fighting — 149

ACKNOWLEDGEMENTS — 151
GLOSSARY — 152
ENDNOTES — 155
INDEX — 164

See the glossary for definitions of underlined words

INTRODUCTION

One of my earliest memories, when I was maybe five or six, is standing with my brother and two sisters, our hands linked around an ancient native tree on the section next door as we tried to stop a bulldozer knocking it down. Although we failed to save it, it was our first united effort to exercise our human right to protest.

Human rights are the basic freedoms and protections that apply to every single one of us. They are based on the values of dignity, equality and mutual respect – regardless of age, nationality, gender, race, beliefs or personal orientation.

These rights are about being treated fairly and treating others fairly, and about being able to make choices in our lives. Such basic human rights are universal – they're there to protect every person in the world. And they're each equally important; there's no ignoring the ones you don't like!

United Nations Declaration on Human Rights Defenders sets out the rights particularly important to human rights defenders and other protesters. They call for:

- the right to freedom of association (being able to meet with whomever you choose),
- freedom of peaceful assembly (meeting or rallying together),
- freedom of opinion and expression,
- the right to access information relating to human rights,
- the right to provide legal assistance, and the
- freedom to develop and discuss new ideas in the area of human rights.

Although the Universal Declaration of Human Rights has been in place since 1948, in 1998 the UN's General Assembly added another layer of protection with the UN Declaration on Human Rights Defenders.[1] This sets out the rights of anyone who protests, actively defends human rights or calls for change. Journalists and whistle-blowers rely on these rights when leaking or publishing vital information to expose hidden crimes or corruption. But these rights only apply if the information is important and it's in the public's best interests to know. I'm grateful for these protections. Speaking out or exposing the wrongs of those in power is a risky business.

You might think it's strange that four small children back in the 1960s felt inspired to protest at such an early age, but it's easy to explain. Both of my parents were born in countries where people were subjected to horrific human rights abuses, and tens of millions were suffering, enslaved or killed. As a result, they believed all decent human beings had a duty to stand up and call something out if it was hurting others or the environment. We grew up observing them putting their beliefs into practice, always helping others and speaking out if needed – so, naturally, their actions rubbed off on us. We all form our values from those who raise us, good or bad; the great news is we can choose to accept those values or not — it's our right! In my family, we all chose to follow in our parents' footsteps.

That's why the subject of this book matters so much to me, and why I've participated in protests throughout my life, including some of the campaigns you'll find in here. Every one of these protests saw ordinary people like me decide to take a stand based on their values. Sometimes it's to protect the people they love and future generations. Sometimes it's to prevent or undo some terrible injustice. For some protesters, it's stopping the destruction of something precious and unique that drives them, or a deep spiritual connection to the land and sea. For some, it's all of these reasons, and more.

The examples here are only a tiny taste of the thousands of protest actions that have taken place around Aotearoa — many changed our lives and nation forever, or the lives of others, including our Pacific neighbours. They are grouped to create a sense of the range, from demanding the return of stolen land or refusing to fight in a war, to protecting a lake or defending the right to earn enough to feed your family or marry the person you love.

Some of these protests failed to achieve what they hoped to, yet their efforts weren't wasted. They planted a seed and helped guide future actions. Others descended into violence, causing disruption right through our society and leaving long-term scars. Many made a real difference, with some now celebrated as defining moments in our nation's growth.

All these campaigns stem from concerns over human rights or the environment, but that doesn't mean all protests have good motives or care about people's rights. We've also seen the ugly side of protest here in Aotearoa, a pick-and-mix of racist, anti- Māori/migrant/ LGBTQIA/Muslim/Jew/Chinese/women and other prejudices given air. That's the tricky thing about the right to free speech: it gives the same protection to everyone, unless they're actively inciting hate or violence. And that's fair, human rights *should* be universal, though it's worth remembering that words have the power to hurt — or heal. One way to judge which side of a debate is respecting human rights is to ask if the intention (and desired outcome) will benefit everyone in society or only a select few (while others suffer).

Fifty-one protests are represented in this book but there are so many more I wish I'd had the space to share. It's not that they're any less important, I simply couldn't stretch my word count any further! I'd like to have included protests over animal rights, surveillance, privacy, plastic pollution, packaging, poverty, domestic violence, homelessness and much more, all worthy of recognition. There are hundreds of inspiring local activists and groups I didn't have room to name, but I'm hugely grateful they donate their time to seek changes that will benefit us all.

Some of these protests involved tens of thousands of people, while others started with a dedicated individual taking a lone stand, eventually joined by like-minded others. Many involved large grassroots movements, where ordinary people gathered together to take on local or central government, large institutions or big business. Sometimes whole communities rallied. Sometimes one specific group stood up, like the students involved in School Strikes 4 Climate. They bring to mind my favourite quote: "Never doubt that a small group of thoughtful, committed citizens can change the world; indeed, it's the only thing that ever has."[2]

Most of these protests followed the principles of passive resistance (also known as non-violent resistance). Some engaged in civil disobedience, refusing to obey certain laws, rules or demands to pressure governments, business or an occupying power. Protesters invested time in raising awareness around each issue, to rally support, and some used creativity to draw attention to their cause and make their point. A few risked their lives or freedoms, clambering up towers, camping in treetops, blockading ships at sea, tying themselves to train tracks. Some were attacked; some even killed.

I've tried to source most of the research online so you can quickly find more information using the endnotes if you wish. In some cases, I swapped notes directly with key people who were involved. But these protests I've chosen, and how I've chosen to tell each story, reflect my own world view. It sets the tone. That's true for everyone; we all see the world through the lens of our own values and history, even if we're not aware of it. Compassion and a belief in social justice and human rights will always colour how I view an issue or action. It's fine if you see it differently, that's your right! I hope, though, that you'll consider the facts, think about how you'd feel in each situation, and ask who was wielding the power and whether their motives were good or bad for the people involved. Consider both sides. Make up your own mind. The important thing is to think the issues through.

There are moments in some of the early examples when attitudes or behaviours seem obviously sexist or racist, or outright wrong to us now. Take note of them and consider how society has changed since then and why. Did the protests play a part in shifting the public's thinking? We're lucky to live in a social democracy where we can voice our opinions and freely debate ideas. But democracy and freedoms are only as good as the people elected to protect them. We've recently seen how quickly even the most powerful democracies, like the US, can descend into chaos. Pay attention to the decisions made by our leaders and consider how they will affect vulnerable people, other animals or the planet. That's a pretty good starting point to unravel any political stance. Keep asking, "But why?" after every answer until you drill down to the issue's core truth.

Finally, a couple of explanations. Througout this book I refer to our nation as Aotearoa, to acknowledge that these beautiful islands were already named before 17th-century Dutch mapmakers labelled them New Zealand, from a desk on the other side of the world. I think the name Aotearoa better represents who and what we are: a collection of people all living together in a land first settled by Māori and Moriori. That's my personal stance, and the kind of individual action we all can take every day to support the rights and values we personally hold dear. It's also why I refer to everyone as Kiwis, to acknowledge that we come from many different ethnicities and cultures, yet we all co-exist together on the only islands in the world where real kiwi roam. That's kind of magical!

What I hope you'll take away from this book, besides an insight into our history, is a sense of inspiration; it *is* possible to make significant change if needed. We are entering uncertain times and it's easy to feel helpless, but all it takes is one person with one voice to ignite the first spark, and others will be drawn to it if the cause is good. And perhaps it might encourage you to become a human rights defender – and a defender of our planet, too. Together we can be, as Gandhi said, "the change we wish to see in the world". Together we can ignite hope.

Kia kaha

Mandy Hager

HUMAN RIGHTS INTRODUCTION
UNIVERSAL DECLARATION OF HUMAN RIGHTS

CIVIL RIGHTS AND LIBERTIES — Right to life, freedom from torture and slavery, right to non-discrimination.	Article 1	Freedom and equality in dignity and rights
	Article 2	Non-discrimination
	Article 3	Right to life, liberty and security of person
	Article 4	Freedom from slavery
	Article 5	Freedom from torture
LEGAL RIGHTS — Right to be presumed innocent, right to a fair trial, right to be free from arbitrary arrest or detention.	Article 6	All are protected by the law
	Article 7	All are equal before the law
	Article 8	A remedy when rights have been violated
	Article 9	No unjust detention, imprisonment or exile
	Article 10	Right to a fair trial
	Article 11	Innocent until proven guilty
	Article 14	Right to go to another country and ask for protection
SOCIAL RIGHTS — Right to education, to found and maintain a family, to recreation, to health care.	Article 12	Privacy and the right to home and family life
	Article 13	Freedom to live and travel freely within state borders
	Article 16	Right to marry and start a family
	Article 24	Right to rest and leisure
	Article 26	Right to education, including free primary education
ECONOMIC RIGHTS — Right to property, to work, to housing, to a pension, to an adequate standard of living.	Article 15	Right to a nationality
	Article 17	Right to own property and possessions
	Article 22	Right to social security
	Article 23	Right to work for a fair wage and to join a trade union
	Article 25	Right to a standard of living adequate for your health and well-being
POLITICAL RIGHTS — Right to participate in the government of the country, right to vote, right to peaceful assembly, freedoms of expression, belief and religion	Article 18	Freedom of belief (including religious belief)
	Article 19	Freedom of expression and the right to spread information
	Article 20	Freedom to join associations and meet with others in a peaceful way
	Article 21	Right to take part in the government of your country
CULTURAL RIGHTS, SOLIDARITY RIGHTS — Right to participate in the cultural life of the community.	Article 27	Right to share in your community's cultural life
	Article 28	Right to an international order where all these rights can be fully realized
	Article 29	Responsibility to respect the rights of others
	Article 30	No taking away any of these rights!

PRINCIPLES OF NON VIOLENCE:

Mahatma Gandhi

Principles with regard to Public Policy
1. **Truth and truthfulness**
   Unconditional commitment to be truthful and authentic
2. **Ahimsa (non-violence) in relationships at all levels**
   One must also accept the fact that all forms of violence cannot be totally eliminated.
3. **Trusteeship**
   Each one of us has a uniqu talent' however, we do not own it but serve as a trustee' our talent must be used as much for the sake of others as ourselves.
4. **Constructive Action**
   Once acknowledged and balanced, we must use our talents to empower others in creating social change as a whole community.

Principles with regard to Personal Policy
1. **Respect**
   To respect others and accept the interdependence and interconnectedness of all life.
2. **Understanding**
   We must begin to understand the 'whys' of being here, both for ourselves and others.
3. **Acceptance**
   Out of respect and understanding, we can begin to accept one another's differences.
4. **Appreciating differences**
   To move beyond acceptance into appreciation and celebration of differences.

Martin Luther King, Jnr

Principles of Non-violence
1. **Nonviolence is a way of life for courageous people.**
   It is active nonviolent resistance to evil.
   It is assertive spiritually, mentally and emotionally.
   It is always persuading the opponent of the justice of your cause.
2. **Nonviolence seeks to win friendship and understanding.**
   The end result of nonviolence is redemption and reconciliation.
   The purpose of nonviolence is the creation of the Beloved Community.
3. **Nonviolence seeks to defeat injustice, not people.**
   Nonviolence willingly accepts the consequences of its acts.
4. **Nonviolence holds that voluntary Nonviolence willingly accepts the consequences of its acts.**
   Nonviolence accepts suffering without retaliation.
   Nonviolence accepts violence if necessary but will never inflict it.
   Unearned suffering is redemptive and has tremendous educational and transforming possibilities.
   Suffering can have the power to convert the enemy when reason fails.
5. **Nonviolence chooses love instead of hate.**
   Nonviolence resists violence of the spirit as well as of the body.
   Nonviolent love gives willingly, knowing that the return might be hostility.
6. **Non-violence holds that the universe is on the side of justice and that right will prevail.**

Process toward Social Change
1. Information gathering.
2. Education.
3. Personal commitments.
4. Negotiation.
5. Direct action.
6. Reconciliation and beginning the healing process.

1. LAND PROTESTS

HŌNE HEKE – FLAG FELLER

You might think a flag is just a strip of coloured cloth, but flags have the power to bring us together – or to divide us. Since early times, flags have been used as <u>symbols</u> to show we belong to a group or nation and that we share their beliefs, customs, lands and rules.

Flags have been used as national symbols for 500 years. They're a way of saying to others "I own the land this flag is on" (<u>proclaiming</u> a possession) and "I rule over these people and this land" (proclaiming <u>sovereignty</u>). Raising a flag is often the first triumphant act of <u>conquerors</u> in staking their claim, whether war heroes, tyrants, sports teams or explorers. The flag sends a message – and sometimes that message is really communicating who holds the power.

When Neil Armstrong first stepped onto the surface of the moon in 1969, he planted an American flag there, claiming that proud moment as belonging to his country. It also announced to the world that America had won the race to the moon. When Sir Edmund Hillary and Tenzing Norgay reached the summit of Mount Everest in 1953, they raised the Union Jack (as the British flag is known), thus claiming the glory for the British, who'd paid for the expedition.

When Captain Cook first anchored in Queen Charlotte Sound in 1770, he climbed to the top of Motuara Island and raised the flag of the British Empire.

"THE TREATY OF WAITANGI IS ALL SOAP. IT IS VERY SMOOTH AND OILY, BUT TREACHERY IS HIDDEN UNDER IT."[313]
HŌNE HEKE

HOME IS WHERE THE HEART IS   1

He formally claimed the island and its adjacent lands (the whole of Aotearoa) in the name of, and for the use of, the sovereign of the British Empire (who at the time was King George III). But planting that British flag here displaced Māori, trampling on their rights and customs. James Cook's symbolic act began a struggle for justice and equal rights that Māori continue to fight to this day.

One of the earliest protesters to understand the symbolic power of the British flag was Māori chief Hōne Wiremu Heke Pōkai of the Ngāpuhi iwi, more usually known as Hōne Heke.[3]

He originally supported Te Tiriti o Waitangi (the Treaty of Waitangi) and was one of the first to sign it in 1840. But he soon grew disillusioned by the colonial government's attacks on his people's way of life and their hunger for control. To express his anger, in July 1844 he sent his right-hand man, Te Haratua, the chief of Pakaraka in Northland, to attack the flagstaff on the hill above Kororāreka in the Bay of Islands.[4] Te Haratua chopped it down.

Toppling the flag was a powerfully symbolic act, protesting against the lack of respect being shown for Māori customary laws. However, the colonial government and settlers viewed this as an act of spite and rebuilt the flagstaff.

That didn't stop Hōne Heke. He was so frustrated with the British, he returned to chop that flagstaff down three more times. Sadly, the fourth and final time, the felling of the flag signalled the outbreak of the Flagstaff War — fighting in the north between British troops and northern Māori.

"Friend Governor — This is my speech to you. My disobedience and rudeness is no new thing. I inherit it from my parents, from my ancestors, do not imagine that it is a new feature of my character, but I am thinking of leaving off my rude conduct towards the Europeans. Now I say that I will prepare another pole, inland at Waimate, and I will erect it at its proper place at Kororāreka in order to put an end to our present quarrel. Let your soldiers remain beyond sea and at Auckland, do not send them here. The pole that was cut down belonged to me, I made it for the native flag, and it was never paid for by the Europeans."
Hōne Heke to Governor FitzRoy, translated by Thomas Forsaith from a letter held at Auckland Public Library.[3][4]

This wasn't simply Māori vs British — two Ngāpuhi groups also took sides against each other. Hōne Heke and Te Ruki Kawiti fought both the Crown and a Ngāpuhi group led by Tāmati Wāka Nene. The fighting ended in January 1846[5] after many brutal battles, with no one winning and with suffering on all sides. Heke finally made peace with Governor George Grey at a meeting in May 1848 at Te Waimate mission. Two years later Heke died.

For Hōne Heke, when he looked at the British flag, he saw the British Empire's domination and control over his people. His act of cutting the flagstaff down expressed this view, and he continued to protest over treatment of Māori until his death. "He resisted the government in battle and in letters," the *Dictionary of New Zealand Biography* says of him. "By the time he retired to Kaikohe, his actions had made a powerful statement about his people's rights to self-determination."[6]

PARIHAKA – THE BIRTHPLACE OF NON-VIOLENT RESISTANCE

"Though the lions rage, still I am for peace."
Te Whiti-o-Rongomai (Parihaka 1881)

"STAY WHERE YOU ARE, EVEN IF THE BAYONET BE PUT TO YOUR BREAST DO NOT RESIST." TOHU

Imagine you are living peacefully in a settlement your ancestors have occupied for generations. Now imagine that strangers from overseas arrive and start to carve up your land, moving you on, tearing down your home. How would you react? Would you fight for your land? Your home? How would you protect it when the newcomers have weapons, soldiers, and new legal powers you do not? In 1881, the people of Parihaka in Taranaki faced just this.

Led by two extraordinary men, Te Whiti-o-Rongomai (of Taranaki and Te Āti Awa descent) and Tohu Kākahi (Taranaki and Ngāti Ruanui), the people of Parihaka showed the colonial government (and indeed the world) a new non-violent way to protest. Their people were drawn to Te Whiti and Tohu's dignity and strength as they were guided through Parihaka's darkest hours. These two men are fully deserving of their place next to other great world activists – Mahatma Gandhi, Martin Luther King Jnr and Nelson Mandela.

"I HAVE NO MONEY, NO RICHES, I NEVER HAD. I ONLY WANT MY LAND."
TE WHITI

What led them to take this stand? It must have been a terrifying time, with many Māori suffering greatly as the new government confiscated their land and drove them off. The actions around Parihaka sparked the Taranaki Land Wars of the 1860s – Māori felt tricked and betrayed, and when they fought back to protect their rights, the Crown took thousands more hectares to punish them. Hundreds of Māori were arrested and thrown in prison – or killed.

By the 1870s, Parihaka was the largest Māori village in the country – refuge to thousands made homeless by land confiscations happening in both islands. Te Whiti and Tohu's aim was to maintain peace while protecting their land and culture. Both men preached non-violence and their peaceful teachings offered Parihaka's people inspiring leadership at a very troubled time. They truly believed it was possible to live alongside the settlers peacefully, but they insisted their land be left alone and their customs respected. It seemed their words weren't enough.

The year of 1879 came to be known as "The Year of the Plough". The settlers demanded that surveyors slice up the land around the village, despite a promise not to. Te Whiti and Tohu's talk shifted to action. Te Whiti ordered his followers to plough the surveyed fields, an act of passive resistance. They could cause disruption but must avoid using violence.

> "GO, PUT YOUR HANDS TO THE PLOUGH. LOOK NOT BACK. IF ANY COME WITH GUNS AND SWORDS, BE NOT AFRAID. IF THEY SMITE YOU, SMITE NOT IN RETURN. IF THEY REND YOU, BE NOT DISCOURAGED – ANOTHER WILL TAKE UP THE GOOD WORK."
> TE WHITI

The villagers built fences across the newly surveyed land and roads, ignoring anyone who tried to stop them, sneaking back if they were moved away. Large squads of armed police swooped down on the ploughing parties. They found them "unarmed, unresisting, and quite unimpressed".[7] The surveyors continued, their men breaking down the fences, only to find them rebuilt again within hours.

Now the settlers called in backup from the police and army. Soon, hundreds of protesters were arrested and held in prisons without trial. Yet, the worst was far from over.

On the morning of 5 November 1881, as more than 2000 villagers sat quietly on the marae listening to a group of singing children, an invading force entered Parihaka.

"Nine hundred and fifty-five armed volunteers and forty-four armed constabulary were sent to deal with people who were peacefully resisting the theft of their land. More than four hundred resisters were arrested before the invasion […] [which] was marked by rapes, the looting of the resisters' property, the burning of their homes and the uprooting of their crops, the forced relocation under armed escort of 1507 men, women and children; arrests which continued for three weeks after the invasion, then imprisonment without trial […] for periods of up to two years."[8]

Te Whiti and Tohu were arrested and led away through their weeping friends and whānau, wearing korowai cloaks about their shoulders. Those from other tribal regions were forced to leave. The village was nearly wiped out. The colonial government built a fort inside the pā and for the next five years it was manned by 70 soldiers and five officers. Maps were redrawn. History was rewritten. The invasion of Parihaka was swept under the colonial carpet, its people left landless, hurt and grieving.[9]

"GATHER UP THE EARTH ON WHICH THE BLOOD [OF ANY PLOUGHMAN] HAS SPILT AND BRING IT TO PARIHAKA." TOHU

"WE LOOK FOR PEACE AND WE FIND WAR. BE STEADFAST, KEEP TO PEACEFUL WORKS, BE NOT DISMAYED: HAVE NO FEAR." TOHU

Te Whiti and Tohu were jailed without a trial, as were hundreds of their followers (some for up to 18 years). They were shipped to overcrowded prisons in the South Island, where on average one prisoner died every two weeks. Conditions were so bad in Dunedin that caves were dug by the prisoners to hide those most unwell from prying eyes. When they were released in 1883, Te Whiti and Tohu returned to Parihaka, but, although they continued to fight for its return, their land was lost. However, their peaceful vision remains strong to this day.

It took 136 years for the Crown to apologise for its invasion and the destruction of Parihaka. On 9 June 2017, people wept as a government minister said sorry for the wrongful arrests and detention of Parihaka's men, and the rape and abuse of its women and girls. He acknowledged it was a shameful moment in Aotearoa's history. It's important we acknowledge this; even now, there are many land claims and much pain yet to be resolved. But one thing is certain: Te Whiti and Tohu's peaceful legacy of non-violent, passive resistance stands as a shining beacon for many, right around the world.

"Theirs was a moral victory, in which they upheld Māori honour and integrity against inconceivable odds." Dick Scott in *Ask that Mountain: The Story of Parihaka*.

THE MOTHER OF THE NATION LEADS THE WAY – DAME WHINA COOPER AND THE MĀORI LAND HĪKOI 1975

Before the arrival of Europeans, Māori held collective kaitiakitanga over their tribal land. No one person had ownership rights — everyone worked together to ensure protection of the land and its future sustainability.[10]

But within a century of Te Tiriti o Waitangi being signed in 1840, the tribal land had shrunk to a few small pockets, mostly in the middle of the North Island. The ongoing effect of sales and land confiscation means that together, Māori today only have exclusive kaitiakitanga over 4.8% of Aotearoa's total land. Such an enormous loss.

Māori have never given up writing letters, papers, petitions, holding hui, speaking out ... they are connected to their land; it's part of who they are. But time after time their pleas were ignored and laws were passed to make the confiscations easier.

In 1953 a new law invited people to report so-called "unused" or "unproductive" Māori land to the Māori Land Court and then apply to "borrow" it for themselves. Another law in 1967 went even further, forcing the compulsory transfer of Māori land with four or fewer owners into a pool of "general" Crown land, which was often then sold.

Early in March 1975, a hui was called at Te Puea Marae in Mangere, South Auckland. They discussed the idea of a protest march from the far north to Parliament, to catch public attention and spread their message that "land is the very soul of a tribal people"[11] and that it was time to give it back. Everyone was called to action: young and old, people from farms, towns and cities came to join the protest. It took four months of planning and fundraising, with offers from marae throughout the country to provide hot food, showers and beds.

On 14 September 1975, 50 protesters left Te Hāpua, on the shores of the Parengarenga Harbour in Northland, on a mission to hīkoi (march) all the way to Wellington, a 1000 kilometre journey. At their head was 79-year-old kuia, Whina (Hōhepine) Cooper, with a scarf on her head and a walking stick in her hand.

"YOU CAN NEVER WIN ANYTHING UNLESS YOU ARE THERE TO DO SOMETHING."
DAME WHINA COOPER

She was the daughter of Heremia Te Wake, a leader of Ngāti Manawa, and she took part in her first act of passive resistance at the age of 18, when she helped save local mudflats from being drained for cattle. In the non-violent spirit of Parihaka, Cooper and her friends filled in the drains to save the delicate ecosystem and then argued their case. Eventually they won.

Sixty-one years later, Cooper's determined figure became the symbol of the hīkoi, her age a reminder of the long battle Māori had already faced to recover their lands, and her dignity a reminder that they had a right to be treated with respect.

As the hīkoi moved south, its numbers grew. In nearly every town and city, people joined them. At night, in each local marae, Cooper and others spoke of the march's purpose and gave out leaflets entitled "Why We March".

Accompanied by two trucks and a bus, the hīkoi travelled to Wellington in 29 days, collecting signatures of support along the way. Their petition demanded an end to monocultural land laws that excluded Māori cultural values. It demanded new laws that allowed communal ownership of land within iwi, as had always been the way for Māori.

By the time the hīkoi approached Parliament on 13 October, 5000 chanting protesters walked with Cooper. They brought with them a petition containing 60,000 signatures, and they handed it to Prime Minister Bill Rowling.

Did this solve all their problems? No. But it did help educate people about the issues and in time it was seen as a powerful symbol of Māori cultural revival. It also inspired others to act, with many hīkoi to follow.

Whina Cooper was called "Mother of the Nation" by the media. In 1981, she was made a Dame, and in 1991, a member of the Order of New Zealand.

At the age of 95, Dame Whina Cooper spoke to her biggest audience yet at the opening of the 14th Commonwealth Games in Auckland 1990. Her message was one that she repeated many times in the last years of her life: "Let us all remember that the Treaty was signed so that we could all live as one nation in Aotearoa."

THE SPARK CONTINUES TO SPREAD – BASTION POINT 1977 TO 1978

Two years after Cooper's hīkoi to Parliament, another huge land protest flared over a piece of coastal land in Orakei (overlooking Auckland's Waitematā Harbour) known as Takaparawhā or Bastion Point. Home to Ngāti Whātua, this site offered views to their fishing grounds and gardens. Although they had welcomed the new settlers and their government, eventually they lost both land and trust.

In 1840, when Ngāti Whātua's chiefs signed Te Tiriti o Waitangi, they invited the first governor to set up his government in Waitematā Harbour. The iwi willingly gifted 3000 acres (1214.057 hectares) for the creation of Auckland township. But within 15 years the tribe had lost all but roughly 700 acres of land in Ōrākei (280 hectares) due to confiscations and punishing laws.

What followed was a steady acquisition of the remaining land, made possible by court and Crown rulings that had been designed so Ngāti Whātua could never win. The government built a military outpost on Bastion Point in 1885. When it was disbanded in 1941, instead of returning the land to the tribe, Bastion Point was given to Auckland City Council as a reserve.

These maps illustrate the gradual alienation of Māori land in the North Island. In 1860, Māori still held on to most of their land except for a few areas, particularly Wellington, Wairarapa, Hawke's Bay and parts of Northland. The 1860s saw confiscations of huge areas by the government and large areas of land began to be lost through the effect of the Native Land Court. The period between 1890 and 1920 saw a boom in government land purchases, despite Māori protests. By 1939, very little land was left in Māori ownership.

The Crown took the last 12.5 acres (5 hectares) of the Ōrākei block in 1951, including the marae and several homes. They destroyed all the buildings except the chapel and cemetery, and built a national marae, cutting Ngāti Whātua out.

The final straw came in 1976, with the announcement of a luxury housing development and park to be built there. Activist Joe Hawke and members of his hapū, along with many others, formed the Ōrākei Māori Action Committee (OMAC). On 5 January 1977, just two days before building was due to start, the OMAC and their supporters occupied the one remaining hectare of land the tribe could access. The protesters refused to move, rebuilding a disused warehouse, which they renamed Arohanui Marae. Over time, they planted gardens to feed their families and built more temporary huts. Living conditions were basic, and it was grim in winter as the site was very exposed, yet the protesters were determined to stay until their demands were met.

Joe Hawke reflected on this thirty years later: **"We had to make sure it was a peaceful protest, and no one resisted or started trouble [...] We got the children away. But people were crying everywhere and old kuia and kaumātua were asking young Māori and Pacific Island police officers why they were arresting their own people."**[315]

On the night of 26 September, five-year-old Joannee Hawke (niece of Joe) died in a fire that could be seen right across Auckland. Her lean-to home, at the centre of the tacked-together village, burned down before her family's eyes. Her tragic death made the protesters even more committed to achieving their goal.

The occupation lasted 506 days – nearly one-and-a-half years. The protest appeared every night on the TV news and many people, both Māori and Pākehā, went to offer their support. Some came from overseas, including the American country singer John Denver.

The following February, the government offered to return some land and houses if Ngāti Whātua would pay them $200,000. The tribe said no. With public pressure building, Prime Minister Robert Muldoon appeared on TV, saying that the protesters "would be gone within a week". Little did anyone know how aggressive this eviction would be.

On the morning of 25 May 1978, around 800 army and police officers dragged 222 people from Bastion Point, and set about destroying all the buildings to stop anyone returning.

While it might seem as though this action was a failure, instead the issue kept smouldering. Nearly 10 years later, the Waitangi Tribunal found that Ngāti Whātua's complaints and claims were fair. Most of Takaparawhā has now been returned to them, along with other lands and three million dollars in compensation. These determined people's non-violent protest proved successful in the end.

Supporter Andrew Robb recalled:
"We heard a voice using a megaphone [… and] skyrockets being fired from the roof to alert Auckland that the eviction had begun […] A ladder went up and we heard footsteps overhead […] As the arrests began, I was overwhelmed with emotion. Tears streamed down my face, not because I was scared or angry, but because, at that moment, there was nowhere in the world I'd rather have been than right there with those people. Ordinary people doing extraordinary things."

NGĀ TAMATOA – YOUNG MĀORI TAKE THE LEAD

Ngā Tamatoa (Young Warriors) was one of many groups that arose to challenge racism in the 1970s. This Auckland-based student movement (which sprang from a conference led by academic and historian Ranginui Walker) took its lead from freedom and indigenous movements overseas, such as the Black Panther Party and the American Indian Movement.

The group consisted mainly of city and university-educated Māori who'd had enough of the continuing confiscation of land and the loss of Te Reo Māori (Māori language). They often worked alongside the Polynesian Panthers, their Pasifika peers.

Ngā Tamatoa initiated an annual protest at Waitangi on Waitangi Day, disrupting events in 1971, staging a walkout in 1972, and again in 1973 after Prime Minister Norman Kirk changed the name of Waitangi Day to New Zealand Day. They wore black armbands to mourn the loss of Māori land, and claimed the "Treaty is a fraud", calling out ongoing betrayals by the government.

In September 1972, they presented a petition with more than 30,000 signatures to the Crown, demanding that Te Reo Māori be taught in schools.[12] They also strongly supported moves to set up Kōhanga Reo (Māori language nests) and Kura Kaupapa (Māori immersion schools). The long-term payoff for their actions saw the Māori Language Act passed in 1987, making Te Reo Māori one of Aotearoa's official languages, and inspiring a rise in Te Reo speakers.

Members of Ngā Tamatoa sit on Parliament's steps in late 1972.

These keen young activists also organised the historic 1975 Land March led by Dame Whina Cooper, and following the march, they created a "Tent Embassy" by camping on Parliament grounds in Wellington, demanding immediate action on land issues. In 1979, they disrupted Auckland University's Haka Party (part of the student capping parade where engineering students painted male genitals on their bodies and performed the haka with obscene gestures), offended by the way they performed it.[13] Māori and Pacific Island students formed a group called He Taua (War Party) and members of He Taua were arrested after a violent attack on the engineering students. Their court case in Auckland sparked anti-racism protests outside the courthouse. One member of He Taua was Hone Harawira, who later became a Member of Parliament.[14]

PĀKAITORE (MOUTOA GARDENS) 1995

For 79 days from February to May 1995, Whanganui Māori and supporters occupied Pākaitore (also known as Moutoa Gardens), beside the river in Whanganui city, to show their frustration over the lack of progress towards a settlement of their Whanganui River claim. News headlines about gang involvement and "radical activists" stirred up many, but proved untrue. Eventually the occupation ended peaceably, with an agreement signed. Their claims were backed by the Waitangi Tribunal in 1999.

> "THIS IS NOT JUST GOOD FOR MĀORI, THIS IS GOOD FOR SOCIETY AS A WHOLE." KEN MAIR, ON OCCUPYING MOUTOA GARDENS IN WHANGANUI.

RAGLAN GOLF COURSE 1978

"All we have is the truth on our side"
Eva Rickard

The Raglan Golf Course land occupation took place because land was taken from Tainui Awhiro Māori by the government to build an emergency military airfield during World War Two. When the war ended, it was not returned to Tainui Awhiro and part of the land (25 hectares) was converted into a golf course for public use in 1969.

Eva Rickard (of Tainui) led over 150 protesters in an occupation of the Raglan Golf Course on 12 February 1978. She believed that a protest action like the one at Bastion Point would force the return of the land. But, once again police were sent in and 18 protesters, including Rickard, were arrested. However, after years of protest, the government agreed to return the land in 1984.

> "THIS IS A TRIBAL ISSUE WHICH HAS NOW BECOME A MĀORI ISSUE."
> EVA RICKARD

FORESHORE AND SEABED PROTESTS 2004

By 2004 there was much wider understanding of Māori issues, thanks to rulings by the Waitangi Tribunal, but it didn't stop politicians using Māori land claims as a way of dividing people — or passing new laws that continued to trample on Māori rights.

After a ruling over customary ownership of the seabed in Marlborough was reversed by the High Court in 1997, a debate broke out about who "owned" the rights to the seabed (land under the sea)

and foreshore (the part of the beach affected by the tide's ebb and flow).

The debate stirred up suspicion that Māori wanted to claim the entire coastline of Aotearoa as their own, banning others from its use, when Māori simply wanted to make sure their customary rights were protected. Until this point, many Pākehā took for granted their access to beaches and rivers and suddenly they feared this freedom was being threatened. Prime Minister Helen Clark announced that her government would pass a law to protect public use of the foreshore and seabed by putting it all into Crown ownership. Most Māori saw that as an attempt to quash their customary rights.

The debate grew openly racist when the leader of the National Party, Don Brash, gave a speech at Orewa, claiming the government was giving away too much to Māori. His remarks drove a wedge between Māori and Pākehā, and encouraged Pākehā voters to support his party. His party erected billboards that whipped up racist fears by setting "Iwi" (Māori) against "Kiwi" (Pākehā) – a divisive message that still angers many people to this day.

When Parliament began to rush a law through, government minister Tariana Turia announced she would vote against it. While politicians argued, Māori once again joined forces and marched on Parliament, hoping to stop the law from passing.

On 5 May 2004, after a 13-day hīkoi from Northland, the group arrived in Wellington, having picked up more supporters along the way. It was estimated there were 15,000 people by the time the hīkoi reached Parliament, the grounds echoing with a thunderous haka. The marchers strongly opposed the government's plans, supporting Tariana Turia's decision.

In 1885 Hōri Ngātai of the Ngāi Te Rangi tribe said that the land below high water immediately in front of where he lived on Tauranga Harbour was "part and parcel of my own land ... as being part of my own garden." He explained, "From time immemorial I have had this land ... The whole of this inland sea has been subdivided by our ancestors, and each portion belongs to a proper owner."[316]

Among the hīkoi leaders was Dr Pita Sharples who, with Turia, would eventually become co-leaders of a new Māori Party, designed to give Māori a stronger voice in Parliament.

But even though thousands of people marched and expressed their fears, including some Māori within the government's own party, the Foreshore and Seabed Act (2004) was passed on 18 November, after government made a deal with two smaller parties. Many Māori felt betrayed, and abandoned their traditional support of the Labour Party by turning to the new Māori Party in the hope that their rights would be better protected.

In 2011 the National-led Government replaced the 2004 Act with the Marine and Coastal Area (Takutai Moana) Act (2011). Crown ownership of the foreshore and seabed was replaced with a "no ownership" system. The new law allowed iwi to apply through the courts or to the Crown for "recognition of customary rights".[15]

Many still think more change is needed and in July 2020 the Waitangi Tribunal ruled that processes within the Act breach Te Tiriti o Waitangi. The Tribunal is investigating whether the entire Act properly recognises and protects Māori customary rights as the Treaty requires.[16]

WAITANGI DAY PROTESTS

Every year on 6 February, Aotearoa marks the signing of Te Tiriti o Waitangi in 1840. The day was first officially honoured in 1934, and it has been a public holiday since 1974. Since the 1970s, the day has been used by Māori to focus on breaches of the Treaty and issues around racism and inequality. Protest actions have ranged from chanting and waving banners, hurling abuse and staging walkouts, to throwing mud and other objects at visiting politicians. A Newshub article in 2019 listed some of the more memorable protests as:

- Queen Elizabeth II and the wet tee shirt
- Tears as Helen Clark is denied the right to speak
- Don Brash gets covered in mud
- John Key jostled by two men at Te Tii
- Steven Joyce and "dildo-gate"

Find out more at: https://www.newshub.co.nz/home/new-zealand/2019/02/a-short-history-of-waitangi-day-protests.html

IHUMĀTAO – A STORY STILL UNFOLDING

"We want a liveable city. We need places to breathe, to dream, to connect to our ancestors, and engage with our history. At Ihumātao we can do this."
Save Our Unique Landscape (SOUL)

Ihumātao, a village three kilometres from Auckland International Airport in Mangere, Auckland (Tāmaki Makaurau), was first settled as early as the 14th century. During the invasion of the Waikato in 1863, the land was confiscated by the government as punishment for supporting the Kīngitanga movement. The land was mainly used for farming until late 2016, when Fletcher Building bought the site as part of a housing development project. Māori group Save Our Unique Landscape (SOUL) opposed the development and have occupied the site and staged protests there since 2016.

At the time of writing this, they were in discussions with the government to have the land returned.

EMPLOYMENT ISSUES STRIKING FOR A BETTER LIFE

2

THE GREAT STRIKE 1912–1913

When people refuse to work in protest against pay or conditions, that's an act of passive resistance too. It's called a "strike". And like the groups that form to protest against the theft of land, workers sometimes join together to form trade unions, to bargain with their bosses using one united, loud voice.

There were several worker actions in the colony's early days. Māori timber workers walked off the job in 1821, wanting to be paid in money or gunpowder rather than food. In 1840, men all over the country joined Wellington carpenter Samuel Parnell in refusing to work longer than eight hours a day. Thanks to him, that's something we take for granted now. A group of schoolboys even went on strike to protest against having too much homework (please don't try this!).

Our first country-wide strike came in 1890, when staff at ports from north to south stopped work in support of Australian unions.

After 1894, employers were expected to bargain with the unions. If they couldn't agree, a special Arbitration Court would help to solve it. Some pay and working conditions improved, and for a time Aotearoa was known as "the country without strikes". It wouldn't last. Workers and their families were still struggling.

The seed of the Great Strike was planted by the Blackball miners' strike of 1908. The coal miners of Blackball, on the South Island's West Coast, went on strike to demand shorter workdays and longer lunch breaks. Funds were raised to support the families of striking miners, who held out for 11 weeks. There was joy and relief when the company agreed to their demands. Word of this success gave others hope.

In 1909, union supporters formed the New Zealand Federation of Labour (NZFOL); joining together to strengthen their power. They claimed the government's courts had failed, and they demanded higher wages and a pledge that their men would be fairly paid for every hour they worked. Their membership grew when the government passed a law that said only registered unions would be allowed to strike. All other strikers would be fined — a lot. Within two years, the Federation of Labour's membership doubled to nearly 14,000 workers. But not all workers or unions were united.

THE WAIHĪ STRIKE 1912

In March 1912, a small group of men who worked the gold-mine engines broke away from the Waihī Miners Union to form their own. The thousand other members of the union they'd abandoned stopped work in protest.

The strike grew violent when a new anti-union government took power in the July, led by William Massey. A large squad of police were sent and quickly jailed more than 60 strikers. That October, strikers watched as hundreds of hired non-union strike-breakers (also known as "scabs") were driven to the mines in horse-drawn wagons, guarded by police. The scabs reopened the mine (no doubt in need of money) and went to work. The strikers had failed to keep the mine shut, and they kept protesting against the employment of scabs.

Tension boiled over on 12 November. Strike-breakers attacked the union hall and one of the striking miners, Fred Evans, was beaten to death. And it didn't stop there. They stormed around Waihī, smashing property, hurting anyone in their path. The strikers were forced to gather up their families and run for their lives. There was nothing peaceful or passive about this. It was ugly.

WAR ON THE WHARVES 1913

Only one year after the terror at Waihī came the most violent strike in our history. Influenced by new ideas spreading from Europe and the US, workers were urged to combine forces into one enormous general strike, involving *every* union, so they could run their places of work without needing bosses. Such ideas made them bolder and two minor disputes — one at the Huntly mine and the other at Wellington's port — spread like wildfire to other ports and mines around the country.

Queen's Wharf during the 1913 strike.

By November 1913, around 16,000 workers had gone on strike, mostly in Christchurch, Wellington and Auckland. Government and management hoped to use it as an excuse to force the most "troublesome" unions back to arbitration courts. To break the strike and get the wharves moving again, the government ordered police to call for volunteers. Thousands of rural labourers and farmers turned up, many riding in from their farms to assist as troops on horseback. They were given the power to act as "special constables" and were called "Massey's Cossacks" by the strikers. The volunteers were armed with wooden batons, some also carrying guns and horsewhips. Elsewhere, armed office workers patrolled the wharves and other important sites on foot.

Wellington Harbour Board building during the 1913 strike.

The arrival of these armed "specials" triggered brutal fighting in the streets and numerous pointless acts of destruction. Threats flew back and forth.

For weeks it looked as though the country was sliding towards a violent revolution. In Wellington, gun shops sold out of revolvers and many stores put notices up stating that scabs would not be served. Two naval ships were sent to guard the wharves, the commander of one sending his uniformed men to parade with bayonets and a machine gun. It was a show of force, a warning, and on 5 November, the specials marched through Wellington's streets to reopen the wharves. The strikers couldn't stop them. They were outgunned – for now.

"If this case can be settled only by setting the country on fire industrially, that is going to be done," roared the Seamen's Union leader, Tom Young. "If the authorities of this country are going to use the police against the working class, I will undertake to mass in this city of Wellington 10,000 or 15,000 armed men."[317]

Meanwhile in Auckland, things continued heating up when more armed volunteers rode down Queen Street to the waterfront. The strike committee were outraged. They called for a general strike and most work in the city shut down in support for several days. Six weeks later, the government arrested the main strike leaders. Eventually it settled down. People needed to work to feed their families.

What good came from all this upheaval? Nothing, in terms of the violence and suffering. But it certainly helped many realise they *did* have a voice – and later two of the strike leaders, Peter Fraser and Michael J. Savage, each served the country as prime ministers – Prime Minister Savage put our social welfare safety net in place. Bernard Freyberg, one of Massey's Cossacks, went on to a celebrated military career and became Aotearoa's first Kiwi-born governor general.[17]

WATERFRONT DISPUTE 1951

T he 1951 Waterfront Dispute was the biggest strike in our country's history. Although not as violent as the Great Strike of 1913, it lasted longer – 151 days, from February to July – and involved more workers. At its peak, nearly 22,000 waterside workers (known as "wharfies" or "watersiders") walked off the job.[18]

Back then, ships were the only way to send our products overseas and shipping was vital for trade. The watersiders set up a union early on and they fought for decades to improve their conditions. Even so, their work was hard, heavy, dirty and dangerous,[19] with some men hefting loads up to 136 kilos. The shipping companies chose cheap labour over safer time-saving machinery — so workers suffered terrible injuries, breaking bones, snapping spines and losing fingers; they were plagued by lung problems, ulcers and hernias. In 1938 alone, there were 1300 injuries on the Auckland wharves.[20]

There was almost no safety equipment, little job training, and inadequate first aid. All that, and they were working dangerously long hours too.

Fathers were hardly ever home to see their children, and their wives had to care for the children alone. Everyone missed out.

It was the time of the Cold War. Soviet Russia was the enemy, and both sides flung about words like "Nazi", "Commie", "traitor" and "terrorist".[21] Government ministers called the strike leaders "communist wreckers". The Waterside Workers' Union, among others, quit the Federation of Labour to form the Trade Union Congress in April 1950. They weren't in a mood to be pushed around.

When the Arbitration Court awarded a 15% general wage rise the following January, waterside workers were offered only 9%. In disgust, they called for a ban on overtime. The shipping companies struck back, refusing to hire union members unless they agreed to work the extra hours. If not, they'd be locked out. Soon, all work on the country's wharves ground to a halt.

The government claimed our country's trade was at risk and declared a state of emergency on 21 February. The next day Prime Minister Sidney Holland warned that the country was "at war" and five days later troops appeared at Auckland and Wellington's wharves to take over the work. The police were sent in to arrest the "wreckers". It was made a crime to help strikers — even giving food to their children was banned. The government hoped to starve the strikers into backing down. But the strikers fought on with the help of their community.

The watersiders and their supporters wrote illegal newsletters and tried to set up freedom radio to fight back. Coal miners, freezing workers, seamen, power workers, drivers and railwaymen, all went on strike to support them. But, with only 8% of all union members taking part, it

"MOST NIGHTS, IF A SHIP WAS IN PORT, THE MEN WOULD COME HOME FOR AN HOUR FOR DINNER AT SIX AND THEN RETURN TO WORK, FREQUENTLY NOT RETURNING UNTIL AFTER 10 OR MIDNIGHT."[318]

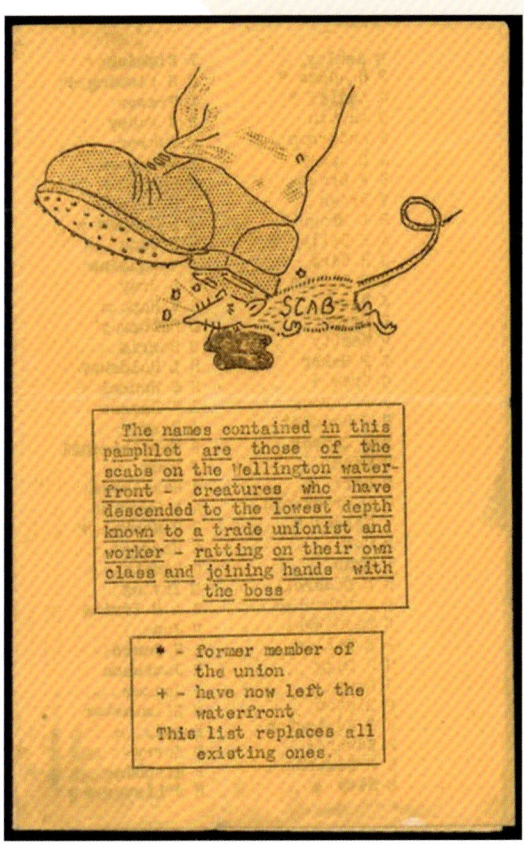

> "Somebody produced a slaughtered sheep to share. I got the impression it was stolen but now I know there were friendly farmers who donated sheep, and market gardeners who gave vegetables, and tradespeople who provided other goods and services for nothing."[319]

wasn't enough. As winter set in, bullying and violent outbursts grew more common.

At the end of April, the railway bridge near Huntly was blown up and the striking coal miners were blamed. Though the train drivers had been warned and no one was hurt, the coal supply was disrupted. Prime Minister Holland called it "an infamous act of terrorism". After that, any man caught at a street protest was attacked by baton-swinging police. The first of June was so violent, it's still known as "Bloody Friday". Police drove 1000 marchers off Queen Street, leaving more than 20 protesters injured.

By the end of May, new unions of strike-breakers started to work at the ports. Finally, after a hard five months, the strikers gave in on 15 July. Many were banned from the wharves for years after. The government called a snap election and won, gaining four more seats.

But this doesn't change the fact that, for many members, the watersiders' loyalty card – stating that its owner "stood loyal right through" – was seen as a prized badge of honour. While they may not have won this fight, they had certainly proven themselves to be determined and brave.

WAR ON WOMEN

Women and children felt some of the worst effects of the emergency regulations introduced during the 1951 waterfront dispute. Labour MP Mabel Howard called the dispute "a war on women", because the wives of strikers had to survive with no income, and it was illegal for anyone to help them. The regulations applied to children too. In Wellington's Clifton Terrace Primary School, strikers' children were separated from other pupils during playtime in case anyone illegally shared their lunches.[320]

SHAKING UP THE SYSTEM

GENDER AND DISABILITY RIGHTS

The world turned upside down? A typical anti-suffrage cartoon warns that tampering with men's and women's "natural" gender roles could cause the breakdown of society – or screaming babies, burnt dinners and cats in the milk jug at least.

WOMEN'S SUFFRAGE – FIGHTING FOR THE RIGHT TO VOTE

These days, the majority of women in Aotearoa have rights only dreamed of in earlier times. Back then, women were not allowed to vote, had limited rights to control their fate and were shamed if they dared speak out against the men who ruled their lives.

The fact that Aotearoa was the first country in the world to grant women the vote is something we should all be proud of. And it wouldn't have happened without the long, hard struggle borne by thousands of women to make their voices heard and their opinions count.

> **"Let the laws be fitted to the people and times. Do you still persecute for religious opinion? Do you still burn for witchcraft? Why, when the broad road of progress is cleared for so many human beings, is the juggernaut car of prejudice still to be driven on, crushing the crowds of helpless women beneath its wheels?"** Mary Müller writing as Fémmina in her 1869 pamphlet *An Appeal to the Men of New Zealand.*

The argument for women's suffrage (the right to vote) was clearly voiced by Englishwoman Mary Wollstonecraft in 1792. She wrote a book that called for equal rights and proper education for all girls and women. This view was very rare! It took another 100 years before the fight for women's voting rights fired up in Aotearoa. It was a visit from Englishman John Stuart Mill and his wife Harriet Taylor Mill that lit the spark. He boldly compared the treatment of women to slaves, and she wrote inspiring essays on women's suffrage. The spark quickly spread, especially among women already working alongside men, those holding their families together while their husbands worked away from home, and those who ran a household or business on their own. They deserved a voice.

The first suffrage pamphlet produced here was written in 1869 by English-born Nelson woman Mary Ann Müller. She published her words under the name "Fémmina". Her husband did not approve.

Another woman, Mary Colclough, (known in print as "Polly Plum") wrote letters to newspapers and gave public lectures in Auckland and Waikato, which was very unusual for a woman at the time. And it wasn't just settler women fighting for their rights. Māori women like Meri Te Tai Mangakāhia, Niniwa Heremaia and Iriaka Matiu Rātana fought for general voting rights *and* for their right to stand for seats in Te Kotahitanga (the Māori Parliament). They achieved both and were hugely respected.

Kate Sheppard

> **"Perhaps the Queen may listen to the petitions if they are presented by her Māori sister, since she is a woman as well."**
> Meri Te Tai Mangakāhia

The most well-known of our suffragists is Kate Sheppard, and her role is celebrated on our 10-dollar note. Born in England, she came to Aotearoa in 1862, married Walter Sheppard at 24 years old and had a son Douglas in 1880. She was educated in science, art and law, and put her talents to good use. She helped start the Women's Christian Temperance Union (WCTU) here, concerned by the impact of alcohol on families. The WCTU fought for a ban on selling it to anyone under 21. They also ran health classes, pre-school centres, and helped "fallen women" to find jobs and homes.

They ran soup kitchens and night shelters, and helped prisoners after their release. As well as all this, they fought for years for women's right to vote, under Kate Sheppard's guidance.

It was no easy fight. When they started, women were in the same class as "children, lunatics and criminals" — all were banned from voting. Women were insulted, shunned, made fun of, arrested, hurt, and many kept their traumas secret, fearing disapproval — or worse.

The first small win was a law change in 1875, giving women who owned property the right to vote in local elections. Suffragists pushed for their right to vote in general elections as well, but they failed to convince Parliament — they were turned down in 1878, 1879 and 1887. They decided a petition might show the size of their support more powerfully, and planned to present the government with long scrolls of signatures, each signature penned by a woman wanting to be heard. They presented their first petition to Parliament in 1891, signed by more than 9000 supporters from eight different regions. It had no effect. Six more petitions were signed by over 19,000 women. Again, they were ignored.

But that didn't stop them. The movement was growing, and groups of supporters sprang up around the country. In 1893, the biggest petition yet was presented to Parliament, with nearly 32,000 signatures from 13 regions. At last, the politicians were forced to listen. The pressure was on.

Sir John Hall put forward a Bill to allow women to vote – and managed to convince Parliament's lower house to pass it. All they needed was the Legislative Council to do the same. But at that very moment, John Ballance, the Premier and a suffrage supporter, suddenly died. The new Premier, Richard Seddon, opposed the idea of women's suffrage. To make sure the Bill wasn't passed by the Legislative Council, Seddon appointed 12 new members, half of whom he knew would vote against it. His plan failed because two of the existing members were so outraged by Seddon's underhanded action that they supported the Bill and it was passed. Phew!

Even then, several members of the Council tried to talk the new Governor, Lord Glasgow, out of signing it into law. Women everywhere fired back, sending telegrams and rallying on 8 September 1893 to hand all members who'd supported the Bill a white camellia (which is the flower on our 10 dollar note), and a red camellia to those who opposed the Bill, to shame them. At a glance, the Governor could see that the Bill had more support. He signed it and the deed was done: women finally had the right to vote, the first of anywhere in the world!

Amid the celebrations, Kate Sheppard said: "It does not seem a great thing to be thankful for, that the gentlemen who confirm the laws [...] have declared us to be 'persons' [...] We are glad and proud to think [...] there is a majority of men who are guided by the principles of reason and justice, who desire to see their womenkind treated as reasonable beings, and who have triumphed over prejudice, narrow-mindedness and selfishness."

The ripples from this spread right around the world, inspiring women everywhere. Today, the only nation where women are banned from voting is Vatican City (where only male cardinals are allowed to vote), although there are several other countries which continue to make it very hard for women to vote. It's a good reminder to treasure this right and use it to benefit all.

MMP – FAIRER REPRESENTATION FOR ALL

Until 1994, Aotearoa voted using the First Past the Post (FPP) electoral system, meaning that the candidate with the most votes was elected. This system favoured the two biggest parties, National and Labour, although in both the 1978 and 1981 general elections, the Labour Opposition actually gained more votes overall, yet National won more seats and remained in government. Smaller parties found it hard to muscle in, and those who voted for them felt their voices were being swamped.

In the lead-up to the 1981 and 1984 elections, Labour promised to establish a Royal Commission into the electoral system. This they did after they won the election in 1984. The commission's 1986 report recommended we adopt Mixed Member Proportional representation (MMP). After nothing was done to action the recommendation, public protest forced another referendum in 1992. When an overwhelming majority voted for change, a second, binding referendum in 1993 asked voters to choose between FPP and MMP.

In 1994, Aotearoa officially adopted MMP as its electoral system, thanks to the people who refused to give up until a change had been made.

WOMAN POWER!

The women's suffrage movement was only one of many times Aotearoa's women have stood up to improve their rights. Every win came after they managed to gain public support, pushing the government to heed their demand for change. Thanks to their efforts we now take many of our rights and protections for granted.

Women-led protests have driven many important changes, each another step towards giving women more control over their own bodies and lives. Examples include:

- Being allowed to stand for Parliament
- The right to divorce
- Access to birth control and safe maternity care
- Welfare support for solo mothers
- Laws against sexual and domestic violence
- Moves towards equal pay with men
- Parental leave (for fathers too)

Women have worked hard to end the silence on issues that affect them, and in the process helped to improve countless other lives. Yet there are issues that have been fought over for centuries which are still not resolved. Let's look at four women-led protests still rumbling along today.

ABORTION RIGHTS

The right for a woman to decide whether she goes ahead with a pregnancy or not is one of the most hotly debated women's issues there is.

It's not surprising this debate draws passionate arguments on both sides — it challenges people's personal values, their morals and beliefs. Whose rights are the most important — the woman or the unborn child? It's an issue people get heated over; it evokes big emotions. There are several organisations in Aotearoa that campaign on each side. Most churches take a strong position against it. Meanwhile, individual women continue to march, debate, write, talk to politicians and fight for law change — both for and against abortion.

A sign promoting the saving of unborn children — Marlborough, 2007. (Alan Liefting)

About 300 protesters march for abortion rights — Parliament grounds, May 1977.

Abortion was outlawed when English law was established in Aotearoa, first via inclusion in Australia's Legislative Council in 1840 and then more specifically after the New Zealand Constitution Act of 1852. Anyone having an abortion, or helping someone else to get one, could be arrested. In the 1930s things eased a little, letting women whose life or mental health was at risk apply for one — but they'd still be thought of as criminals if people knew.

The law has changed over the years, tweaked by different governments with different views.

Badge produced by the Abortion Law Reform Association of New Zealand (ALRANZ) in 1973.

Between 1965 and 1970, the number of abortions performed in public hospitals in Aotearoa had jumped from 70 in 1965 to more than 300 by 1970. Following the legalisation of abortion in Britain in 1967, and court decisions in 1967 and 1970 legalising abortion in Australia, public debate increased in Aotearoa. With legalised abortion next door in Australia, Kiwi women (who could afford to) travelled there to have abortions.[22] In the 1970–80s, some women were helped to travel to Australia by action group Sisters Overseas Service (SOS).[23]

Growing public awareness and debate about abortion led to the rise of anti-abortion and pro-abortion groups. Early anti-abortion groups included the Society for the Protection of the Unborn Children (SPUC) and REPEAL, while early abortion rights groups included the Abortion Law Reform Association of New Zealand (ALRANZ) and the Women's National Abortion Action Campaign (WONAAC).[24]

The first abortion clinic in Aotearoa was the Auckland Medical Aid Centre (AMAC), which opened in 1974. By the end of its first year, it had provided 2288 women with abortions. By 1975, this figure had risen to 4005. AMAC attracted opposition from anti-abortion activists including arson attacks, attempting to burn it down. The police also raided AMAC in 1974, leading to the prosecution and acquittal of one of its doctors.[25]

The most recent change in our abortion laws came in March 2020 and was only passed after more heated debates and protests. The change allowed women to have an abortion at up to 20 weeks pregnant, (or more, under special conditions). With the passing of this Bill, abortion was removed from the Crimes Act (1961), the first time since 1840. The debate continues around the world – violently in some countries.

WOMEN RECLAIM THE NIGHT

"For most of us it was the first time we have felt safe and secure at being out on the street at night."[26]

"Reclaim the Night" marches were held at night and moved through nightclub districts or places women usually avoided out of fear. They were first held in Aotearoa in the 1970s after the movement began in England. Marchers demanded that the streets be made safer for women, who feared attack after dark (and often were). The 1979 protests in Wellington were organised after several women were raped in Mt Victoria.

These marches carried on throughout the 2000s, raising public awareness. Sadly, it's a message that still needs repeating, and issues around women's safety keep bubbling up, as the following examples show.

SLUTWALK RALLIES – "YES MEANS YES AND NO MEANS NO."

Have you ever heard of "victim blaming"? In this case, it's when women make a complaint of sexual assault, rape, stalking, undesired touching or remarks, and the blame is turned back onto them: it was caused by what they wore, how they acted, what they said or drank, where they went. Women quickly realise the way they dress and how they act is judged differently to boys and men.

In 2011, women around the world called "Stop!" on this. Victim-blaming was unfair and dangerous. They organised "slutwalks" – protest marches declaring that *every* person has the right to be free from violence, no matter what they wear or how they act. Marches were organised around the country, with women asserting the right to go out at night without fear, and stressing that it's never the victim's fault; nobody deserves it. These actions helped bring the issue into the open, but little has really changed.

"I SAW A CARTOON THAT SUMMED IT UP REALLY WELL, THAT SAID, BASICALLY, SOCIETY SAYS TO WOMEN, DON'T GET RAPED! WHY DOESN'T IT JUST SAY TO MEN, DON'T RAPE!?" [321]

Marchers walk down George Street during the Dunedin Rape Crisis "Slutwalk" rally against sexual violence. (Craig Baxter)

#METOO

The #MeToo movement began in 2017 when American actress Alyssa Milano posted on Twitter that if every women who'd been sexually harassed or assaulted wrote #MeToo as a status, people would see the size of the problem. The hashtag went viral and within a day, half a million #MeToos came back in reply. Women all over the world shared their stories, and for many it was the first time they felt listened to and believed.

In Aotearoa, stories emerged about sexual harassment and abuse in law firms, among politicians and political parties, in universities, the film industry, police, the defence force, even the Human Rights Commission. Broadcaster Alison Mau began #MeTooNZ and the news outlet Stuff set up a hotline. They heard from thousands of women and published dozens of stories. Within two months of #MeToo going viral, helplines saw a 50% increase in the number of people contacting them. Recently, several powerful men have been named and shamed. This isn't over yet ...

"WHEN I GREW UP, THEY USED TO SAY, 'SHE WAS RAPED BUT NOT INJURED'. NOW WE KNOW THAT THE INJURIES ARE FAR MORE LIFELONG THAN A PHYSICAL BEATING. WE NOW KNOW THE INVASION OF YOUR BODY IS JUST HUGE." FRANCES JOYCHILD QC[322]

Sharon Murdoch – Stuff Limited

RAINBOW ROMANCES AND ACCESSIBILITY ACTIVISTS

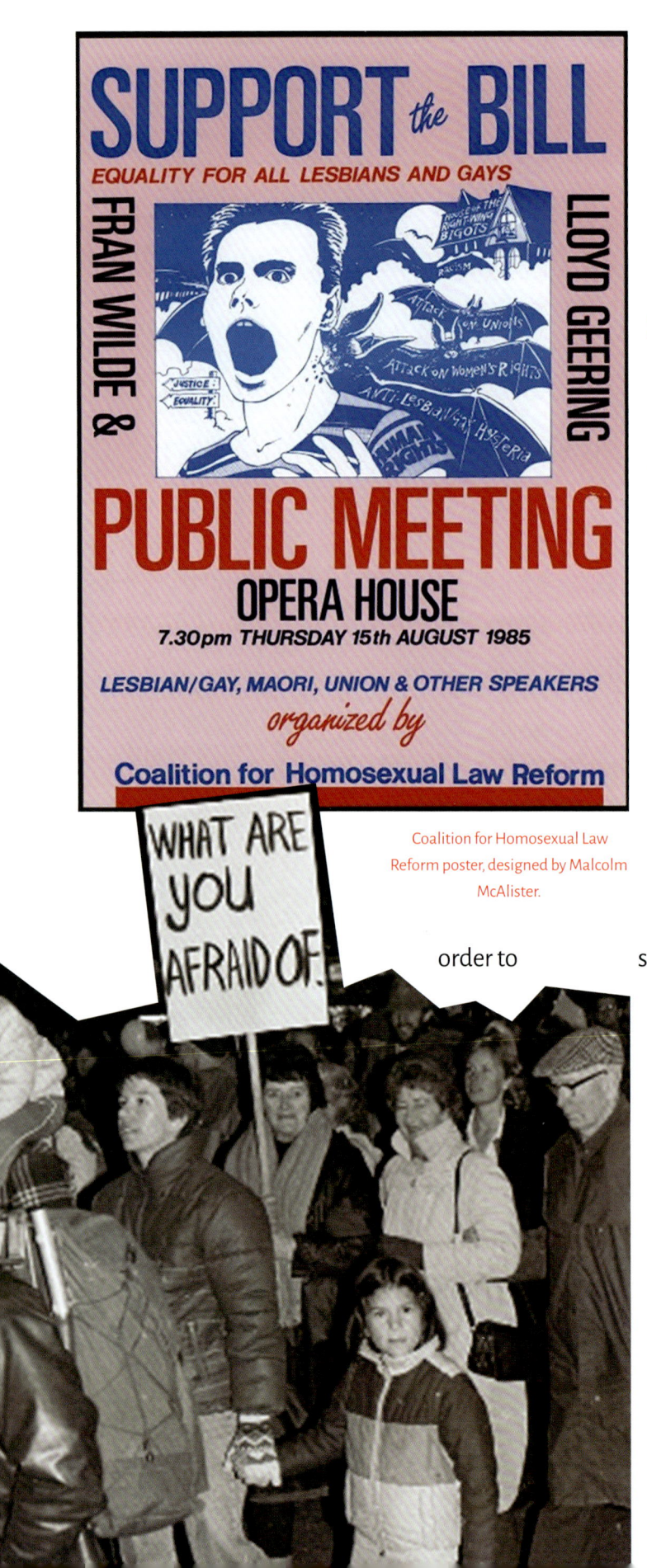

Coalition for Homosexual Law Reform poster, designed by Malcolm McAlister.

"Go back into the sewers where you come from," yelled National Party politician Norman Jones to gay rights protesters outside the Wellington Town Hall in 1985. This comment sums up one side of the bitter public and political debate that swept Aotearoa, during the homosexual law reform campaign in the mid-1980s.[27]

It's hard now to understand the very real anger, hate and fear that was piled on gay people and their supporters at that time. After 1840, any man caught having sex with another man risked the death penalty in Aotearoa. Later, in 1861, England replaced the death penalty with life imprisonment, and Aotearoa followed six years later. Yet men convicted of any sexual act with another man (of any age) faced flogging or whipping and hard labour. Gay men had to pretend not to be gay, denying who they were in order to survive.

An attempt in 1959 to reduce such severe punishments failed. In 1961, the term of life imprisonment was dropped, though it remained a crime that put men in jail. Oddly, lesbians (women in same-sex relationships) were not mentioned under the law at all – as if they didn't exist. The same goes for other diverse genders.

The first local organisation for gay men was formed in 1962. The Dorian Society started as a social club where men could meet in safety, and in 1963 it set up a committee to provide legal advice for members.

In 1967, 150 people met in Wellington with protest action in mind. This group, later called the NZ Homosexual Law Reform Society, organised a petition, signed by 75 well-known citizens. It was presented to Parliament in 1968 – and was rejected. But having been established, these groups kept fighting.

As gay rights protests started to spring up overseas in the mid-1970s National MP Venn Young put forward a Bill to legalise private homosexual acts between consenting adults over 21 years old. It failed. Several other moves also failed due to lack of support. What the gay movement needed was another politician to stand up on their behalf, and in the early 1980s, Labour MP Fran Wilde did exactly that. She consulted with gay groups and wrote the Homosexual Law Reform Bill, introduced to Parliament on 8 March 1985.

The bill had two parts. The first was about removing sexual acts between men from the Crimes Act and protecting minors (those under 20 years old). The second part would make it illegal to discriminate against gays and lesbians – in the workplace, when looking for somewhere to live, or in the supply of goods and services.

Gay and lesbian groups were promised the campaign would be "short, political and carried out in Parliament".[28] But angry sections of the public, and some politicians, were deeply opposed to the proposed Bill. From the moment of its introduction, a heated public campaign quickly turned abusive. Gays were attacked in the street. Organisations like the Salvation Army loudly opposed it, and anti-gay speakers were brought from overseas to argue that homosexuality was unnatural and that the Bible condemned it.[29] They feared it would encourage others and cause the "collapse of the family unit". New awareness of AIDS also fuelled fear, leading to government-funded education programmes delivered by the NZ AIDS Foundation.

> "Everyone is equally entitled to human rights without discrimination. Discrimination happens when someone is treated unfairly or less favourably than another person in the same or similar circumstances. Discrimination can be direct or indirect, and generally takes the form of exclusion or rejection from something." NZ Human Rights Commission[323]

Many groups – the NZ Homosexual Law Reform Society, the Gay Task Force, Heterosexuals Unafraid of Gays (HUG), the Lesbian Coalition and the Campaign for Homosexual Equality – all tried to offset the fear whipped up by anti-gay messages. They handed out information at nationwide street marches and rallies, and disrupted anti-law-reform meetings, arguing for their human rights, freedom of choice and an end to discrimination based on sexuality.

On 24 September 1985, a petition against the Bill was presented, with 91 boxes (one for each electorate) delivered to the steps of Parliament. The petition claimed to contain over 800,000 signatures, but it was found some boxes were nearly empty, and several petition sheets were forged by the same person. The petition was rejected.

It took 14 months before the bill's final vote was held on 9 July 1986. It passed by 49 votes to 44 and came into effect on 8 August that year. For the first time in 146 years, men could enter into same-sex relationships without fear of arrest. The gay and lesbian communities were jubilant. Their opponents predicted doom and gloom.

It wasn't until 1993, with the passing of the Human Rights Act, that it became illegal to discriminate on the grounds of sexual orientation. That took further protest action to achieve.

Still more campaigns led to gay and lesbian couples being able to form a Civil Union in 2005, and the Marriage (Definition of Marriage) Amendment Bill (2013) saw us become the 13th country in the world (and the first in Asia-Pacific) to allow same-sex couples to marry.

None of this would have been possible if people hadn't joined together to fight for change. Like abortion, homosexual law reform is an issue that continues to divide the population.

ACCESS FOR ALL – RIGHTS FOR THE DISABLED

Those of us who are able-bodied (don't have a disability) take moving around, using public transport, and accessing shops and buildings for granted. It simply doesn't occur to most of us that there may be people who find these everyday activities hard. Those of us with a disability know that trying to navigate an uneven footpath or supermarket in a wheelchair or as a blind person can be a real challenge.

In the 1980s and 1990s, the disabled community (in a joint campaign with the gay and lesbian community, called "Common Ground") took on the government, requesting that disability specifically be added to the Human Rights Act. It took 16 years of protest action before they saw any change. There were sighs of relief when, finally, disability was added to the Act in 1993.

In the 1990s and early 2000s, the community used the changes they had fought for to demand buses, trains and taxis be made accessible for disabled people. They held protest marches, wrote letters, and finally were asked to help draw up new public transport guidelines. Their actions made life easier for the 24% of Kiwis[220] living with some form of disability, and these champions continue to fight for change.

"WE WERE COMING FROM A PLACE OF DIRECT LIVED EXPERIENCE OF DISCRIMINATION, SO WE WERE ALL PRETTY HOT AND STRONG." ROBYN HUNT[221]

THE PEACEMAKERS

"ALL WE ARE SAYING IS GIVE PEACE A CHANCE ..."

4

Those of us lucky enough to live in a country free from war only know the horror from images and stories. We talk of glory and heroes, yet each death, sometimes millions, leaves a family grieving.

There have always been people who strongly feel that taking any life is wrong, and therefore, war is wrong, no matter the reason. This belief is called "pacifism" and those who live by it are "pacifists" – like the Moriori, who lived on Rēkohu (Chatham Island) and Rangihaute (Pitt Island), whose unique culture was based on a lore of peace. Other pacifists include "conscientious objectors", who refuse to fight in wars when called upon by their leaders.

War Resisters' International, for instance, is a global pacifist and anti-war network with over 90 similar groups in 40 countries. Each member lives by their founding declaration, first devised in 1921, which says: "War is a crime against humanity. I am therefore determined not to support any kind of war, and to strive for the removal of all causes of war." They claim all wars lead to suffering, destruction, and new forms of control.

> "I CAN ONLY SPEAK FOR MYSELF, BUT I DO FEEL THAT I AM FIGHTING FOR A WARLESS WORLD WHERE PEOPLES CAN LIVE TOGETHER IN PEACE AND FRIENDSHIP, AS MOST OF THEM REALLY WANT."
> ARCHIBALD BAXTER

Some say refusing to fight on behalf of one's country is cowardly, but for the men from our nation who *did* refuse, it was a very personal protest and involved a very particular type of courage. These men stood up for what they believed in and were horribly punished as a result, some killed. Most refused to fight for moral, ethical or religious reasons (such as the Quakers), but many Kiwis despised them for it and at the time few saw their stand as brave. Most believed our fighting men were heroes, showing loyalty and love for their country by protecting its values – and no doubt this was also true. But, looking back, it's clear that both sides of this divide were fighting for peace, they simply approached it differently, and both sides suffered hugely.

WORLD WAR ONE – THE WAR TO END ALL WARS

At the start of World War One, 14,000 men, mostly territorials, volunteered to fight. Overall, 72,000 men volunteered, roughly 80% of all who served.[30] But that wasn't enough. In addition, our government conscripted (ordered) 138,034 men into training for military service, with roughly 32,000 actively fighting. Just over 18,000 men were killed (equal to the whole population of a town like Rangiora in Canterbury) and nearly 41,000 were injured over the four years (same as the population of Upper Hutt city).[31]

Only 73 men of around 600 who refused to fight were exempted (let off). Others were pushed into non-fighting roles, like being thrust into battle to drag the wounded out on stretchers. Those who still refused were charged in a military court (court-marshalled). Many more were arrested for refusing to show up at all, others ran away.[32] Their fears were real: somewhere between 8.5 and 11 million men in total died as a result of battle wounds or disease in World War One. Around 7 million civilians were killed, with millions more suffering terrible hardship.[33]

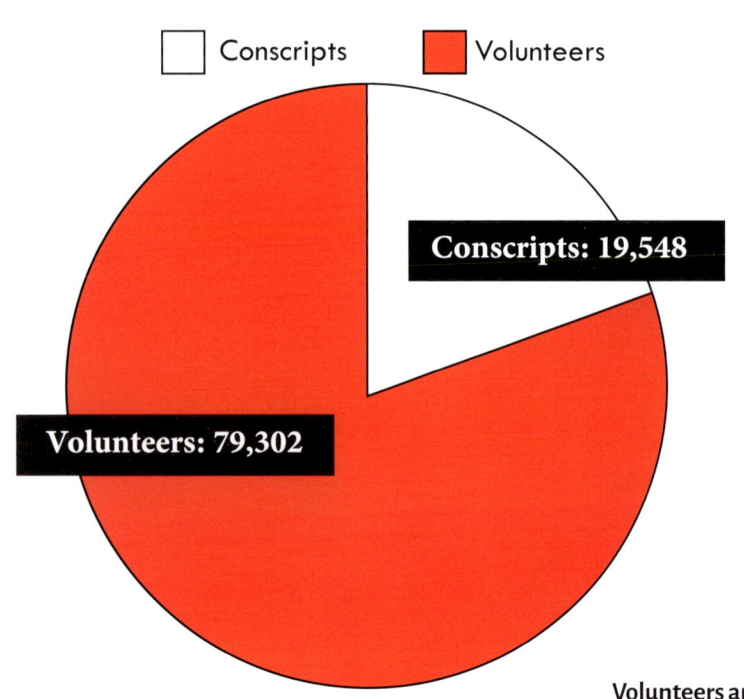

Volunteers and conscripts who embarked for overseas service, 1916–18

ARCHIBALD BAXTER AND THE FOURTEEN

Of the 600 Kiwi men who officially declared themselves conscientious objectors in World War One, 286 of them were thrown in jail. Fourteen of those arrested were locked up on the troopship *Waitemata*, stripped and forced to put on uniforms, with those who refused thrown just a towel to wear. On arrival in England, they were jailed in conditions so harsh that most fell ill. Eventually three men agreed to fight and one was ruled a genuine objector and was returned home to Aotearoa. That left 10.

Those 10 men were sent to France between late 1917 and 1918, where four were talked into fighting by the French. (Note: you may notice that these numbers don't add up, but they are the official figures on record, and referred to in this way.)

Three of the 10 were jailed at Dunkirk in a military prison so brutal they signed up as stretcher-bearers to escape it. One of them, William Little, was killed in action.[34]

Four objectors — Archibald Baxter, Lawrence Kirwan, Mark Briggs and Henry Patton — were sentenced to the feared "Field Punishment No. 1". They were tied to a pole for up to two hours at a time, arms raised, so blood couldn't flow to their hands, day after day. The pain was unbearable.

Out of desperation, Patton signed up to be a stretcher-bearer. The other three were ordered to the front-line trenches. When Briggs refused, he was tied by wire, dragged for over a mile across splintered walkways, with jagged nails tearing into his flesh, and then he was thrown down an old bomb crater full of water. He nearly died. Kirwan was so violently bullied he, too, risked lugging stretchers.

That left Archibald Baxter to face the torture alone. He later described it in his book *We Shall Not Cease*:

Archibald Baxter

"He took me over to the poles, which were willow stumps, six to eight inches in diameter and twice the height of a man [...] I stood with my back to it and he tied me to it by the ankles, knees and wrists [...] he knew how to pull and strain at the ropes till they cut into the flesh and completely stopped the circulation [...] my hands were always black with congested blood [... They] were taken round behind the pole, tied together and pulled well up it, straining and cramping the muscles and forcing them into an unnatural position [...] causing a large part of my weight to come on my arms, and I could get no proper grip with my feet on the ground, as it was worn away round the pole and my toes were consequently much lower than my heels. I was strained so tightly up against the post that I was unable to move body or limbs a fraction of an inch. Earlier in the war, men undergoing this form of punishment were tied with their arms outstretched. Hence the name [...] crucifixion [...]

"A few minutes after the sergeant had left me, I began to think of the length of my sentence and it rose up before me like a mountain. The pain grew steadily worse until by the end of half-an-hour it seemed absolutely unendurable. Between my set teeth I said: 'Oh God, this is too much. I can't bear it.' But I could not allow myself the relief of groaning as I did not want to give the guards the satisfaction of hearing me [...] I felt I was going mad. That I should be stuck up on a pole suffering this frightful torture, a human scarecrow for men to stare at and wonder at, seemed part of some impossible nightmare that could not continue. [But] at the very worst, strength came to me and I knew I would not surrender. The battle was won, and though the suffering increased rather than decreased as the days wore on, I never had to fight it again."[35]

Baxter was also starved. Eventually his body and mental health broke down and he was moved to a hospital in England. Once the war was over, he returned to his farm in Otago. Baxter married Millicent and had two sons who became pacifists as well, Terence and James (also known as James K. Baxter, one of our great poets and writers). He and Millicent set up the Dunedin Branch of the New Zealand No More War Movement in 1931 and remained actively involved. In later years they protested against nuclear weapons and the Vietnam War. Baxter remains a hero to many and his writing helped to open hearts and change minds.

In 2014, the Archibald Baxter Memorial Trust was set up to honour Baxter's memory and the courage shown by all Kiwi conscientious objectors in all wars, with an annual peace lecture and ongoing educational work. In 2021, construction of a memorial peace garden in the heart of Dunedin has begun, where the centrepiece will be a rock sculpture depicting Field Punishment No. 1.[36]

TE PUEA HĒRANGI AND MĀORI ANTI-WAR RESISTANCE

In Waikato meanwhile, up rose a woman whose protest in support of her people took great personal courage. At that time, a number of Māori from Taranaki and Tainui-Waikato resisted calls to serve in the war. Many were hurting, their land taken as punishment for their "rebellion" against the Crown in the 1860s. Why should they fight for the British, they asked, when they'd been so betrayed?

Kīngitanga leader Te Kirihaehae Te Puea Hērangi (Tainui) defended their decision to object. She quoted her grandfather King Tāwhiao, who said at the time of making peace with the Crown in 1881: "The killing of men must stop; the destruction of land must stop. I shall bury my patu in the earth and it shall not rise again [...] Waikato, lie down. Do not allow blood to flow from this time on."[37] How could they possibly disobey him? Besides, Waikato had its own king, she declared, though if their land was returned, then *maybe* they'd reconsider.

The government didn't accept her argument. When the men ignored their call to serve, police were sent. Te Puea gave the men refuge at Te Paina pā. When the police came, she stood her ground, saying she feared no law, or anything "excepting the God of my ancestors".[38] It was a brave stand, but the men were still arrested.

The prisoners were sent to an army training camp at Narrow Neck in Auckland. Those who refused to wear a uniform were punished with the other objectors, fed only bread and water, and given scant bedding. Some were sentenced to two years' hard labour at Mount Eden prison.[39] Te Puea took food to the jail but it never reached those intended. She tried many times to visit, sitting outside the gates so they could glimpse her when they went to the toilet block. Her support inspired them and gave them strength.

Te Puea continued to serve her community throughout her life and is seen as crucial in securing the survival of the Kīngitanga movement.[40]

WORLD WAR TWO – HARD LABOUR

Conscientious objectors at Hautu Detention Camp, near Tūrangi on the Desert Road, 1943.

Twenty-one years after World War One ended, World War Two broke out. In total, 312,000 of Aotearoa's men were called upon to serve, with almost 5000 objecting this time. After their appeals were heard, nearly 800 men were classed as military defaulters. They were rounded up and imprisoned in purpose-built camps for the duration of the war – remote, out of the public eye and despised.

These men were worked hard under guard, farming and labouring. A few escaped. Some wouldn't follow orders and were jailed elsewhere. After the war they were further punished by being banned from voting for 10 years.[41] Many remained family outcasts, or their actions were kept secret.

"MY UNCLE WAS A CONSCIENTIOUS OBJECTOR, REJECTED BY THE REST OF THE FAMILY FOR OVER TWENTY YEARS. HE WAS DETAINED AT A CAMP IN HOROPITO, THE CONDITIONS WORSE THAN THE GERMAN CAMP WHERE TWO OF HIS BROTHERS WERE PRISONERS OF WAR." B. LAIRD[324]

WOMEN PEACEMAKERS

Although women weren't expected to go to war, they were the mothers, wives, aunts, sisters and grandmothers of those who did, and many had strong feelings about the issue.

Women helped start the National Peace Council (NPC) in 1911 and some worked as volunteers. They supported conscientious objectors, wrote letters to newspapers, made public statements, wrote and handed out flyers, attended court hearings and visited those who resisted in prison. They also wrote to politicians. The Canterbury Women's Institute organised public meetings and two of its members, Ada Wells and Sarah Page, became well known as anti-war public speakers.

THE HIDDEN COST FOR OBJECTORS' FAMILIES

Of course, a man's decision to object also affected his family — his wife, children, siblings and parents. Some were sent white feathers through the mail — the symbol of a coward. Some were handed feathers in person.

When their loved ones came home, families had to cope with their physical and mental state as a result of their treatment — they'd been broken, humiliated and scorned. Families fell apart, many lost friends, some were rejected by their churches, sports groups and clubs. One boy was denied the top school prize because of his father's pacifism. Many families suffered greatly, relying on their friends and workmates to survive; invisible victims — but also heroes.[42]

OTHER PEOPLE'S WARS – VIETNAM

These days, the number of people who question the need for Kiwis to fight in overseas wars has grown. This first became visible during anti-Vietnam War protests (1965 to 1971).

These protests may have been inspired by the 45 deaths of our servicemen in the Korean War, where Kiwi troops fought under command of the United Nations (UN) from 1950 to 1957.

Kiwi troops were sent to Vietnam to support the United States, our superpower ally, in the first war when we didn't fight alongside our traditional ally, Great Britain, or under the umbrella of the UN. This action reflected our stronger ties with the US and Australia and a shift

WHEN PROTEST GOES WRONG – FEATHERSTON MASSACRE 1943

In World War Two, Aotearoa had a local tragedy connected to war and protest. A detention camp just outside the Wairarapa town of Featherston held up to 800 Japanese prisoners who had all been captured in the South Pacific. Kiwis were hostile towards them as they feared Japan planned to invade us — their ruthless reputation stoking real panic.

In early 1943, a group of new Japanese prisoners staged a sit-down strike, refusing to work. Guards fired a warning shot and a Japanese lieutenant was said to have been hit. The prisoners rioted and the guards opened fire.

When the dust settled, 48 Japanese men and one guard lay dead, a shameful end to any protest. Today, at a memorial ground created by Aotearoa and Japan, a plaque commemorates the site with a haiku:

BEHOLD THE SUMMER ALL THAT REMAINS OF THE DREAMS OF WARRIORS.[325]

4500 anti-Vietnam War protesters gather in Cuba Street outside the Wellington Town Hall, on May Day, 1 May 1971.

in focus. It caused a huge public outcry here. Protesters were inspired and the peace movement really picked up pace thanks to the hippie era's focus on peace and love. This resulted in a very organised anti-Vietnam War campaign, with many groups and churches involved.

Hundreds of thousands of people with banners and megaphones took to the streets in towns and cities around Aotearoa. In Wellington's largest protest (and there were many held there), "5000 screaming protesters" stormed Parliament grounds in August 1967.[43]

They argued the conflict was a civil war in which Aotearoa should play no part, wanting this country to follow an independent path in foreign policy, not take its cue from the United States.[44]

The depth of resistance to having a Kiwi presence in Vietnam weighed heavily on the government of the time, and Prime Minister Keith Holyoake took note of the opposition, sending the smallest possible military response he could while still honouring our alliance commitments.

Of the 3900 soldiers sent to fight, 37 Kiwis lost their lives and 187 men were injured.[45]

In the end, it wasn't protest but a change in American policy that led to our troops coming home. Yet, the protests inspired many young people to engage in politics and stay politically active from that time on. Perhaps most importantly, the influence of the growing anti-war movement resulted in Keith Holyoake's reluctance to send more soldiers. Aotearoa's values were changing.

It's important to note that due to the protests, the soldiers who *did* serve in Vietnam weren't welcomed home as heroes when they returned to Aotearoa. They faced hostility; one group was attacked with red paint to represent "the blood of innocent Vietnamese". They were shunned, with many suffering from poor mental health after the brutality of their mission.

Their physical health was badly affected too. This was overlooked for years before a report in 2004 finally admitted they'd been exposed to a "toxic environment"[46] while in Vietnam. One of the worst chemicals was the deadly Agent Orange, a powerful herbicide that destroyed millions of acres of forest and farmland, and was linked to cancers, diabetes, birth defects and other disabilities.[47]

"It's in our DNA so therefore it's in our children's DNA and it's going to be in their childrens' DNA," one soldier said.[48] In 2006 our government acknowledged the health impacts of Agent Orange and apologised.[49] But the consequences continue to impact lives today and our Vietnam veterans continue to need support.

However, as anti-war protesters feared, our forces did take part in the brutal and systematic destruction of North and South Vietnam – and their people. An estimated four million Vietnamese were killed or wounded in the war, including as many as 1.3 million civilians in South Vietnam. The US military detonated more than 14 million tons of explosives, mostly in the South Vietnamese countryside. The bombing destroyed thousands of buildings too, and damaged 4000 villages. Bombs occasionally hit schools, churches, and hospitals. The poverty, desperation, and destruction of the war years – along with the US troops' influence – devastated Vietnamese families, culture and society for decades after.[50]

American planes dropped more than twice as many bombs as US forces used in the whole of World War Two – all on an area about the size of California. They also sprayed millions of gallons of chemicals on South Vietnam, killing or burning crops, forests, and other vegetation, making huge numbers of peasants homeless.

Unidentified Vietnamese women and children were killed in the Mỹ Lai Massacre, 16 March 1968.

In one of the most terrible acts of the war, known as the Mỹ Lai Massacre, US troops mass-murdered unarmed South Vietnamese civilians. Up to 500 innocent people were killed – men, women, children, even infants. Some women were gang-raped and their bodies mutilated, as were children as young as 12.[51] Only one man was ever successfully charged for this, and he had his sentence quietly reduced from life to three-and-a-half years under house arrest (not in a cell).

THE IRAQ WAR 2003 – "COALITION OF THE WILLING"

Sadly, every year we see dozens of deadly conflicts around the world, affecting tens of millions of people. Many are fights for power within a country (civil, religious, tribal, etc), but there are others fought between groups or smaller countries that are really dictated

by the interests of bigger powers. Often, it's about getting control of the country's resources, particularly minerals – especially oil. Sometimes conflict is used by one big power to attack another big power by stealth, fighting it out in a third country, destroying it and killing its people instead of their own (a proxy war). Sometimes it's prompted by the vanity or greed of a corrupt leader.

In response to the terror attacks in the US on 11 September 2001, a US and UK coalition led an invasion of Afghanistan. This attack and its aftermath caused enormous suffering, with nearly 57,000 people killed, more than 60,000 seriously wounded, and any sense of safety or security gone from the country.[52] Ten Kiwi soldiers involved in peacekeeping later died there.

Protests began in Aotearoa with approximately 10,000 Kiwis marching up Auckland's Queen Street on 15 February 2003 to protest against the coalitions next move: the planned invasion of Iraq. Hundreds more marched in more than 20 centres around the country.[53] Their message was clear: they did not want to see Kiwis fighting in other people's wars, especially a war based on unproven claims. So how did Kiwi soldiers end up there?

One year earlier, while in Britain for the funeral of the Queen Mother in April 2002, our Prime Minister Helen Clark, Australian Prime Minister John Howard and Canadian Prime Minister Jean Chrétien were pulled aside at a post-funeral reception by UK Prime Minister

Tony Blair for a "private discussion". It was revealed that Tony Blair and US President George W. Bush were plotting another invasion – this time of Iraq.

Blair told them, "The Americans are going to war [in Iraq]. We will have to go with them. Are you with us?" John Howard spoke up straight away: "I'll be with you, Tony." But Helen Clark and Jean Chrétien were aghast. They said, "No, you can't." Clark took the position that "you can't do anything that doesn't have UN backing" and Chrétien agreed. She came away from the meeting shaking her head.[54]

This was truly astounding. For the first time Aotearoa did not join its military partners when called upon to do so, walking its own path instead, backed by a population who'd seen the suffering that rained down on the people of Afghanistan and didn't want to see our troops involved in another bloodbath.

As Iraq's invasion seemed more likely, anti-war protests sprang up around the world. They did not believe George Bush and Tony Blair's claims that Saddam Hussein had weapons of mass destruction and ties to Al-Qaeda and must therefore be stopped. It turned out they were right to be suspicious; it would eventually be revealed that the claims were false. Iraq had the second-largest reserve of oil in the world and the US wanted control of it.

By early 2003, polls found 86% of Kiwis opposed our troops joining the invasion unless it was approved by the UN (who did not support it). Only 10–20% of Kiwis believed there was enough evidence and 58% were sure George Bush was misleading the world. We were correct to be concerned. When the invasion went ahead, more than 125,000 Iraqis died, and more than four million were made homeless (roughly the entire population of Aotearoa at the time). Two-and-a-half million fled the country as refugees, with many more living in desperate conditions.[55]

The toppling of Saddam Hussein's statue in Firdos Square, shortly after the capture of the city of Baghdad, April 2003.

But Helen Clark *did* eventually agree to send 61 troops, including 35 army engineers to help with reconstruction efforts in September 2003 – under pressure by Foreign Affairs to support our allies. We later sent more troops in a joint training mission with Australia, under the lead of the coalition. North of Baghdad, 106 Kiwis were based at Camp Taji, with a further 37 stationed in coalition headquarters and key logistical positions in Baghdad and other undisclosed locations.

As a country, we stood up to foreign pressure and did what we thought was morally right. In light of Aotearoa's previous war history, this was a huge change.

PLOUGHSHARES PROTEST – THE WAIHOPAI THREE

This anti-nuclear protest was led by children as a symbol of innocence and the world's future – Queen Street, Auckland, 1961.

In the quiet backroads of the Waihopai Valley, near Blenheim, two massive satellite dishes appeared between the late 1980s and 1990s, covered by white radomes – weatherproof structures that look like giant puffballs on the landscape. They were fenced and guarded 24/7. What on earth was their purpose?

It turns out Waihopai Station is an "interception" facility run by our Government Communications Security Bureau (GCSB) and these two dishes were bigger and better "ears" for our spies. They intercept communications relayed by satellite, capturing every signal that passes through – and we pass the information on to the US, UK, Canada and Australia, as our part in a security network known as Five Eyes.

In 1996, the book *Secret Power*[56] (researched and written by my brother Nicky Hager) exposed Waihopai's strong links to the USA-led ECHELON system, another network of similar spy stations around the world. Waihopai's job is to catch what is said or shared via phone or internet between different countries, basically spying on our people and our Pacific neighbours to help other countries' intelligence operations and inform issues around trade.

Radomes at Waihopai Station, Marlborough.

As a result, Waihopai has been the target of numerous protests demanding people's right to privacy and protesting against the station's military links. Members of the Anti-Bases Campaign continue to protest outside the gates to Waihopai Station every year.

In April 2008, three men broke into Waihopai Station. Teacher Adrian Leason, Dominican priest

Peter Murnane and farmer Sam Land described themselves as The Waihopai ANZAC Ploughshares. They released the following statement:

"This morning, 30 April 2008, we entered the Waihopai Spy Base near Blenheim. Our group [...] cut through three security fences surrounding the domes – these are armed with razor wire, infrared motion sensors and a high voltage electrified fence. Once inside we used sickles to cut one of the two 30-metre white domes, built a shrine and knelt in prayer to remember the people killed by United States military activity."[57]

Their group was part of a global Christian movement known as Ploughshares, the name taken from the Bible: "They shall beat their swords into ploughshares, their spears into pruning hooks; nation shall not lift sword against nation; and there shall be no more training for war." Isaiah 2:4

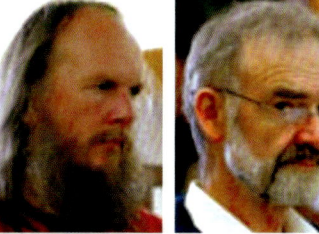

Adrian Leason   *Peter Murnane*   *Samuel Land*

At the time, Prime Minister Helen Clark called the attack "a senseless act of criminal vandalism". The three men were arrested and charged with intentional damage and unlawful entry. As they were escorted into a police van, Sam Land announced he was going on a five-day hunger strike, and Adrian Leason said he would pray for those in Iraq, where one million people had died.[58]

In court, they freely admitted breaking into the spy base and slashing the radome, saying they felt driven by the "unspeakable evil caused by activities enabled by spy bases, such as torture, war and the use of weapons of mass destruction".[59] They claimed they attacked the radomes to save human lives and prevent suffering, a defence used by Iraq-war protesters overseas. The jury agreed and they were let off on all charges. The government sued for $1.2 million in damages but, in another extraordinary win for the protesters, the fine was dropped. To some, these three men are modern-day heroes.

BAN THE BOMB
– ANTI-NUCLEAR PROTESTS

After World War Two, Aotearoa and Australia signed a pact with the United States to join the ANZUS Treaty. It was one of the reasons we felt obligated to send troops to Vietnam. The treaty required that we accept the protection of the United States' so-called "Nuclear Umbrella", meaning that our government agreed to the possible use of US nuclear-powered vessels or weapons in the event of an attack on us. Those already concerned by the idea of nuclear weapons considered this move deeply troubling.

THE COLD WAR

By 1959, concerns were growing as the Cold War between the US and the Soviet Union turned the building of nuclear weapons into a competition – an "arms race" where each side rushed to stockpile more and bigger bombs. In a US report not released until 2015, it was revealed that the US nuclear plan during the Cold War stated that nuclear bombs would be "used against priority 'air power' targets in the Soviet Union, China and Eastern Europe". Major cities in the Soviet Union, including East Berlin, were seen as high priorities for "systematic destruction" by nuclear bombs.[60] Targets included industrial and communication centres, transit hubs and major military installations, with long-range bombers intended to deliver the bulk of the strikes.[61] All these targets would have involved catastrophic civilian deaths and injuries.

THE "ARMS RACE"

The arms race saw the nuclear weapons stockpile grow globally from more than 2400 nuclear bombs in 1955 to 12,000 in 1959. By 1961 it had reached 22,229. The number of countries with nuclear weapons or reactors climbed too. In 2021, the US, UK, Russia, France, China, India, Pakistan, North Korea, and Israel are cited as having or developing nuclear weapons, and a total of 455 reactors are generating power in 35 countries.[62]

In response to this threat, the Campaign for Nuclear Disarmament (CND) was set up in Christchurch in 1959. It was co-founded with the help of Elsie Locke and Mary Woodward. The CND formed just in time to protest against the first nuclear-powered vessel arriving in Aotearoa — nuclear submarine, the USS *Halibut*, arrived in our waters in 1960.

The first Hiroshima Day commemoration was held here in 1961, with anti-nuclear marches taking place throughout the country. The bomb that fell on Hiroshima in 1945 killed or wounded nearly 130,000 people, with intense fires destroying everything within a two kilometre radius. Of the 286,000 people living in Nagasaki (which was bombed three days later), an estimated 74,000 were killed and another 75,000 had severe injuries.[63] More people died of their injuries in the following months. The damage to health from the radioactive fallout would affect survivors for decades after the initial blast — *and* their children and future generations.

CND drafted a petition in 1963 titled *No Bombs South of the Line*. It was signed by 80,000 Kiwis and called for a nuclear-free southern hemisphere.

FRENCH TESTING IN THE PACIFIC

Then things took an unexpectedly bad turn when France moved its nuclear testing location from Africa to the Mururoa atoll in French Polynesia — our back yard. And it wasn't only one test; they would carry out approximately 198 explosions on Mururoa and Fangataufa in the 30 years between 1966 and 1996. One Pacific reporter wrote in 2013 that "radiation levels frequently rose in New Zealand 4700 kilometres away following each test", and the leftover plutonium-239 was "extremely toxic and

Members of the Campaign Against Nuclear Warships (CANWAR) stand aboard the yacht Phoenix in Wellington Harbour, awaiting the arrival of the USS Long Beach — 1976.

has to be contained for 240,000 years before it can enter the wider environment".[64] Two-hundred-and-forty-thousand years. Take that in.

By 1972, anger over French nuclear testing was widespread in Aotearoa. The 38ft yacht *Vega*, flying a Greenpeace banner, set sail for Mururoa to protest. It was captained by one of Greenpeace New Zealand's founders, David McTaggart. Several other Kiwi yachts joined him, including one which carried Māori MP for Northland and Cabinet Minister Matiu Rata. He later said, "We represented small people from small countries who felt powerless in the face of events beyond the comprehension of our own government." Meanwhile, 10,000 people signed a petition calling for a halt to all French nuclear testing in the South Pacific. The French ignored it.

AOTEAROA TAKES ACTION

In 1973, the *Vega* sailed into the test zone again. The French Navy boarded the yacht and beat up David McTaggart. Photos of the attack went viral, opening the world's eyes to France's actions. At the same time, the Aotearoa and Australian governments took France to the World Court over their continued testing – and they sent the navy frigate *Otago* to the test zone, followed by the *Canterbury*, accompanied by the HMAS *Supply*, a fleet oiler of the Royal Australian Navy. Other local yachts, including the *Fri*, *Spirit of Peace*, *Boy Roel*, *Magic Island* and the *Tanmure* also set sail to join the protest. But the testing went on. A year later, the Aotearoa arm of Greenpeace, Greenpeace New Zealand, was officially founded, intent on stopping nuclear testing in the Pacific and helping the local people.

Widespread protests greeted the arrival of the nuclear-powered frigate *Texas* in Auckland in August 1983. These protesters on Mercer Street, Wellington, wore grotesque masks and carried a papier-mâché Statue of Liberty wielding a nuclear missile.

Photographer: Stuart Ramson

The next election brought a change in policy and in 1976 the new National Government announced it would welcome nuclear-powered and nuclear-armed warships. There were massive street rallies in response. The USS *Truxton* was brought to a halt by a spectacular protest fleet of 80 vessels, and the fleet took to the water again to halt another arrival of the USS *Long Beach* in 1976.

By 1978, after yet another protest over the USS *Pintado*, the frequent visits were starting to alarm people, concerned about the risks posed by their nuclear technology and the possible weapons aboard. The US refused to confirm or deny whether the vessels were armed. Many Kiwis believed that every port the vessels entered was potentially at risk should something go wrong. A new campaign declared cars, houses, boroughs and city council areas nuclear-free zones. Four years later, Wellington City would declare itself a nuclear-weapon-free zone in a move initiated by Councillor Helene Ritchie.

Between 1978 and 1983, public opposition to nuclear-powered or nuclear-armed ships rose from 32% to 72%. The largest anti-nuclear march to date happened in 1983, when 25,000 women marched up Queen Street in Auckland.

NZ Prime Minister Norman Kirk said at the time: "I believe that to base our foreign policies on moral principles is the most enlightened form of self-interest. What is morally right is likely to be politically right."

NUCLEAR-FREE AOTEAROA

In 1984 an election loomed, and under intense public pressure the Labour Party declared that it would (a) work for a nuclear-free Pacific, (b) ban nuclear-powered or nuclear weapon-carrying ships and (c) renegotiate the ANZUS Treaty. Labour was swept into power.

The US decided to test Labour's position. They asked that the ship USS *Buchanan* be allowed to visit. David Lange, the new Prime Minister, stuck to his word and refused them. Furious, Washington severed all visible military ties with Aotearoa and downgraded all diplomatic and political exchanges. US Secretary of State George Shultz said the US would no longer guarantee our security, although the ANZUS Treaty remained in place.

In 1985 the campaign to stop testing at Mururoa was dealt a shocking blow: the Greenpeace flagship, *Rainbow Warrior*, was bombed while docked at Marsden Wharf in Auckland. Crew photographer Fernando Pereira was killed. After an intense police investigation (helped by an angry public), it was announced that the bombers were French government secret agents! It was an astounding moment. It seemed unbelievable the French would do such a thing, but it became clear the attack was linked to Greenpeace's campaign to stop the testing at Muruoa.

Prime Minister David Lange channelled his anger into arguing that "nuclear weapons are morally indefensible" in a widely televised Oxford Union Debate in England. He drew thunderous applause when he quipped in reply to an American student, "Hold your breath for just a moment. I can smell the uranium on it as you lean toward me."

After a final push, the New Zealand Nuclear Free Zone, Disarmament and Arms Control Act (1987) came into force, writing our country's nuclear-free state into law. The US Congress hit back with the Broomfield Act, downgrading Aotearoa from "ally" to "friend". Their stand only further alienated Kiwis. By 1989, 52% of the population said they'd rather break

> "THERE'S ONLY ONE THING WORSE THAN BEING INCINERATED BY YOUR ENEMIES, AND THAT'S BEING INCINERATED BY YOUR FRIENDS."
> DAVID LANGE.

defence ties with the US than admit nuclear-armed ships into our waters — a huge shift from our adoration for all things American after World War Two.

Such was the pride in our anti-nuclear status that by 1990, just prior to the next election, the National Party also committed to keeping Aotearoa nuclear-free if they won.

Lange with the Bill to declare New Zealand nuclear-free in 1985. (Fairfax NZ)

In 1994, we were the only Western nation to come before the UN General Assembly and vote in favour of a resolution to ask for a ruling on whether it was legal to threaten with or use nuclear weapons.

Protesters were feeling confident, until the eve of the 10th anniversary of the Rainbow Warrior bombing in 1995, which coincided with the anniversary of Hiroshima and Nagasaki. French President Jacques Chirac announced France's plan for further nuclear testing at Mururoa, triggering a massive flotilla to Mururoa in protest. Two Greenpeace ships were seized. By this time, all our political parties declared unanimous opposition to French nuclear testing — we were now a whole nation of anti-nuclear campaigners!

CALLS FOR NUCLEAR DISARMAMENT

The following year the International Court of Justice finally gave its opinion — they said that nuclear weapons should be illegal. A year later, the Model Nuclear Weapons Convention was drafted and circulated by the UN Secretary-General as a UN document (one of the two drafters of this document was Kiwi activist Alyn Ware). Foreign ministers from eight countries including ours, released a declaration in 1998 seeking a new timetable for nuclear disarmament.

In the year 2000, the Nuclear Non-Proliferation Treaty Review Conference adopted 13 steps for disarmament, which was agreed to by the nuclear nations. Aotearoa's Disarmament Ambassador Clive Pearson chaired the subcommittee responsible for negotiating these steps, and in 2002 the Aotearoa section of the Parliamentary Network for Nuclear Disarmament was established. We were helping to lead the way.

These moves had a significant effect on the number of nuclear warheads around the world. Global stockpiles have dropped, since peaking in 1986 when there were almost 64,500 nuclear warheads in existence (enough to destroy us all many times over). The largest reductions have been made by the US and Russia, although the UK and France have also reduced their stockpiles.[65]

As of 2020, the world's nuclear powers have 13,400 nuclear warheads in their arsenals.[66] While the reductions are good news, these remaining weapons still have the capacity to kill millions directly and, through their impact on agriculture, probably kill billions.[67] Yet they're not illegal.

Modern nuclear weapons are much more powerful than those dropped on Japan. Just 50 could kill 200 million people – or the combined populations of Britain, Canada, Australia, Aotearoa and Germany.[68]

The radioactive waste created in the making of an average nuclear bomb includes 1814.369 tonnes of uranium mining waste, 3.62874 tonnes of depleted uranium and 50 cubic meters of "low-level" waste.[69] Many of these storage facilities are degrading with age or are threatened by climate change and other natural disasters, as are some of the nuclear power reactors currently operating.[70]

FUKUSHIMA AND CHERNOBYL MELTDOWNS

While the most obvious and urgent reason to protest against the use of nuclear technology related to weapons, the potential risks around the growing number of nuclear power stations also drove people to protest.

Two particular incidents would further feed their fears.

- The 1986 meltdown of the Chernobyl nuclear power plant in the north of Soviet Ukraine is considered the worst nuclear disaster in history.
- Within the first three months, 257 people suffered acute radiation sickness, and 31 died.[71] A 2007 Russian report concluded there were 985,000 premature deaths because of the radiation released in the meltdown. Many believe the real figure is much

On 4 February 1985 the Labour Government refused the USS *Buchanan* entry to New Zealand ports on the grounds that the United States would neither confirm nor deny that the ship had nuclear capability. This cartoon shows the *Buchanan* in Sydney Harbour.

higher. Estimates for when the land around Chernobyl will be safe to enter again is anywhere from 320 years to 20,000 years.[72]

- The 2011 meltdown of the Fukushima nuclear power plant in Japan caused by a post-earthquake tsunami.

154,000 residents were evacuated to escape the radiation but a screening programme in 2012 found that more than a third (36%) of children in Fukushima had abnormal growths in their thyroid glands as a result.[73] A large amount of water contaminated with radiation was released into the Pacific Ocean (almost 1.2 million litres).[74] Unhealthy levels of radiation have been detected in fish stocks far beyond Japan. Over one million tonnes of contaminated water are still held in Fukushima, with management warning it will run out of space by the summer of 2022.[75] They plan to dump this waste water in the ocean.

It's sobering stuff. All we can do today is pay attention and try to prevent repeating the mistakes from the past.

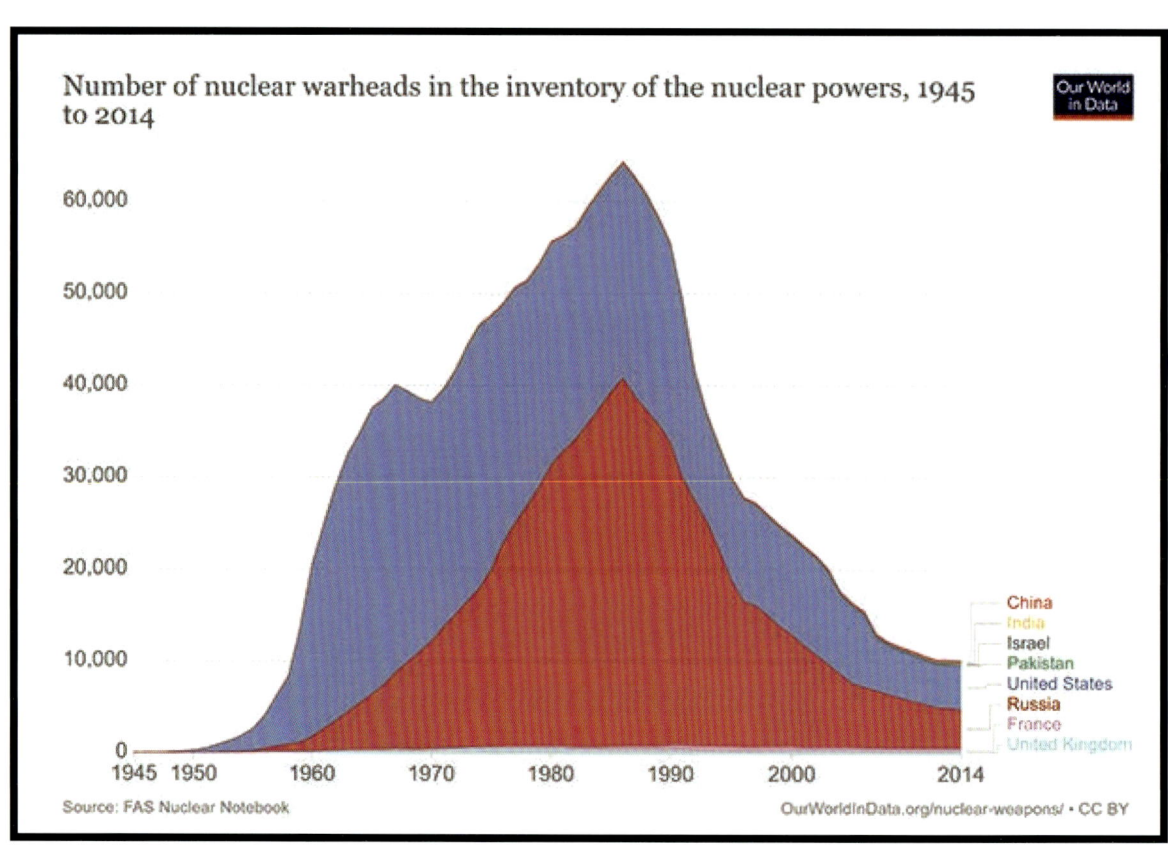

CALLING OUT RACISM AT HOME AND ABROAD

5

1981 SPRINGBOK RUGBY TOUR – THE GREAT DIVIDE

Protests against the 1981 Springbok Rugby Tour were among the most violent and painful in Aotearoa's recent history. The tour divided families and friends, inspiring a depth of feeling so strong that it still prompts reactions of anger, pride and shame in some Kiwis.

For 56 days between July and September 1981, Kiwis fought each other in our biggest civil uprising since the 1951 Waterfront Dispute. More than 150,000 people took part in over 200 demonstrations in 28 towns and cities. Around 1500 civilians were charged with offences and the police spent close to $15 million on Operation Rugby, defending the tour. The experience proved traumatic for the police as well.

Protest badges from the 1981 Springbok tour.

At its heart, the divide was between those who believed we should refuse to engage with South Africa until it changed its racist apartheid laws, and others who thought politics had no place in sport or argued that direct engagement would be a better pathway towards change through leading by example.

As a rugby-loving nation, the rivalry between the All Blacks and the Springboks was legendary, with many players claiming their games against the Springboks were among the best of their careers. The first official series between the two countries took place here in 1921, before the worst of the apartheid years in South Africa. By 1928, the first All Black tour of South Africa excluded all Māori players, causing us great offence. On their next tour of Aotearoa in 1937, although several Māori played for the All Blacks, the Springboks refused to play an all-Māori team. It prompted outraged complaints in reports back to South Africa:

"Bad enough having to play officially designated New Zealand Natives, but [the] spectacle [of] thousands [of] Europeans frantically cheering on [a] band of coloured men to defeat members of [their] own race was too much for the Springboks, who frankly [were] disgusted." South African Journalist Report[76]

The Te Arawa tribe called for a cultural and sporting boycott (ban), supported by most Māori, accusing the New Zealand Rugby Football Union (NZRFU) of putting "cash before conscience". The NZRFU wouldn't budge.

By 1960, Kiwis were also starting to voice their discomfort more loudly. There was outcry when another white-only team was selected to tour South Africa. There were calls of "No Māoris – No Tour" and 160,000 Kiwis signed a petition supporting this. Thousands marched in the largest protest against racially-selected sports teams anywhere at that time.[77] Despite this, the tour went ahead without any Māori players.

The next few years followed the same pattern: the Rugby Union and government allowed our teams to play South Africa on their racist terms, with thousands protesting against it. By the time the 1981 Springbok Tour was announced, several groups were already in place, committed to stopping it. Other Kiwis were excited about the tour and were keen to welcome the Springboks. These two opposing viewpoints were at the root of the tension.

What followed involved an incredible feat of planning by both police and protest groups. They had to activate and control thousands of people with different backgrounds, cultures, ages, and levels of commitment. From the moment the Springboks touched down in Aotearoa until they departed, the protest leaders had planned almost every hour. The people who took part would find it life-changing – often terrifying but ultimately rewarding. Several leaders who rose up during the protests continued to fight for social justice throughout the rest of their lives.

Reverend George Armstrong addresses police in Hamilton.

SOME OF THE MAIN ANTI-TOUR GROUPS:

ACCORD – Auckland Committee on Racism and Discrimination

CABTA – Citizens All Black Tour Association – started in the late 1950s.

CARE – The Citizens Association for Racial Equality-formed in Auckland in 1964.

CATHOLICS AGAINST THE TOUR

COST – Coalition to Oppose the Springbok Tour – a Wellington-based group.

HART – Halt All Racist Tours – set up by Trevor Richards of the NZ University Students Assocation in 1969. It became an umbrella group including CARE and a range of student, church, Māori and other left-leaning groups.

MĀORI ORGANISATION ON HUMAN RIGHTS – led by Tamatekapua Poata.

MOST – Mobilisation to Stop the Tour – an Auckland-based group.

NAAC – National Anti-Apartheid Council

NGĀ TAMATOA – anti-racism group made up of young Māori, who also campaigned on issues such as loss of land, language and Treaty breaches.

SCHOOL STUDENTS AGAINST THE TOUR (secondary school students)

STUDENTS AGAINST THE TOUR (tertiary students)

WOMEN AGAINST THE TOUR

PRO-TOUR GROUPS:

NZRFU – New Zealand Rugby Football Union

SPIR – Society for the Protection of Individual Rights

THE TOUR AND THE PROTESTS: A TIMELINE

12 September 1980 – The New Zealand Rugby Football Union (NZRFU) formally invites the South African rugby team to tour Aotearoa.

1 May 1981 – The first organised mass protests take place throughout the country. Numbers were estimated at around 75,000, all demanding the invitation be withdrawn.

14 May – Prime Minister Robert Muldoon is presented with a demand by the Commonwealth to cancel the tour or lose hosting rights to the Commonwealth Finance Ministers Conference, which was due to take place in Auckland. He ignores this.

3 July – The second round of mass protests are held throughout the country and the opposing sides firm up.

10 July – The NZRFU meet one final time to decide whether the tour should go ahead. They say "yes".

19 July – The Springboks arrive in Auckland and 2000 angry protesters greet them, tearing down fences and storming the runway.

22 July – On the night before the first game in Gisborne, a Land Rover smashes into the park and the unknown driver scatters broken glass across the field. On the day of the game, a no-fly zone is declared over the park after it is rumoured a light plane is going to attack to disrupt play. Protesters break down the perimeter fence when the game starts, wrestling with angry rugby supporters. The Springboks beat the All Blacks 24 to 6.

25 July – For the Hamilton game, 535 police are on hand, including the dreaded Red Squad, who use their long batons to attack protesters. Four thousand marchers converge in Hamilton's Rugby Park, after over 500 of them spent the night chanting and singing freedom songs outside the Ambassador Hotel where the Springboks are staying. When the game starts, 400 protesters break through the boundary fence and rush onto the field, chanting, "The whole world's watching!" and "Shame! Shame! Shame!" It stops the game and is broadcast around the world. The game is abandoned and angry rugby supporters attack the protesters, some of whom fight back. It quickly becomes a riot, with vehicles overturned, windows smashed, objects thrown and many injured. Protest leaders are attacked in their homes and badly beaten.

Meanwhile in a South African jail, Nelson Mandela (who becomes South Africa's first president after the fall of apartheid) hears of the Hamilton game's cancellation and says it was "as if the sun came out".

27 July – The government declares it won't back down in the face of violent protests and threatens to bring in the army.

29 July – The Battle of Molesworth Street (also known as The Night of the Batons). The evening after the Springboks play in New Plymouth, 2000 protesters meet outside Parliament, planning to march up Molesworth Street to the home of the

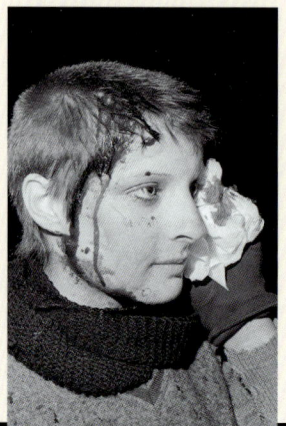

South African Consulate-General. They move the women, children and elderly to the front to indicate that the march is peaceful. Five lines of police block the protesters, warning them not to proceed. Those at the back of the march continue to push forwards. The police start chanting "Move! Move! Move!" and attack the marchers with their batons. Photos of battered and bleeding protesters, including a 16-year-old high school student, shock the nation.

1 August – Cars, buses and vans full of protesters converge in Palmerston North. They are prepared for violence, wearing crash-helmets and padding for protection. Two-metre-high barbed-wire barriers and lines of rubbish skips greet them on the field. Protesters are faced by 1100 police and the Red Squad, who brutally club them. Muldoon claims the protests are led by "extreme left-wing agitators" and presents a list of 20 named "subversives". This is later proved false.

13 August – Two days before the first rugby test, the grandstand at Christchurch's Rugby Park where the Springboks are due to practise, is destroyed by fire. No arrests are made.

14 August – A bomb blast wakes residents near Lancaster Park in Christchurch where the first test will be played the following day. Police confirm an explosive device was placed by the perimeter but caused no damage or injuries.

15 August – At the first test match, 1473 police patrol Lancaster Park. Seventeen protesters who run onto the field are "savagely dispatched".[78] Rugby fans cheer the Red Squad and pummel protesters with anything they can throw. One policeman claims it's "sheer luck" no one was killed. "The batons thudded. People were injured and screaming. Heads were bleeding again. A man in his 40s was staggering around with his teeth punched out."[79] The All Blacks win 14 to 9.

19 August – The game scheduled for Timaru's Fraser Park is cancelled. The police argue the grounds are too difficult to guard.

29 August – For the second test in Wellington, 7000 protesters gather. Concern for the Springboks' safety is so grave that they sleep under the grandstand on the night before the test. One thousand six hundred and eleven police are on duty, and 37 officers from a special police surveillance squad go undercover in the crowd (along with 14 from another intelligence unit). Protesters block the motorway offramps into the city, as well as road and foot access to Athletic Park. Fighting between rugby fans and protesters breaks out. Batons are used again. The Springboks win 24 to 12.

12 September – The third and final test in Auckland is the bloodiest and most violent of all, with 2134 police standing between thousands of fans and protesters. It quickly turns into an all-out brawl. Over 200 protesters are arrested and dozens injured. A light plane flies over the park and drops flour bombs, one knocking over All Black Gary Knight. Meanwhile, other groups further south sabotage the TV transmitters on Mt Studholme and Mt Cargill, cutting the live broadcast to nearly half the South Island. The All Blacks win 25 to 22.

WHAT DID ALL THIS ACHIEVE?

The Springboks flew from here to the US, where they were met with more protests. Several games were cancelled, and the headquarters of the Eastern Rugby Union was bombed.

The pressure was on the South African government and it continued to grow. The country was isolated more and more, until the apartheid regime began to crumble under the strain. In 1991 South Africa's apartheid laws were abolished and the country had its first fully free election in 1994. Nelson Mandela was sworn in as president, and when he visited Aotearoa the following year, he said, "The people of New Zealand played a crucial role in the international campaign against apartheid. I wish to express our gratitude for that generous support."

Apart from loudly voicing support for those oppressed by South Africa's racist laws, perhaps the most significant consequence was the spotlight the protests shone on our own race relations here in Aotearoa. As Trevor Richards, spokesman for Halt All Racist Tours (HART), said afterwards, "[We] helped shift New Zealand into a different national and international consciousness … ultimately [the issues] were more about us than they were about South Africa." [80]

We are yet to properly address the racism on our own soil with the same resolve we displayed on behalf of South Africa. Sometimes it's easier to see injustice from the outside looking in, especially if you're in the majority. If you're one of the oppressed, however, then you live with it every day.

But, just like the Kiwis who educated themselves about apartheid, we all can learn about our colonial history, examine ourselves, and commit to stamping out racism at home as well. Imagine the lives we could change if we did.

Schoolchildren protesting against the 1981 Springbok tour.

THE DAWN RAIDS – RACISM NEVER SLEEPS

It's easy to be shocked by the obvious racism of South Africa's apartheid laws, but in the early 1970s there was an obvious example of targeted racism here at home. In what became known as the Dawn Raids, police descended on people from the Pacific Islands in the early hours of the morning, plucking them from their beds, demanding proof that they were legally allowed to stay in Aotearoa. They dragged people away in their pyjamas, broke up families, some were sent back to the Islands without even being able to say goodbye. What was going on?

A family of Tongan overstayers deported from Porirua were forced to leave most of their belongings behind in the rush. Anna Likio surrounded by the luggage they had to leave behind. 6 June 1991 (*Evening Post* staff photographer Ray Pigney)

In the years after World War Two, Aotearoa enjoyed a period of huge economic growth, which left employers desperate to fill the many jobs created by this. By the 1960s, this boom saw labour shortages in many factories and unskilled jobs. To fill the gaps, people from nearby Pacific nations were encouraged to come to Aotearoa with their families, helped by a government-backed scheme. They were promised a new and improved life here, with more work opportunities and better pay than back at home. Many Tongan, Samoan and Fijian families made the move, as did people from Niue, Tokelau, and the Cook Islands (all already citizens of Aotearoa). Most of them settled in Auckland.

From 1961 to 1971, Pacific Island populations in Aotearoa rose from 12,000 to 48,000,[81] and by the 1976 census there were almost 65,700 Pacific Island people living here, making up 2.1% of the total population.[82] This figure reached 90,000 by 1981.[83] They came seeking better lives for their families and they wanted the best education for their children. Between 1972 and 1978, as many as 25,000 permanent migrants came here from all over the Pacific, making them the third-largest group after migrants from Britain and Australia. Many more came on short-term work permits, intending to bank some savings and then return home. Some stayed on after their permits ran out, but employers and government turned a blind eye – we needed their labour. They'd do the jobs for less, worked hard, and never complained; they didn't dare.

But by the early 1970s, a troubling theme was emerging in letters to newspapers and editorials: "Fit In or Get Out".[84] The attitude spread, with 62% of Auckland company managers in 1978 saying that people from Pacific nations should reject their traditional cultural practices and adopt the local (Pākehā) lifestyle.[85] Between 1972 and 1978, a total of 130 anti-Pacific Islander letters were published in two newspapers alone, with 28 letters of complaint sent to the Minister of Immigration.[86] Accusations ranged from lack of assimilation (failing to adopt Pākehā ways), to blaming Pasifika for increased crime and unemployment, housing shortages, breeding too fast, clogging hospitals, bringing disease and being "overstayers" (those with expired permits).[87]

The issue of overstaying led to the most obvious racist attacks. By 1973 the economy was struggling, after Britain's entry into the EU reduced demand for exports and a global oil shock shot oil prices from US$3 per barrel to nearly $12.[88] Our economy spiralled down and we saw the first real wave of unemployment since the Great Depression in the 1930s. Rather than look at the underlying global causes, many Kiwis blamed the economy on too many Pacific Islanders living here – conveniently forgetting they'd been actively encouraged to come here during the economic boom. They were an easy target. The jobs they'd filled when no one else wanted them were now demanded back.

As the recession worsened, Pacific migrants found their basic human rights kicked out from under them. They were blamed by politicians and many Pākehā Kiwis for more and more of the country's ills. The use of racist language also increased, as reported by W. G. Copwell in the *Pacific Island Monthly*: "It comes as a shock to hear a friend, headmaster of a large primary school, refer to the Polynesian pupils under his control as 'Coconuts', and to be everywhere assaulted with the use of racist names such as 'headhunter', 'tar pot', 'spear-thrower', 'wog' and 'wop'."[89]

Accused of overloading the welfare system, some Pacific migrants were detained and deported (sent back to their home country). Dawn raids by police on the homes of suspected overstayers began in 1974 and intensified in October 1976. Homes were forcibly entered in the early hours of the morning, doors kicked in, snarling dogs set free; children cried as a parent or sibling was marched away.

Samoan and Tongan overstayers especially were singled out, people were stopped in the street and ordered to produce paperwork or they'd be detained. Māori were also harassed, based on their skin tone. If they weren't carrying proof of identity, they were carted off too – a triple-dip of racism: harassed for the colour of their skin, not recognised as tangata whenua and ordered to prove their birth right by the very colonisers who stole their land.

Those speaking out likened these police checks to South Africa's "pass laws", this obvious racism underlined by the fact that most real overstayers were actually from Europe and North America … and were white.[90]

THE POLYNESIAN PANTHERS

On 16 June 1971, a group of young people, mainly ages 17–19, came together in Auckland, inspired by the Black Panthers, a US Black-empowerment movement. This mixed group of Polynesians – many born in Aotearoa – joined forces to challenge the racist attitudes they saw around them. Founded by a group of young men (particularly Fred Schmidt, Nooroa Teavae, Paul Dapp, Vaughan Sanft, Eddie Williams, Ta Iuli and Will 'Ilolahia)[91] the Polynesian Panther movement wanted to show the true essence of Pacific people and their culture, and to undo the damage caused by the constant harassment. They also desired empowerment for their people and were driven to show others how to stand up to unjust laws and treatment through the power of peaceful protest.[92] Other chapters were formed in South Auckland, Christchurch, Dunedin, several prisons and in Sydney, Australia.

With a membership of around 500, they shared a clear vision of what they wanted. Their motto was, "Educate to liberate."[93] They encouraged Polynesian children to make use of the education system and become capable, engaged citizens. They promoted Polynesian culture within Pacific communities, to stay connected to their roots, but also to share their culture with Pākehā – and to learn about Pākehā culture, too – believing this would lead to better understanding on both sides ("Educate to liberate" in action).

They wanted to wipe out all forms of racism in Aotearoa, protesting for equal rights – including the right to housing fit for human occupation.[94] Many Pacific migrants at that time were trapped by poor pay and unethical landlords into living in overcrowded, decaying houses, some without inside toilets, hand basins or running water.

The Panther's leader, Will 'Ilolahia, a former member of a gang of youths called the Niggs, fought hard to shake off the "gang" label and established the Polynesian Panthers as a force for good, stressing non-violent action.[95]

> "WE HAD TO SPEND A LOT OF OUR EARLY TIME PERIOD TRYING TO DISPEL THE GANG MYTH, SO WE ENDED UP DOING PROGRAMMES LIKE TAKING ELDERLY FOLKS ON BUS TRIPS AND DELIVERING COMMUNITY NEWSPAPERS [...] JUST TO KILL THE IMAGE THAT WE WERE A GANG." WILL 'ILOLAHIA'[96]

Only a few women joined, their membership was more difficult due to their strict culturally defined roles. Those who overcame this included Melani Anae, Miriama Rauhihi, Etta Gillon, and Vicki Mae. They provided a good balance to the all-male leadership, though they often ended up in the kitchen, catering for meetings and events. Dr Melani Anae went on to become a respected and powerful voice as an academic, recently writing of her experience in a book called *The Platform: The Radical Legacy of the Polynesian Panthers*, published by Bridget Williams Books.[97]

The Panthers honed their activism skills by supporting Māori at Bastion Point and Waitangi Day protests, joining forces with many other local groups, including the Tenants Aid Brigade, churches and community workers, and anti-racist groups such as Ngā Tamatoa, HART, CARE, ACORD and the Ponsonby People's Union. They roped in others to establish better social supports for the Polynesian community, held after-school homework centres with the help of CARE and local high-school teachers, started petitions, lobbied for traffic lights on dangerous intersections, fought racist and negligent landlords, ran food programmes, organised prison visits so families could see their loved ones, and supported those caught up in the random checks and dawn raids.[98]

With the help of lawyer David Lange (who would go on to be Prime Minister from 1984 to 1989), they produced Aotearoa's first legal aid booklet, which spelt out people's rights if they were stopped or arrested. They distributed these throughout the community. As the random police checks and raids grew worse, they set up the Police Investigation Group (PIG), and (along with groups like CARE and the People's Union) began following the paddy wagons as the police went about their checks, ready to record any wrongdoing or assist those stopped. They also followed police into bars and pubs, taking photographs as evidence and distributing advice.[99]

Despite the good they were doing, many older Pasifika community members and family were uncomfortable with their actions. They were used to obeying authority and were reluctant to make a fuss. Some within the community even reported others to the police as overstayers, not liking how the controversy was "ruining it for everyone".[100] But the Panthers persisted, eventually winning most people over with their pro-community, peaceful actions.

By 1976, they came up with a powerful new strategy at a time when politicians were loudly denying the brutal truth about the checks and raids. They began "dawn raids" on politicians' houses, banging on their doors, spotlights blazing, demanding to see passports, and running away as the politicians stumbled out.[101] Unsurprisingly, MPs weren't too happy about this taste of their own medicine.

Tigilau Ness, one of the original Panthers and a legendary musician, recalled the night the Panthers went to the home of National MP Bill Birch: "We were calling out on loudhailers at three o'clock in the morning — Bill Birch, come out with your passport now!"[102]

Another time, they surrounded the house of North Shore MP George Gair and turned their spotlights on. Through loud hailers they yelled for Gair to come out and show his passport. As soon as the house lights came on, they jumped in their cars and fled. The next day George Gair responded to a question about the raid from Radio Hauraki, "How dare these people come at such an ungodly hour?" The radio announcer retorted, "Well, surely that's what they're complaining about?"[103]

The Panthers' point was made and two-and-a half weeks later, the government finally backed down and the raids were stopped. It was a tremendous effort.

The Polynesian Panthers also supported Ngā Tamatoa and others in championing Māori rights and the anti-Springbok Tour campaign. They continue to work in their communities and to inspire new generations. Musicians Ladi6, Scribe and Che Fu — as well as All Blacks Ben Atiga and Benson Stanley — are just a few Pasifika achievers whose parents were involved with the movement.[104]

Some of the pivotal Polynesian Panthers today.

"THE MEMBERS OF THE PANTHERS HAVE GONE ON TO GOOD THINGS: TEACHERS, LECTURERS, MINISTERS [...] WE HAVEN'T ALL BEEN KILLED OFF AS REVOLUTIONARIES. OUR MAIN AIM WAS THEN, AND STILL IS NOW, EQUALITY AND A MORE PEACEABLE AOTEAROA. SO UNTIL THAT HAPPENS, WE WILL ALWAYS BE GOING." TIGILAU NESS[105]

STOP PRESS: at the time of printing this, the Government have indicated they will give a formal apology for the Dawn Raids in the near future.

PEOPLE NOT

THE OCCUPY MOVEMENT – "WE ARE THE 99%"

Aotearoa's Occupy movement began after the rise of the Occupy Wall Street movement in the US in 2011, which focused on social and economic inequality, greed, corruption and the unfair influence of corporations on government – particularly from the finance sector. They declared, "We are the 99%," referring to the huge income and wealth gaps between the richest 1% and the other 99% of the world population. They set up tents and occupied public spaces, talking to passers-by about fairer systems for sharing wealth and other social justice issues.

At the time, Aotearoa was listed as the second-worse country in the OECD for economic inequality; America was first. In 2011 alone, our 150 wealthiest Kiwis' income increased by seven billion dollars, while real income fell for almost everyone else.[106] While some drank champagne on the decks of their holiday homes, other Kiwis lived in real poverty (and still do).

Occupy protests began here on 15 October 2011, when over 2000 Aucklanders marched from Britomart to Aotea Square. Other occupations took place in New Plymouth, Wellington, Lower Hutt, Christchurch, Dunedin, and Invercargill – all these groups set up tents in public spaces like Dunedin's Octagon. In Auckland, the group settled in Aotea Square and at its peak 350 people camped there. Occupy Wellington began with a rally of 300 or so, although only 50 people camped in Civic Square.

The groups involved a wide range of Kiwis, including long-time activists, social justice groups, unions, students and political organisations like the Mana Party. Those participating saw their role as highlighting inequality and gathering different groups together for united action, though they had no set protest goals. Their events were generally family-friendly,

PROFIT

free of drugs or alcohol, and attractive to local homeless people, who were housed and fed.

Instead of pushing one key message, protesters invited discussion through "assemblies". Anyone could talk, and care was taken to stop the usual voices from dominating the conversation. Although democratic, this system led to criticisms that their messages were too diverse, diluting any action.

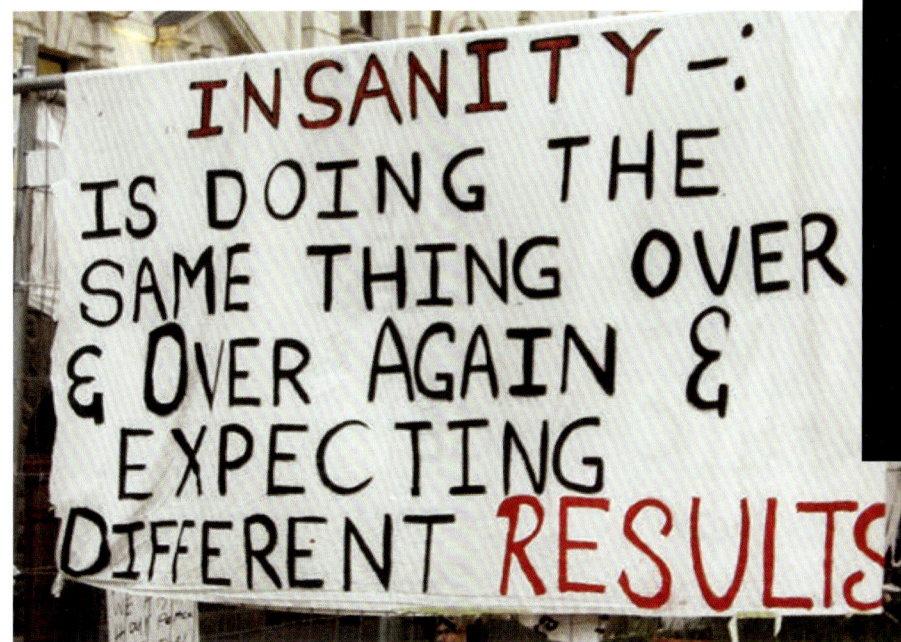

Yet on 16 October, the first political resolution was passed in Aotearoa, rejecting anti-Semitism, Islamophobia, racism, and sexism. It called for unity between the 99% to fight inequality and injustice. While this worked to unite the people involved, it had no practical effect beyond this.

The Declaration of the Occupation of Auckland[107] was announced on 3 November. It was addressed to the people of Aotearoa and listed issues that covered a range of social ills. It ended with the plea:

> "THE OLD IDEAS, THE OLD SYSTEMS, THE OLD WAYS OF THINKING HAVE SET OUR SOCIETY ON AN UNSUSTAINABLE PATH. WE NEED TO SET A NEW COURSE THAT ENSURES US AND OUR CHILDREN A FUTURE. WE ARE HERE, AND HERE WE STAY, TILL WE HAVE FINALLY ROUSED THE 99% FROM ITS LONG AND TROUBLED SLUMBER."

On 17 October, around 200 student activists occupied the clock tower of Auckland University for several hours, until the police arrived with dogs and threatened to arrest them. Although this ended peacefully, the patience of the police and council was wearing thin. In the new year, police moved in to dismantle the tents and end the occupations. Several arrests were made and there were accusations of illegal spying on the movement's leaders.

The campsite of the Occupy Auckland protest, Aotea Square, 9 December 2011.
(Photograph taken in the evening, by Connor McKee)

Despite a seeming lack of focus, the Occupy movement certainly worked to bring like-minded people together to share ideas — and it fired them up with a desire to make positive change. Most importantly, from that time forward, the notion of the 1% vs the 99% has become shorthand for the huge wealth gap between the very rich and the rest of the human population, and has brought conversations about this imbalance into the open.

"WE POLITICISED A WHOLE GENERATION OF YOUNG PEOPLE WHO DIDN'T QUITE KNOW WHAT TO DO WITH THEIR ACTIVISM AND THEIR FEELINGS OF ANGER."[108]

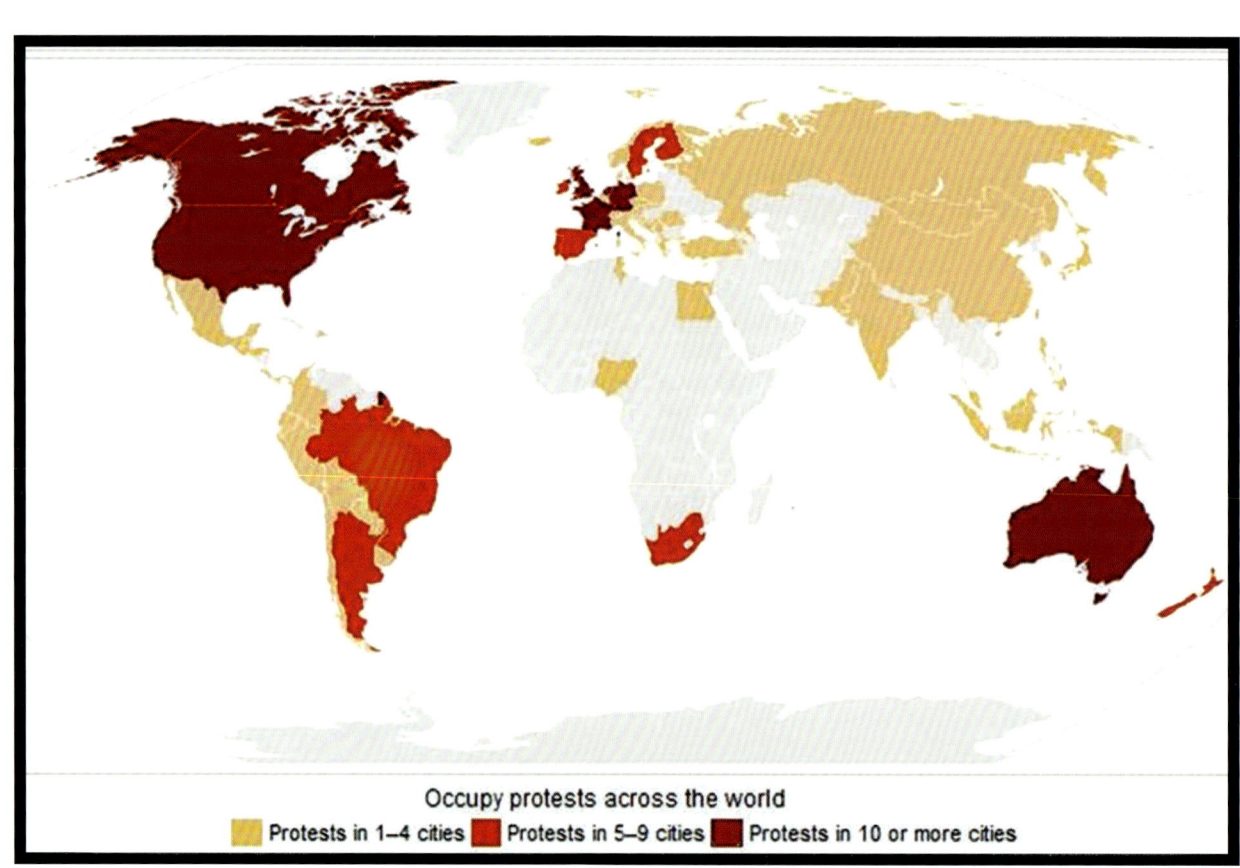

PEOPLE NOT PROFIT
– ANTI-TPP(A) PROTESTS

A round 2015, the public started hearing talk of a new trade deal that some commentators worried would favour Big Business and undermine Aotearoa's ability to make our own laws and walk our own path. Originally called the Trans-Pacific Partnership Agreement (TPPA), then shortened to the Trans-Pacific Partnership (TPP), the agreement was sold to the public as freeing up trade and investment between 12 Pacific-rim countries: Aotearoa, Australia, Brunei Darussalam, Canada, Chile, Japan, Malaysia, Mexico, Peru, Singapore, the United States and Vietnam.[109] Protests flared, drawing large and diverse crowds, from anarchists to academics.

PROTESTERS' CONCERNS

One of the most pressing concerns was the possibility our sovereignty might have been eroded. Under the agreement, overseas corporations would have the right to directly sue our government if it passed any new laws or regulations that hurt their profits. For example, if we were to ban cigarettes to protect Kiwis' health, overseas tobacco companies could sue the government for billions because this new law would affect their sales. Such lawsuits would be decided in international trade tribunals, not our own courts. Also any judgments would be binding and would overrule any decisions made by our Parliament and courts.

March and demonstration against the TPPA, Wellington, 14 November 2015.

The agreement could make environmental protection more difficult too. Similar trade agreements have challenged laws or public decisions relating to environmental protection (particularly mining, fracking, oil and gas production, regulation of toxic chemicals, waste dumping and renewable energy). This means our action on climate change could have been greatly hampered. Te Tiriti o Waitangi could also be undermined – the TPP could affect how our government honoured Te Tiriti obligations, affecting Māori tino rangatiratanga, culture, indigenous knowledge, biodiversity and opportunities for economic development.

Medicines might have become more expensive, with big overseas pharmaceutical corporations challenging the right of our state-run government agency (PHARMAC), to decide what medicines and health products are funded in Aotearoa.

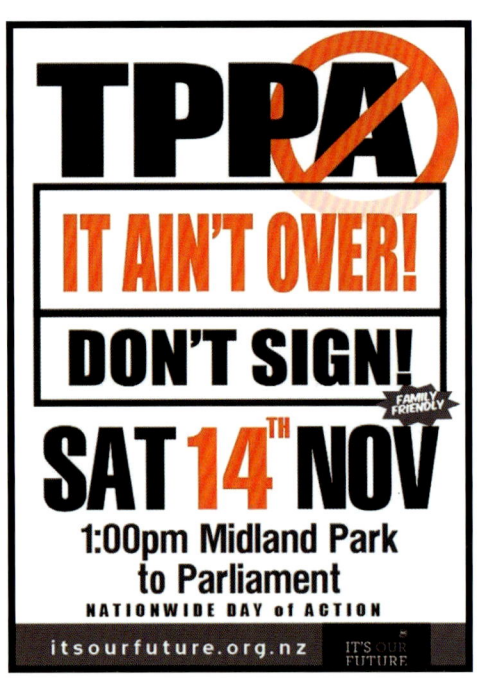

There were concerns around copyright law and the privatisation of state assets. As well, local businesses predicted a loss in competition with large multinationals, and economic analysts said that the TPP might result in 5000 fewer jobs in Aotearoa and increased inequality.

Despite all protest, our government passed the Bill, but it more or less died in 2017 when the United States withdrew from the agreement after the election of Donald Trump.[110] Yet, before protesters could even draw breath, a new version without the US, known as the Comprehensive and Progressive Trans-Pacific Partnership (CPTPP), was ratified by our government on 25 October 2018, in agreement with Australia, Brunei, Canada, Chile, Japan, Malaysia, Mexico, Peru, Singapore and Vietnam.[111] Our government claimed all the protesters' concerns had been addressed. However, University of Auckland law professor Jane Kelsey, a prominent critic of the agreement, said: "It's widely recognised that the benefits of these deals are uneven, and instead they've just been continuing with business as usual and doing it in secret."[112]

THE PROTESTS – SOME EXAMPLES

29 March 2014 – Several thousand protesters converged on downtown Auckland, one of 15 similar events held around the country, including Wellington, Hamilton, Nelson, Whangārei, Tauranga, Napier, Christchurch, Dunedin, Palmerston North, New Plymouth and Invercargill. The Auckland protest was addressed by speakers from several political parties, unions and advocacy groups. Former Green Party Leader Jeanette Fitzsimons' speech received the loudest cheers. She said the agreement was "an extremely dangerous initiative" and that, "At the heart it is a huge lie […] It's not about trade, it's about allowing foreign corporations to override the decisions of democratically elected governments […] The] specific clause in it to allow investor corporations to sue our government […] is the most anti-democratic thing that has ever happened in my lifetime."[113]

7 March 2015 – Protesters took to the streets in rallies in 22 towns and cities. More than 3000 people marched in Auckland alone, with a symbolic TPP Trojan horse pulled by "corporate" teams and an Uncle Sam who represented US interests. In Christchurch, almost 3000 people gathered in Addington before a march to Hagley Park.[114]

22 May 2015 – 1500 people marched on Dunedin's Octagon as protesters gathered in up to 23 centres, including all our largest cities.[115]

15 August 2015 – Thousands of people across the country rallied. In Wellington, an estimated 8000 protesters marched to Parliament grounds, some pushing through barricades. A thousand more protested in Christchurch's Hagley Park, with 1500 marching up Dunedin's George Street.[116] In Auckland, an estimated 5000 people joined the rally at Aotea Square then marched to the US Consulate building. They called on the government to walk away from the agreement, with placards declaring, "Don't trade our needs for corporate greed", "Enough is enough", "TPPA locks in climate change", and "Aotearoa is not for sale". Singers Tiki Taane and Moana Maniapoto performed for the crowd, with Taane covering Bob Marley's *Get Up, Stand Up*. Maniapoto told the protesters: "We are academics, jurists, lawyers, politicians, opposition parties, environmentalists, Māori leaders, ordinary people, parents, across the board who're saying we're going to stand for something."[117]

14 November 2015 – Nationwide Day of Action against the TPPA, with protests held in Kerikeri, Auckland, Hamilton, Tauranga, Rotorua, Gisborne, Palmerston North, Wellington, Christchurch, Little River (Banks Peninsula), Dunedin and Invercargill.[118]

4 February 2016 – An anti-TPP protest in Auckland saw roads blocked and protesters jumping in front of cars. The 10,000-strong crowd marched through Auckland's streets as 12 ministers from across the world met at SkyCity to sign the TPP.[119] Other protests were held around the country.

2020 – Although the movement is not currently active, concern about the current CPTPP remains, and following the election of Joe Biden as president in the US in late 2020, talk of reviving a similar trade deal with the US is back on the table.

PROTECTING THE ENVIRONMENT

DAMN THE DAM – THE "SAVE MANAPŌURI" CAMPAIGN

Manapōuri hydropower plant. Access to the engine room is through a tunnel.

On 20 October 1969, five Southlanders kick-started a decade of environmental campaigns. Invercargill Deputy Mayor Norman Jones and his wife Marjory met with sheep farmer Ron McLean, dentist Bill Bell, doctor Bill Reekie and Dipton farmer Alister McDonald to plot how they could protect the beautiful Lake Manapōuri, one of the jewels in Fiordland's National Park.[120] What were they worried about?

To understand, we need to look back to 1904, when a government engineer noted that Lake Manapōuri would be perfect for generating electricity and, therefore, smelting aluminium. The environment was viewed as an unlimited resource to plunder at the time, but even he noted that the lake was already one

PART ONE: LAKES, FORESTS, WETLANDS AND RIVERS

of Aotearoa's most loved tourist attractions. "It is not likely, for scenic reasons, that a high dam would be built at Manapōuri. The present beauty of the lake is worth preserving to the fullest extent," he said.[121] But it was too late. A seed had been planted …

In July 1956, the Electricity Department announced it could be possible to harness Manapōuri's water in an underground power station, with an underground tunnel to discharge the water into Doubtful Sound. By 1959, the Ministry of Works' Chief Engineer was speaking to Southland's business leaders. Aotearoa needed to expand the ways money could be made off the land, he said. It was time for "exporting our rainfall in some other form than meat and wool". We needed to turn one of our major resources — water — into electricity, he told them, and "farm" that electricity to make industrial materials we could sell around the world.[122] The audience eagerly embraced his vision.

What he didn't tell them was that the government already had a draft agreement with the Commonwealth Aluminium Corporation (known as Comalco) for a hydroelectric power scheme to generate electricity for a new aluminium smelter at Tīwai Point in Bluff, 160 kilometres away. This agreement, written behind closed doors with no public input, granted Comalco a 99-year water right over both Lakes Manapōuri and Te Anau — and gave permission for the company to raise the level of Lake Manapōuri by up to 30 metres, merging it with Lake Te Anau. The more water storage there was, they reasoned, the better the power station would be able to generate electricity around the clock, even in droughts. This was great news for Comalco and the local economy, but an unimaginable loss to everyone else.

While the government seemed to brush aside the destruction of such outstanding landscapes as if they didn't matter, the truth was that 33 of the lake's islands would be drowned, 22 of them covered in lush native forest. And the surrounding native forests, crowned by giant matai and rimu, would be flooded for kilometres inland. The townships of Manapōuri and Te Anau would be at greater risk of flooding, too, and Māori interests hadn't been considered.

This deal was signed in January 1960 and reported as a win for progress. The government minister in charge, Hugh Watt, described it as "the most important single step in industrial development taken in New Zealand's history".[123]

By the time construction began in 1964, public concern was skyrocketing. Word had leaked out that the proposed dam would raise Manapōuri's level by 26 metres (equivalent to a seven or eight-storey building). Angry meetings were held. Letters were written. Noisy protests involving hundreds took place. In the end, so much pressure was put on the government that they reduced the proposed rise to 8.4 metres. That was still more than three times the height of a single-storey house, enough to drown whole forests and all the creatures who lived there. Protesters feared there could be up to 7000 hectares swallowed whole.[124]

By 1969, the power station was running, and construction of the smelter was rapidly progressing. The date was announced when the lake would be raised – 1971. There were only two more years for protesters to stop the destruction of Manapōuri's "glacier-carved beauty".[125] The clock was ticking.

The Forest and Bird Protection Society and the New Zealand Scenery Preservation Society spoke out, demanding the plan be dropped. But their voices weren't enough; they needed more people power – and that's where the private meeting at Norman Jones' house in Invercargill comes in. It was vitally important.

The group at his table agreed they had to act. They called a public meeting in Invercargill and the Save Manapōuri campaign officially started that October. Those who joined were warned it'd be a hard fight – government and industry were certain to push back – but they loved the lakes and forests so much they refused to stand by and watch humanity commit such a crime against nature. These people's determination created our first modern environmental movement.[126]

"At its simplest, the issue was about whether Lake Manapōuri should be raised by as much as 30 metres. But there was much more at stake than that. There were strong economic and engineering arguments opposing lake raising, and there were also legal and democratic issues underlying the whole debate. What captured the public's imagination across the country was the prospect that a lake as beautiful as Manapōuri could be interfered with, despoiled and debased." Neville Peat, in his book *Manapōuri Saved!*[326]

Some opposed raising the lake based purely on the ecological impacts. Others grieved for the loss of the outstanding landscapes. Some were concerned that the electricity needs of an overseas corporation were given priority over Kiwi interests (indeed, even now Comalco/Rio Tinto continues to pay much less for their electricity than ordinary Kiwis).

The Save Manapōuri campaign started a petition in January 1970 and within two months they'd collected more than a quarter of a million signatures (264,907 in fact!). That was about 10% of the country's population back then. It was the largest petition ever presented to Parliament at the time, a tremendous effort.

To help collect signatures, sheep farmer Ron McLean and his college-age daughter Jill organised a road trip. They held public meetings that led to 19 further Save Manapōuri committees being set up around the country. "I put the slides into the projector and Dad did the talking," Jill recalled. "I couldn't believe how passionate and ready people were to join the campaign. They had been working in isolation, and here was a chance to be part of something national."

Sir Edmund Hillary joined the Auckland branch and many other notable Kiwis helped pressure the government. Ron McLean was named *The Dominion*'s 1970 Man of the Year.[127] That May, Forest and Bird presented the petition to Parliament. Hopes were high.

Although the government said they were ready to listen, they declared their hands were tied; they'd already signed an agreement guaranteeing supply of electricity to Comalco and that meant building the dam. A commission of inquiry found they had no option but to raise Manapōuri and Te Anau's lakes. The public felt differently.

With an election looming in 1972, protesters made sure Manapōuri was the number one talking point. After Norman Kirk pledged the Labour Party's support for the campaign, they won with ease.

Kirk fulfilled his pledge in 1973 and created an independent group called The Guardians of Lake Manapōuri, Monowai, and Te Anau to ensure the lake levels were well managed. The Guardians focused on preserving the environment and they still do this today. All six of the original Guardians were respected Save Manapōuri leaders, including Ron McLean. There was great relief; it seemed the lakes were saved ... then, suddenly, everything changed.

In 1984, the Labour Party shifted direction and announced a new policy to sell off power stations and other state assets to private companies. Many feared Manapōuri's power station would be offered to Comalco and were worried by the thought of an overseas owner who had no personal sense of responsibility for Aotearoa's environment. Save Manapōuri

Staff of the Royal Forest and Bird Protection Society display boxes of the Save Manapōuri petition, shortly before it was presented to Parliament, 1970.

was rebooted in 1991, led by the same passionate leaders and helped by a growing network of public support. They renamed the campaign Power For Our Future and opposed selling off Manapōuri Station. It was time to ensure the lakes could never be threatened again.

The government had no intention of caving in to pressure, but they hadn't reckoned on the impact of a hugely popular song that had become the unofficial protest anthem for the Save Manapōuri campaign and wormed itself into the nation's subconscious. Dam the Damn, an award-winning hit by Kiwi singer-songwriter John Hanlon, captured people's hearts, putting nature firmly at the centre of this debate.[128] Power For Our Future's campaign was so successful the government was forced to agree that the Manapōuri station would not be sold to Comalco — or anyone else. Music is a powerful form of protest — it expresses thoughts and feelings creatively, in a way that connects people to ideas and emotions. That is music's superpower.

In July 2020, Comalco (now known as Rio Tinto) announced they would close the Bluff aluminium smelter in August 2021. It's not the first time they've done this. Six years earlier, John Key's National Government gave Rio Tinto $30 million to keep operating when they threatened to close. However, in early January 2021, Meridian Energy announced that Rio Tinto accepted a new contract to keep the smelter open for another four years.[129] This temporary reprieve was welcomed by most locals, who estimate that up to 3500 Southland jobs could be lost when the smelter finally closes.[130]

There's also serious concern over the toxic waste from the smelter that's currently stored in the town of Mataura. More than 8500 tonnes of a waste product from making aluminium — ouvea premix — is stored in a building at risk of flood and fire. When wet, the waste releases ammonia gas, poisonous to humans. Rio Tinto are supposed to clean this up but there's no sign of it happening yet. Mataura business owner Lynette Webb made her feelings clear, telling Rio Tinto: "Be responsible. Don't just pack up and run, put on your big boy pants and clean up [the] mess you've left."[131]

Looking back, it's clear the Save Manapōuri and Power For Our Future campaigns achieved even more than they first set out to. Most importantly, they saved the lakes (a win for us all) and ensured Manapōuri Station remained in state ownership. But it's also been said the campaigns helped shape the thinking behind our Resource Management Act, so all new developments must be forced to consider environmental impacts. The secrecy over the government's plans for the lakes also helped the creation of the Official Information Act, which means Kiwis have the right to access information held by government departments and ministers. Maybe best of all, it changed our view of the environment, from a thing to exploit for profit until it's gone, to recognising it has immense value in its own right — and is vital to the whole planet's wellbeing and every living thing upon it.

Monument to the Save Manapōuri Campaign, in Manapōuri. (James Dignan, 2008)

DAMN THE DAM – AN ANTHEM TO NATURE

First written in 1973 as part of a campaign designed to promote compulsory insulation in new homes, Aotearoa singer-songwriter John Hanlon's song *Damn the Dam* became the anthem for the Save Manapōuri campaign. It was released commercially and reached No. 5 on the national charts. Later that year, John won a RATA award for Single of the Year. You can hear him singing it online.

Leaf falls to kiss the image of a mountain /
the early morning mist has ceased to play /
Birds dancing lightly on the branches by a fountain /
Of a waterfall which dazzles with its spray /
Tall and strong and aged, contented and serene /
The kauri tree surveys this grand domain /
For miles and miles around him, a sea of rolling green /
Tomorrow all this beauty won't remain

Damn the dam cried the fantail,
 As he flew into/
as he flew into the sky,
 To give power to the people
 All this beauty has to die

Rain falls from above and
splashes on the ground /
Goes running down the mountain to the sea /
And leaping over pebbles makes such a joyful sound /
Such as Mother Nature's meant to be /
I have grave reflection, reflection of a grave /
Trees that once lived green now dead and brown /
The homes of tiny animals and little birds as well /
For the sake of man's progression have been drowned

Damn the dam cried the fantail,
 As he flew into/
as he flew into the sky,
 To give power to the people
 All this beauty has to die

© John Hanlon. Reproduced with thanks.

THE CLYDE DAM

The Clyde Dam is Aotearoa's third largest hydroelectric dam. It was built on the Clutha River near the town of Clyde in Central Otago and construction was finished in 1992.

There was considerable controversy over the plan, as it meant flooding many houses and orchards upstream at Cromwell, as well as the scenic Cromwell Gorge, a highlight of the growing tourism industry. Part of the government's Think Big policy, the government pushed it through.

Local orchardist Kevin Jackson said in 2020, "while some considered Cromwell benefited from the new lake, that had to be measured against the loss of orchard land, the loss of the pristine river, the loss of the railway line through the gorge and the loss of much tourist potential for both Cromwell and Clyde."

THE FIGHT TO SAVE OUR FORESTS

The friction between those who think the environment is there to serve the economy and those trying to preserve it, impacts on the protests to protect our native forests too.

Over 80% of Aotearoa was forested when humans first arrived here. Now only 23% survives, most of it at high altitudes. Only scraps of native lowland forest are left; magical places, precious and unique.

Lowland forests are easier to clear and good money-spinners, with fertile soil, and they are generally found in warmer climates (which suits agriculture and managed plantations). The trouble is, these forests also support more varieties of life than forests higher up.

Losing so much lowland forest has already caused the extinction of some of Aotearoa's native birds. This makes the few lowland forests left hugely important to our native wildlife. Small patches were protected, many as scenic reserves, but most large forests disappeared long ago.[132] The efforts to protect our remaining native trees have taken decades of protest action, often led by younger Kiwis, who used their energy and passion for nature to save what we can still enjoy today.

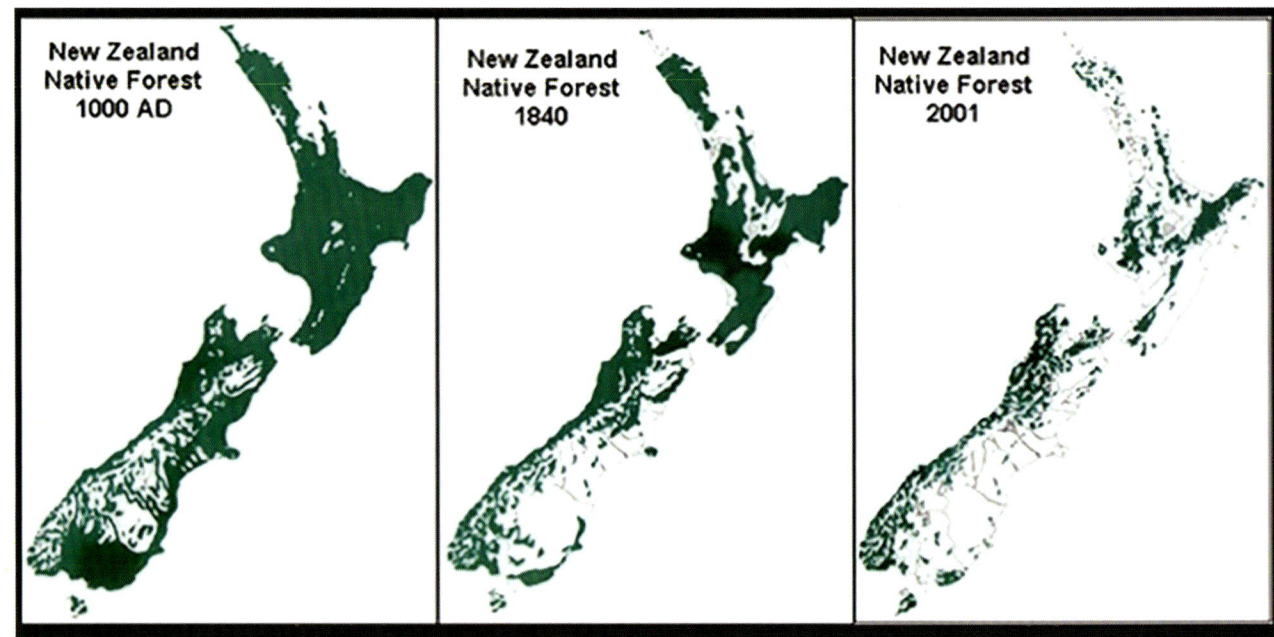

"WE WILL FIGHT THEM ON THE BEECHES"

If you've ever been in a beech forest, you'll never forget it. They're beautiful places, with not much woody undergrowth so it's easy to clamber over the snaking roots of the rough-barked beech trees. The forest floor has a deep carpet of leaf litter, a mosaic of tiny leaves, soft cushions of pale-green milk moss between the roots, set off by masses of translucent kidney fern. Filtered light makes it seem tranquil and magical, the perfect place to meet patupaiarehe or Tolkien's elves! There's a wealth of lichens, mosses and liverworts, and filmy ferns creeping across the forest floor and up trunks and branches.[133] This is why these forests are so loved, along with the precious native wildlife that lives in them. They were definitely worth saving — what we have left needs ongoing protection.

In October 1971, a government paper set out a plan for large-scale logging of the South Island's lowland beech forests to feed pulp mills that munch wood into chips. Half of the proposed block would be clear-felled (every single tree cut down) and the bare land replanted with exotic pine trees (*Pinus radiata*). Part of the remainder would be "selectively logged" (plucking the best trees out and leaving others) and planted with gum trees (Eucalypts). Selective logging was a system designed to silence the critics of clear-felling — yet it still caused long-term damage to the forest by removing the strongest trees. Many of the oldest and biggest were cut down, affecting the lives of everything around them.

In 1972, six months after the paper's release, the Forest Service launched their beech scheme. It put at risk up to 400,000 hectares of lowland forest in Nelson, Westland and Southland, with only 60,700 hectares considered worth saving. Another 173,205 hectares were pencilled to be clear-felled and replaced by pine plantations. Most of the native logs would be pulped and exported.

At the time this scheme was announced, only Forest and Bird were actively speaking out. They had around 11,000 members but they couldn't shout down the spin coming from the Forest Service, who claimed that planting pines would be the "salvation of NZ native trees."[134] This is sadly not true. These days wild pines are a pest if left to spread – invading farmland, native ecosystems and sources of water.[135]

In June 1973, 17 keen greenies, mostly university students, officially set up the Beech Forest Action Committee (BFAC) to stop the logging. Their first campaign slogan messed with the spelling from one of Winston Churchill's war speeches: "We will fight them on the beeches." A great pun but also deadly serious; they were fighting to save the trees. Tim Shadbolt (more recently Invercargill's Mayor) led the first protest in Auckland. It didn't take long before others signed up to the mission to save the beech forests. They gathered 33,000 signatures to add to a Forest and Bird petition that had collected 110,000 overall. It called for a reduction in the area to be replaced with pines.

Rush to Destruction: An Appraisal of the New Zealand Beech Forest Controversy, by Graham Searle.

The movement grew, especially among younger Kiwis, with BFAC branches forming in Auckland, Nelson, Wellington, Christchurch and Invercargill. They tapped into Save Manapōuri's supporters and signed them up, wrote dozens of media statements and articles, held meetings, organised protests, dressed up and did stunts and street theatre to grab media attention.

UK founder of Friends of the Earth, Graham Searle, visited Aotearoa in 1974 and was so upset when he saw the devastation caused by logging, he wrote an anti-logging book: *Rush to Destruction*. It criticised the Forest Service, challenging their statements that forests had multiple uses, noting that most needed logged trees. Searle argued that forests should be saved for their natural ecological value which, he said, was more important than what they could earn.[136] He spoke at public meetings and drew big audiences, matching those of the Save Manapōuri campaign. The message was spreading.

The BFAC decided a new petition was due – but it would have to be a record-breaker so the government was forced to take note. They focused on the Maruia Valley, on the west side of the Lewis Pass, where "thousands of hectares of virgin forest" were set down for "cutting and gutting".[137] It was an area so beautiful it would grab the media's attention and the public's heart.

BFAC produced the Maruia Declaration, signed on the banks of the Maruia River on 4 July 1975. It demanded legal recognition of native forests and an end to all native logging by 1978. This was circulated as a public petition and it *did* break records, with over 340,000 Kiwis signing. They submitted it to the government in 1977.[138]

It didn't change things immediately, but it built a good foundation for future action — and now, 45 years later, most of the Maruia Declaration's demands have been met. Once the petition was handed over, the BFAC transformed into the Native Forest Action Council (NFAC), broadening their focus. It would evolve into one of the most effective environmental groups in the country's history, using peaceful, direct action to make their point. Many of the leaders still dedicate their lives to conservation at the highest levels, including government. We owe them our thanks.

The Maruia Declaration, signed in the Maruia Valley on 4 July 1975, called for legal recognition of native forests and an end to their milling.

THE FIGHT FOR ŌKĀRITO

The fight for Aotearoa's forests moved from Maruia to the coastal rimu and kahikatea forests of Ōkārito in South Westland. The area is home to a precious colony of kotuku (white herons) in Ōkārito's lagoon, and by the late 1970s another 63 species of birds had been identified in the surrounding forests. This made it the richest concentration of species in Aotearoa.[139]

Despite this, the Forest Service made a deal with the West Coast's biggest sawmill to supply them with 250,000 cubic metres of rimu and miro over the following 14 years. Rather than clear-felling, they would selectively log a much wider area, including taking ancient rimu from the few patches of untouched lowland forest around the country. Conservationists argued that selective logging damaged the complex structure of the surrounding forest.

CLEAR-FELLING

Christchurch's Native Forest Action Council (NFAC) started hiring buses and taking interested people over to the Ōkārito area, into logged and threatened forest to see the devastation for themselves – a great way of activating people. A Westland National Park ranger flew NFAC members over the forests to photograph the extent of the logging and to record the beauty of the untouched trees. They were so angry by the end of the trip, they called a meeting and insisted on a big campaign to protect the threatened forests.

NFAC's Wellington partner, Action for Environment, began meeting with government ministers face to face, and set to work writing letters that highlighted the issues, forest by forest. NFAC wrote a 2000-word letter to Minister Venn Young arguing for Ōkārito to be included in the Westland National Park. One of the movement's key leaders, Guy Salmon, wrote a feature article for the *Christchurch Star* with the headline, "Ōkārito: the chainsaw threat", and a week later the newspaper's editor wrote that "a fistful of dollars is apparently of more concern to the Minister of Forests […] than the protection of the habitat of the white heron."[140] A meeting in Christchurch to support the national park proposal drew over 700 people.

Meanwhile, forest workers bulldozed a road into Ōkārito State Forest and large amounts of money were spent to equip the loggers and local industry. A $100,000 sawmill was put in at Whataroa and another half-a-million dollars was invested in work buildings and houses for the 35 workers. Already between 70 and 80 ancient trees were being cut down *every day*.

Many West Coast locals relied on logging for their livelihoods and were furious about NFAC's campaign. There was talk of "taking a shotgun to the herons", describing the precious birds as "bloody scavengers" and "bloody cannibals". Greymouth Mayor Oswald Jackson, whose goldfish had been eaten by herons, said, "They want their necks cut off […] and you can quote me." The activists, he said, were "a bunch of crackpots".[141]

NFAC held their first four-day nationwide hui in 1976 at Franz Joseph, but their hopes were knocked when Forest and Bird's President, John Jerram, announced they were supporting the Forest Service, saying, "We are content that little harm will occur by the proposal to log selectively," and boasting of Forest and Bird's excellent relationship with government ministers. He claimed they were the only responsible organisation the Crown should deal with. All Forest and Bird asked of government was one small band of forest left on the coast (for tourists) and a slightly expanded kotuku sanctuary. Minister Venn Young could now declare that the largest conservation group in Aotearoa backed the logging scheme.

NFAC were so frustrated they switched from writing submissions to street protests, to raise awareness and rally public support. Several groups made white heron costumes and paraded through the streets. In Nelson, a truck decorated with logs and native plants blasted out recordings of native bird calls, the buzz of chainsaws and the thump of axes. They drew nearly 300 people to a public meeting in Nelson, with larger events planned for Dunedin and Wellington.

But all these plans to conserve even a small part of the forest came to a crashing halt when the president of Forest and Bird again changed direction, now saying he believed only a one-mile buffer zone around the lagoon was necessary and nothing more. He effectively doomed the coastal forests. After a bitter disagreement with NFAC over tactics, NFAC's Wellington branch worked to heal the rift, and Forest and Bird who, three months after saying that selective logging in the Ōkārito region would do "little harm", finally backed the NFAC plan to include Ōkārito and Waikūkūpa in Westland National Park.

A North Island kōkako.

Together they kept up the pressure (along with many other groups) until the Forest Service finally dropped its plans to log the southern Ōkārito and Waikūkūpa regions. Instead, it shifted work to 65 hectares in northern Ōkārito and plucked ancient rimu from an area already partly logged in Saltwater State Forest. This wasn't ideal, but NFAC used it as a chance to draw breath before they took the fight to a higher level, intent on halting all native logging and nothing less.

PUREORA AND THE RISE OF THE TREE DWELLERS

Another major anti-logging protest was prompted in 1978, this time over Pureora Forest in the central North Island, between Lake Taupō and Te Kuiti. It was home to the rare blue-wattled kōkako, plus many magnificent trees, including 1000-year-old rimu, kahikatea, miro, matai and tōtara.

In the years after World War Two, 83% of the Tongariro-Taupō region's rainforest was logged,[142] small sawmills operated away from the public eye and large areas were closed to public access. NFAC members snuck into the area in a "series of daring missions [...] dodging

Te Pureora forest, South Waikato District, Waikato, NZ.

Colin Fox, aged 18, (standing) and Bernard King, 17, (sitting) protest against the clear-felling of Pureora Forest, 1978. (Morrie Peacock of 20th Century Photography studio)

roadblocks and logging gangs, then hiding and camouflaging cars on bush tracks or behind shingle piles".[143]

One NFAC member, 23-year-old Stephen King (named "Young Conservator of the Year" when he was 17) went door to door in Prime Minister Robert Muldoon's electorate to talk about the impact of logging. He and his younger brothers Sam and Bernard ran stalls showing pictures of Pureora's giant trees and other North Island forests. "I called out, 'A hundred acres cut down a day!'." Bernard King recalled. "Most people were shocked."[144]

Worried that more of these beautiful trees would be logged within months, King decided it was time to act. He hitchhiked to Pureora and discovered, behind a small unlogged strip along the roadside, a "wasteland – smashed tree stumps some eight to 10 feet in diameter, broken branches, churned earth. Flocks of kākā were screeching in protest and, from the few remaining tōtara still standing in that raped landscape, the song of the kōkako poured out like a great lament."[145]

Although around 50 of the largest tōtara had been left by the Māori logging gang, believing these trees were rangatira (noble), King came across a lone logger whose boss had sent him to fell those last trees and burn them. He also found that several hundred hectares had been clear-felled in the past five years, including a block of 1000-year-old tōtara that the Wildlife Service had tried to save for a kōkako sanctuary in 1971.

At first, King reacted by writing reports and trying to influence government policy. But he grew so frustrated by the delays and the continued logging that, in 1978, while an NFAC protest planted dozens of native seedlings across the logging road and others chained themselves to trees and logs to divert attention, King and several others secretly brought timber, provisions and ropes into the forest and climbed up into the trees, intending to camp there.

PROTECTING THE ENVIRONMENT

FRANKENFISH AND TOAD POTATOES – ANTI-GE PROTESTS

The decision over whether Aotearoa should embrace or reject genetic engineering (GE) has been hotly debated right from the start — with strong feelings stirred up on both sides. To some, GE could be the saviour of the planet's global food crisis and a wonderful opportunity to do good. To others, GE is the slippery slope towards an as-yet unknowable global disaster.

When first developed, little was known about long-term effects of GE, whether good or bad. In 1978, our government took a cautious approach and placed a 10-year moratorium (halt) on releasing any genetically modified organisms (GMOs) into our environment, even for tests. However, shortly before the ban was lifted, an Interim Assessment Group was set up to assess applications for field testing or release of GMOs. It was clear the government intended to allow it into the country. The moratorium ended in 1988 and those already concerned about GE grew fearful.

In August 1998, Jeanette Fitzsimons, then Aotearoa's Green Party Co-leader, began a national speaking tour denouncing GE. In March the following year, the party launched a petition calling for a royal commission of inquiry. The Greens believed there wasn't enough evidence to prove this biotechnology was safe for humans or the environment. Their petition, presented to Parliament in October 1999, had 92,000 signatures.[160]

The money and publicity created helped build a national campaign that attracted support from artists like Ralph Hotere, as well as conservationists and heritage researchers. Many Otago artists, writers and performers contributed to the successful campaign to save Aramoana. This was campaigning at its most creative – engaging hearts and minds. Other people around the country, who were concerned about rising electricity prices, got together in 1980 under the Campaign Power Poll banner to oppose the smelter plans too.[157] The campaign even had an international component – activists wrote to the international companies listed as possible smelter partners and advised them that, if they got involved, they would face persistent and well-organised non-violent direct action against their business interests.

Meanwhile, residents' worst fears were confirmed when they were hand-delivered letters to tell them their leases were being terminated (all the houses were built on land leased by the Otago Harbour Board, not privately owned by the occupiers). They were given the option of compensation (money) or resettlement at Long Beach.

The government, eager to keep the smelter project moving, passed the National Development Act, thinking another smelter would justify building the Clyde Dam (part of its Think Big programme at the time). Two district councils merged so they could rewrite the by-laws in a way that would be more sympathetic to industrial land use (especially regarding a smelter at Aramoana). These slippery provisions were fought by the SAC at both council and Planning Tribunal levels – and they won the case! The court directed that "all reference to industrial development at Aramoana is to be deleted".

Because the campaign was so highly visible and successful, the government couldn't risk losing votes by forcing anything through, as it had with the Clyde Dam. The tide had turned against Think Big and, to the protesters' delight, the smelter proposal disappeared without trace. The village of Aramoana was legally divided into freehold titles, allowing the residents to own the land beneath their houses.[158] Today, Aramoana saltmarsh is a reserve, recognised as an area of national significance.[159]

"WE HAVE ACHIEVED EVERYTHING WE SET OUT TO DO," A SAC SPOKESPERSON SAID, ADDING, "THE DECISION EXCEEDED OUR WILDEST DREAMS." [328]

Official flag of the Independent State of Aramoana.

into another major aluminium smelter by a consortium (partnership) of three companies: Aotearoa-based Fletcher Challenge, Australia's CSR Limited and Swiss firm Alusuisse.[154] This proposal was withdrawn after several public meetings and protests revealed how poorly it was planned, helped along by a change of government. But those who'd joined together to oppose the development were now on alert. When surveyors were spotted on the land over the summer of 1979–80, activists were ready, uniting under the banner of the Save Aramoana Campaign (SAC). They were determined to stop the smelter and protect the saltmarsh by having it named a reserve.[155]

At the time, the land sat within the Waikouaiti District Scheme and had zoning conditions the group believed were illegal. The SAC took the District Council to court and asked for a ruling on the zoning. Once the case was accepted, no work could take place on the site until a judgment was made.

Now they'd committed to this battle, the SAC took their campaign to the public, quickly followed by industry putting out press releases, keen to argue their side. On 2 April 1980, the SAC held its first public meeting at the Regent Theatre in Dunedin and around 1000 people attended. Later that month, they set up the first non-Dunedin branch of the SAC in Christchurch, and later held a hui at Ōtākou Marae, opposite Aramoana, to discuss the smelter. The consortium was invited but didn't attend, though they did visit shortly afterwards and met with worried residents and other concerned groups, including the SAC. One local resident said afterwards she and her neighbours were hit hard as they realised how serious the threat was to their homes and community. That December, the Wellington City Art Gallery hosted Aramoana: Tapu Land, an exhibition by Otago artists and others protesting against a smelter at Aramoana.[156] Word was spreading.

December 1980 brought the official announcement that Aramoana had been chosen as the site for the smelter. The plan called for the destruction of the villages of Aramoana and Te Ngaru, as well as the saltmarsh. The SAC was ready and sprang into action. The next day a march took place from Logan Park to Aramoana, where opponents held a rally. They declared the area the "Independent State of Aramoana", complete with its own flag. A border post was set up at Otafelo Point and manned for 48 hours, and every weekend until mid-February 1981. People were issued with passports and granted citizenship. A set of collector's stamps were issued, with original artwork donated by leading Kiwi artists. They raised the equivalent of nearly NZ$500,000 today.

SAVE ARAMOANA CAMPAIGN

"The beautiful Aramoana has been rescued from the smelter of Think Big and we are now putting it in the right hands. Today's decision is the last step in a story of how a community took on the government and won." Peter Dunne, Associate Minister for the Environment.[152]

Aramoana is a small coastal settlement, 27 kilometres north of Dunedin. Its name means "pathway of the sea" and the area includes marshlands (wetlands) considered to be "biologically significant", as a vital habitat for wading birds and as the most extensive (and least altered) saltmarsh in Otago. As well as providing a home to 80 species of moths, the birds commonly found in Aramoana saltmarsh include eastern bar-tailed godwits, South Island pied oystercatchers, pied stilts, spur-winged plovers, banded dotterels, white-faced herons, and various species of ducks and gulls.[153]

After the smelter opened at Tīwai Point in Bluff in 1971, Otago business interests fancied a similar project for land owned by the Otago Harbour Board at Aramoana. In 1974, they proposed that the site be turned

showing how they were undermining conservation groups and manipulating local people and media — among many other things;

- West Coast native forest logging became a defining election issue in 1999 where Labour won and National got dumped — in large part for their support for the logging of ancient native forests. After the election, Helen Clark and Pete Hodgson worked to end the logging, first stopping the massive planned expansion of beech forest logging, then the (mostly) rimu logging (known rather nicely as 'the Buller Overcut');

- 130,000 hectares of native forests (including Orikaka Forest, Charleston Forest, Hochstetter Forest, North Ōkārito and Saltwater Forests) were eventually added to Kahurangi, Westland and Paparoa National Parks and other protected reserves;

- The West Coast got a $135 million 'regional development' compensation package."

"SO EVENTUALLY WE WON. WE SAVED THOSE 42 ANCIENT FORESTS, HOME TO THREATENED SPECIES LIKE ROWI/ ŌKĀRITO BROWN KIWI, KĀKĀ AND KĀKĀRIKI. THESE FORESTS ARE ABSOLUTELY INCREDIBLE PLACES OF INTERNATIONAL SIGNIFICANCE."[327]

RIVERS AND FRESH WATER

Water is life. Without water, no living thing, human, plant, fish or animal can survive. In Aotearoa, swimming in rivers, gathering freshwater kai and drinking pure water is our way of life. Yet our freshwater is increasingly polluted by industry, and our rivers and lakes are dying. In "100% Pure" Aotearoa, 70% of our rivers are so polluted we can't swim in them. Three-quarters of our native freshwater fish are threatened with extinction and in some areas the drinking water is so polluted it's unsafe for us to drink. Our precious freshwater faces threats from industrial agriculture, big irrigation schemes and toxins.

Many environmental groups over the years have fought to protect and clean up our water and waterways, including (but not only) Greenpeace, Choose Clean Water NZ, Action Station Aotearoa, Bung the Bore, the Green Party, the Environmental Defence Society, Save the Waitaki, Extinction Rebellion, Fish and Game, Waiau Rivercare Group, the Land and Water Forum, Federated Mountain Clubs, Aotearoa Water Action, Forest and Bird, Water New Zealand, the Public Health Association, Recreation Aotearoa, Whitewater NZ, Kāhui Wai Māori, Freshwater Leaders Group, plus many local iwi and community groups, and freshwater scientists, such as Dr Mike Joy.

For a good overview, go to the National Library's webpage on Freshwater Issues in NZ.

"In the forest we had food rations for a few weeks, friends in a kombi van far out at the road-end that we would contact a few times a day and others at a 'media base': a ramshackle local bach. From here we got the message out to the world.

"We were pretty naive. We thought that based on the fact that Stephen King and friends had saved Pureora Forest in 1979 from destruction after a three-day tōtara treetop occupation, that the Jim Bolger/Winston Peters (National/NZ First) Government of the day would have stopped the West Coast rimu logging within three weeks max [...] No such luck! In the following five to six years, our bid to save those forests became an arm wrestle of national proportions. All sorts of people were involved in large and little ways across the country.

"A coalition of the Buller Conservation Group, Forest and Bird, ECO and Native Forest Action campaigned hard. A funky Native Forest Action office was set up in Nelson which ran on love and donations from people who cared. In Wellington the poor little fax machine I was given got a thrashing (you didn't email media releases back then; you'd fax them to reporters one at a time!).

"Over years, the core group of activists from around the country had wonderful planning meetings sitting around campfires in the Pelorus bush and elsewhere planning for our next flurry of activities. The main cities came alive with creative campaign posters that often changed and were pasted up in the middle [of the] night (we were pretty messy by the time we got home).

"We didn't realise some of us would risk arrest and life (in one case), be pitted against a vicious well-funded (by the taxpayer) dirty tricks anti-environmental PR campaign, and a determined new Prime Minister Jenny Shipley who wanted the logging to go ahead.

There were many twists:

- Sticks of dynamite were planted on a logging helicopter and blamed on Native Forest Action;
- Somebody leaked Timberlands' beech forest logging plans to Nicky Hager, then to Forest and Bird, ECO, Jeanette Fitzsimons of the Green Party and Helen Clark, Labour Party Leader (Leader of the Opposition at the time);
- A judicial review of the West Coast Accord was carried out;
- Nicky's book *Secrets and Lies (The Anatomy of an Anti-Environmental PR Campaign)* helped turn the 1999 election into chaos and forced political parties to declare their positions on the logging. This book was based on the biggest leak at the time (even internationally) of a sleazy global public relations company's internal documents

Accord also came into being in 1991, designed to put an end to years of hostility between conservationists and foresters.[150] But it didn't please everyone.

In 1997, dissatisfied members of NFAC split to form Native Forest Action (NFA), holding firmly to their aim to stop *all* logging in publicly owned native forests on the West Coast. Many were current or recent students in their early 20s, with a core group of 21 members. They were ready to take on Timberlands West Coast, a state-owned company that was preparing to expand their logging operations at that time. They'd already logged an extra 50,000 rimu trees — which had been protected under the West Coast Accord, until a new National Government in 1991 broke the agreement. In preparation for this protest, the NFA spent six months of careful planning, doing courses on tree-climbing, media training, legal rights, bushcraft, map-reading and the use of two-way radios. (No mobile phones in those days!)

On the night of 8 February, they crept into Charleston State Forest, tramping in the dark, in silence. The famous West Coast rain was so bad it was too dangerous to climb the trees that night, so they set up a secret camp nearby.[151]

One of team, Dean Baigent-Mercer, tells what happened in his own words: "Around 20 of us had sneaked into Charleston Forest under dark and drizzle, to the call of great spotted kiwi [...] A few navigated by compass and maps, the rest of us had no idea where we were, whether we'd get lost, be attacked, fall down a bank or be successful. It wasn't glamorous. It got the heart racing and was bloody wet. It was the beginning of something that changed everyone who was involved.

"We were hidden and had pitched tents across uncomfortable roots on a steep slope [...] The other side of the ridge was where Timberlands' loggers had been felling centuries-old rimu and kahikatea the week before, on a downhill slope to Madman's Creek (yes, its real name!).

"The next day some of the keener activists scrambled over the treacherous broken forest to standing trees. Here they tied white ribbons around the impressive rimu trunks and stapled notices warning that the forest was occupied and chopping down trees could endanger people's lives. The forest stunk of rimu sap bleeding from ancient stumps and logs.

"As the loggers drove up to go to work they were greeted by some friendly Native Forest Action crew who gave them boxes of chocolates and explained our issue wasn't with them personally but with the government — and that they wouldn't be logging today.

FOREST OCCUPIED
Trees tied with white ribbons mark some of the areas of forest being occupied by people who believe these native forests should not be logged. Any logging in this area, as well as destroying the forest, would put people's safety at risk.

When loggers returned from their Christmas break on January 18, they found King and 13 other protesters camping out in the treetops. The loggers demanded they leave. A police squad arrived, and loggers began marking trees with spray-paint as a warning. The protesters refused to come down. By then, they were making headlines in all the major newspapers: "Forest protesters face death as logging commences." Worried by possible injuries or worse, the district ranger in charge of the logging called a halt.[146]

By this time, they had the support of local Māori too, although their livelihoods were at risk. Kaumātua Pakira Tutaki sent a telegram to politicians saying: "Too much of our heritage has been lost [...] my people do not want to cut any more native trees at Pureora."[147] Their support was the final push that was needed. The Crown halted all logging and established Pureora Forest Park shortly after, a real victory on behalf of us all.

King, Shirley Guildford and others approached the Forest Service with a further request, and were allowed to replant a small piece of failing pine plantation at Pureora with native trees. Seeds from giant tōtara, kahikatea and matai were collected and nurtured in a special nursery, and 3000 native seedlings were planted amid the pines. One section of restored forest is named the "Shirley Guildford Grove" in memory of her efforts.[148] This group formed the Native Forest Restoration Trust and they continue to replant native forests and surrounding scrubland.

Two treetop protesters. (John McCombe)

NATIVE FOREST ACTION AND THE TIMBERLANDS DISPUTE

Although the protests to protect West Coast beech forests had made some progress, battles continued over the logging of rimu forests. Some were saved, such as Whirinaki in 1985, but others were cleared and replaced with pine.[149] In 1986, the government drew up the West Coast Forest Accord and convinced several environmental groups to sign it. It stated that 180,000 hectares of native forest would be preserved, while 120,000 hectares would be logged. More radical protesters, including members of NFAC, rejected the Accord, saying it was too generous to logging interests. They continued to pressure government to protect the forests and stop the logging — with some significant successes.

In February 1989, the Labour Government announced it would protect 311,000 hectares between Fox Glacier and Jackson Bay, to form part of Aotearoa's biggest reserve — 2.6 million hectares in total. This land was named by UNESCO as Te Wāhipounamu South West New Zealand World Heritage Area on 1 January 1991 — a wonderful achievement. The Forest

PART TWO: GE, MINING AND OCEANS

After the election, seven new Green MPs put pressure on the newly elected Labour Government for the royal commission and another moratorium on any GMO releases. This was agreed on 1 December 1999, and in March 2000, the Environment Minister took charge of the inquiry and an elective moratorium was put in place, halting the release and field testing of GMOs until 2003. Experts, "interested parties" and 10,904 private individuals made submissions. Māori held 28 regional workshops, ten regional hui and one national hui to gauge feelings across iwi.

When the inquiry weighed the evidence, they declared that Aotearoa should proceed down the GE path with caution, while still "preserving opportunities" for future use. In late August 2001, the Auckland GE-Free Coalition organised a rally up Queen Street with 10,000 protesters, timed to pressure the government as they mulled over their response to the commission's report.[161]

At the same time, 3000 Kiwis pledged they'd help remove GE field trials in a campaign run by the group Green Gloves. At a rally in an Auckland park, they demonstrated how to destroy GE crops in an "environmentally responsible" way.

Green Gloves spokesperson Logan Petley said that the government had betrayed the majority of Kiwis who didn't want GE field trials or preparation for commercial GE releases:

"They sold out to the GE lobby. That leaves the public no option but civil disobedience to protect our country from GE accidents and contamination [...] This is an astonishing number of New Zealanders prepared to make a stand. It shows how wrong Helen Clark is when she denies there is strong public feeling about genetic engineering [...] Each of those 3000 people represents many other people who also care deeply about the issue. Some New Zealanders might think these plans are irresponsible, however we believe we are acting to defend our country. If the first boat load of possums were arriving in New Zealand tomorrow, and we could still stop them, we would do the same. Keeping the

New Zealand environment GE free, before something goes horribly wrong, is a socially and environmentally responsible act."[162]

Two significant marches took the form of GE-free hīkois, with protesters travelling from Northland to Wellington. The first took place in October 2001, with over 200 people arriving at Parliament on 1 November. They were fired up over GE tamarillo trials by the state-run HortResearch in Kerikeri – and it didn't help that the moratorium on GE applications was lifted the day before their hīkoi reached Wellington. Protesters called for the resignation of Māori MPs, furious they'd failed to stop the government allowing such field tests. Later that day, 15 protesters from the Tino Rangatiratanga movement conducted a "sit in" at the offices of the Environmental Risk Management Authority (ERMA) and refused to leave.

In a speech Janette Fitzsimons gave at the Greens' conference in 2002, she reminded them: "What is it about GE? Once organisms are released into the environment they cannot be recalled; our GE-free marketing status is lost; the organics industry is doomed."[163]

Prior to the 2002 general election, my brother Nicky launched a book called *Seeds of Distrust*. It highlighted possible GMO contamination of imported corn seed and claimed that the government had covered up the planting of GE corn.[164] The book said thousands of GE sweetcorn plants had been grown in Gisborne, Hawke's Bay and Marlborough via a contaminated batch of seeds imported from the United States.

During the election campaign the book caused friction between Labour and the Greens, referred to as "Corngate" in the media. Prime Minister Helen Clark attacked the Greens, accusing them of gutter politics although they'd played no part, and she snarled at a journalist on live TV that he was a

"sanctimonious little creep ".[165] The facts in the book proved largely accurate, according to the Environment Ministry's Chief Executive, although he disagreed with the conclusion that the government had "botched" its testing of the seeds.[166] Shortly after, another GE seed controversy came to light, with similar levels of contamination. This time the government ordered all the crops to be ripped out. Under the gaze of a suspicious public, they couldn't back down.

On 12 October 2003, 35,000–40,000 protesters marched in Auckland, Wellington, Christchurch, New Plymouth and Timaru against lifting the moratorium.[167] Some 9000 protesters marched through central Auckland in a last-ditch effort to convince the government to keep it in place. The protesters, including Mothers Against Genetic Engineering (MAdGE), accused PM Helen Clark of ignoring the fears and voices of a huge section of the population. There were shouts of "We want to be GE free!" and placards that read "What part of 'no one wants it' don't you understand?" and "Don't cell us out". Nearby, a group of pro-GE supporters carried banners arguing: "You see hurting, I see helping" and "It's my body I'll eat GE if I want to."[168]

In 2004, a Greenpeace activist dressed as Ronald McDonald walked into McDonald's on Queen Street in Auckland and handed over his "resignation" in protest against their use of chicken fed with GE soy meal. He urged McDonald's customers to send messages demanding that they stop using it and commit to using only non-GE poultry, eggs and ingredients. Greenpeace claimed the imported soy feed was the biggest source of GE contamination in Aotearoa's food chain. Ronald McDonald was accompanied by a flock of protesters dressed as chickens, with bibs that bore the message "Say NO to McGE — GE fed chicken". They handed out mock Happy Meal packs with crayons, stickers and colour-in postcards, and urged customers to write to McDonald's demanding they shift to non-GE feed.[169] The stunt did its job, gaining media attention, and a McDonald's spokesman responded saying the company was "aware of concerns" over the use of GE animal feed and had asked its suppliers to identify sources of non-GE soy.[170]

GREEN GLOVES PLEDGE OF NON-VIOLENT DIRECT ACTION TO KEEP AOTEAROA NEW ZEALAND FREE OF GENETICALLY ENGINEERED LIFEFORMS

- Because it is my right to live in a world free of genetic experiments,

- and because it is my duty to protect life on this planet from violation of its genetic heritage created over millions of years,

- and because it is a matter of survival for this and future generations that we protect the integrity of the ecosystems we live in,

- and because ...

I,_____
therefore pledge

- to take non-violent but direct action to prevent the irreversible release of genetically engineered lifeforms into the New Zealand environment whether
this is deemed illegal or not,

- and to take all possible steps to avoid the use of genetically engineered foods and products.

Signed:

Date:

(Source: https://www.scoop.co.nz/stories/PO0110/S00186/green-gloves-direct-action-pledge.htm)

By the 2008 election, GE was no longer a key issue. Labour had defused it by quickly passing regulations that required all proposed releases of GMOs to detail exactly how they intended to keep them separate from other plants and animals, as well as how they planned to trace them. Communities and regions changed tack, shifting the fight closer to home. They focused on creating GE-free zones as a local way to manage the risk. Many regional and district councils considered this, but only the Whangārei District Council area, Auckland and Hastings regions officially declared themselves GE-free. A GE-Free Register was created, which now lists 5693 properties covering a total of 145,712 hectares.

As of 2004, no GE food has been grown in Aotearoa, and no medicines containing live GMOs have been approved for use. However, medicines manufactured using GMOs that do not contain live organisms have been approved for sale and imported foods with GE components are sold. Food Standards Australia New Zealand (FSANZ) must approve any food made from GE crops or using GE enzymes before it can be sold in Aotearoa or Australia. Meanwhile, arguments continue over safety and those concerned are advised to read the labels on everything they buy.

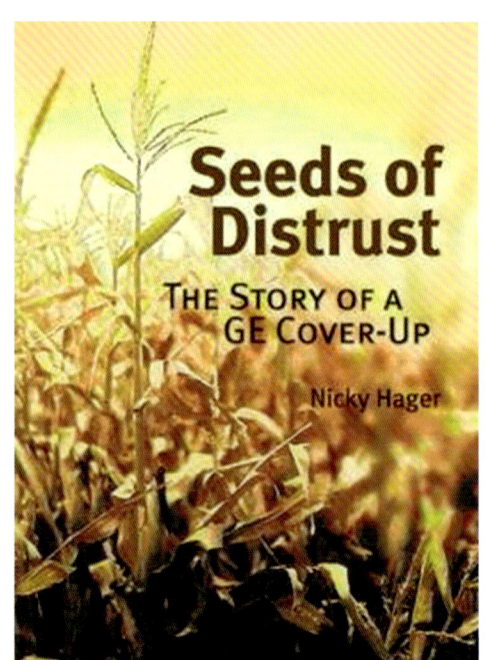

RISKS VERSUS BENEFITS

GE, also called genetic modification (GM), is the science of adding new DNA in an existing living organism or altering its existing DNA. This allows the organism to be given new traits that can protect or improve it in some way – or disable those genes not wanted. Uses for GE include crop enhancement (making crops resistant to diseases and drought, producing greater yields), medicinal uses, and livestock improvements.

In fact, humans have bred plants and animals for these same reasons since agriculture began. The difference is, GE fundamentally changes the host plant or animal in a way not possible before. Some successful attempts have led to increased protein in white corn (the most common food eaten in tropical Africa), allergy-free milk and a new breed of salmon that grows to twice the size in half the time.[171] But many worry the potential risks far outweigh the benefits, including long-term impacts we're yet to fully understand.

The following risks are already known:

- Accidental transfer of the selected gene into other species, with unknown consequences.
- Unbalancing ecosystems (what benefits one organism may harm another).
- GE seeds are often so expensive many farmers and growers in developing countries can't afford to buy them — and commercial seeds often produce infertile crops (on purpose), so seeds can't be saved for future use. This locks people into poverty and debt.
- We still don't know if GE could be harmful in the long term — though toxins from the crops have been detected in human blood.
- Possible allergic reactions.
- Pollen produced by the plants could be toxic and harm insects like bees that transfer between plants (and without bees the whole ecosystem collapses).[172]

Many who oppose GE also believe it's not moral or ethical to interfere with nature in this way.

Asa Budnick, a biology student from the US, expresses her continued concern about GE like this:

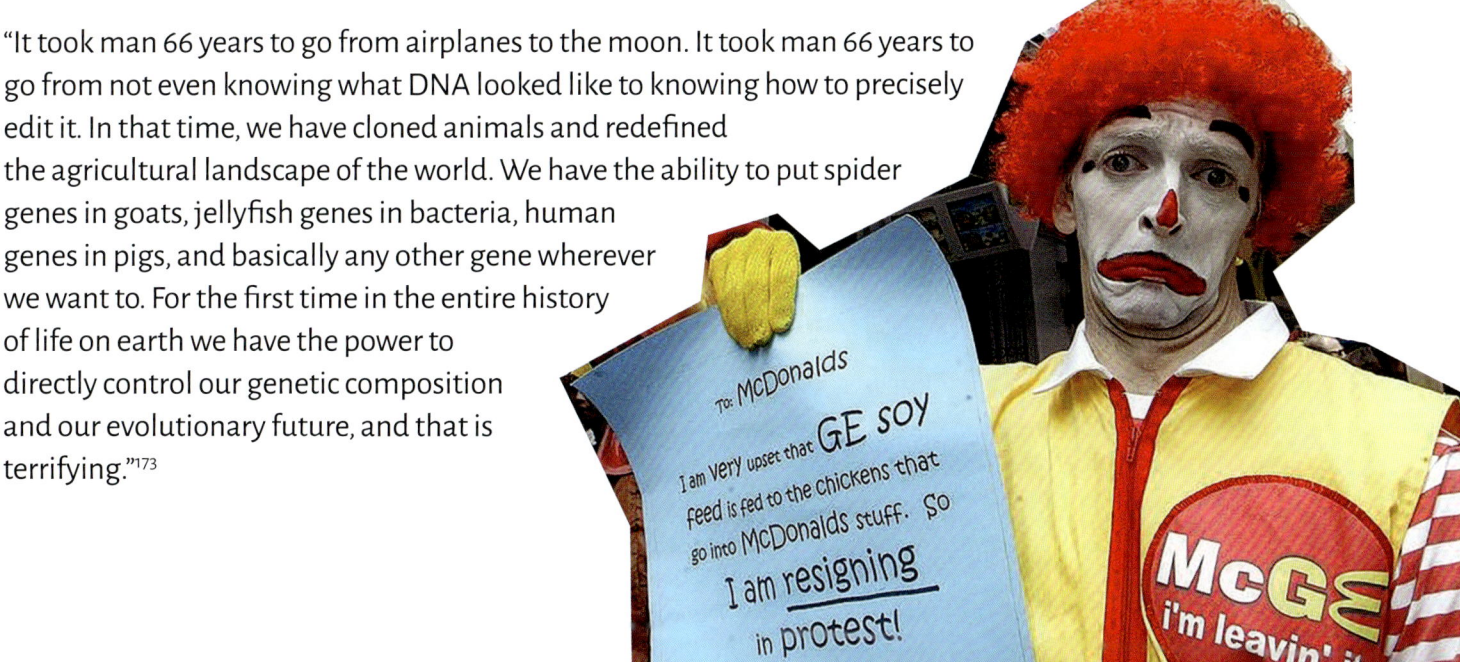

"It took man 66 years to go from airplanes to the moon. It took man 66 years to go from not even knowing what DNA looked like to knowing how to precisely edit it. In that time, we have cloned animals and redefined the agricultural landscape of the world. We have the ability to put spider genes in goats, jellyfish genes in bacteria, human genes in pigs, and basically any other gene wherever we want to. For the first time in the entire history of life on earth we have the power to directly control our genetic composition and our evolutionary future, and that is terrifying."[173]

The Martha Mine at Waihī, 1991. (Chris Jenkins)

MINING – DIGGING IN TO PROTECT OUR LAND AND OCEANS

Mining has been part of Aotearoa's history since Europeans first landed here, from the gold rush in Otago in 1861, to high-tech deep-sea drilling for oil and gas off our coasts. The same questions arise regarding mining as for every other environmental debate: What do we value most? A healthy profit or a healthy planet? Is it possible to balance both sustainably?

Whether gold, coal, other minerals, or oil and gas, those opposing the mining of these resources worry about damage to the environment and native habitats, and how the removal and continued use of fossil-fuels will impact the climate. As with other environmental issues, there's a clash between the people needing the work and those trying to shut it down. It's never straightforward; lives are affected either way.

Let's explore a range of examples across the mining spectrum and why campaigns emerged against them. Keep in mind, they're only a sample of dozens of anti-mining protests Kiwis have been involved in. They continue today and the onset of climate change makes the ongoing mining, particulary of fossil fuels, more unsustainable every day.

GOLD RUSH! MINING FOR SHINY TREASURE

When gold was first discovered in Otago, on the South Island's West Coast and the Coromandel district, it led to gold rushes throughout the 1860s and it wasn't long before surface deposits dried up. By the 1870s, larger scale gold mining was developed to reach the less accessible deposits. Even then, gold output peaked about 1905 and gradually declined.[174]

The opencast mining of today is very different. A large pit is formed by removing all surface rocks to reach the gold-bearing rocks below. In the 1990s and 2000s, large opencast pits were dug at Martha Hill in Waihī in the Coromandel and Macraes Flat in Otago. These two sites account for nearly all our recent gold production. The rock is blasted and loaded onto dump trucks that haul it to processing plants.

At Macraes Flat, trucks capable of carrying over 190 tonnes are filled by a 350-tonne excavator in around 140 seconds.[175] The destruction of the environment and the associated pollution is an ongoing issue for those who oppose these mines.

From the 1880s to 1952 Martha Mine was solely underground. In its early days it was one of the world's most important sources of gold.[176] The modern Martha Mine was converted to an opencast pit mine in 1987 and connected to a series of three underground mines in 2004, all accessed by the same entrance, the Favona portal. These mines (Favona, Trio and Correnso) run under much of Waihī township. They produce approximately 100,000 ounces of gold each year. Total earnings for the first half of 2020 were $234 million, with profits going to shareholders around the globe.[177]

In 2001, a sinkhole suddenly appeared, swallowing a house, a van and two cars. It was found to be caused by voids created by the old underground mine (pre-1952) and warnings were given that there could be more unexpected ground collapses. A 2002 report assessed 174 Waihī properties as at either high, medium or low risk for further subsidence, and 64 properties were red-flagged. Their owners had to walk away – it wasn't safe to stay.

In August 2017, another 20-metre-wide sinkhole appeared, found after the power went out in several nearby pensioner flats. Council staff visited the residents and assured them they were safe[178] and the mine operator filled in the hole.

Given scares like this, it is not surprising that Coromandel locals have been protesting against Martha Mine and others nearby for years, particularly in the 1980s and 1990s. They weren't only worried about the environmental impacts, but also concerned for their own long-term health and safety.

In the early 1980s, a flurry of prospecting licences were approved. Most of the Coromandel Peninsula was pegged out and at risk of being mined if gold was found. Local communities and environmental groups fought courageously, trying to defeat all the applications or get stricter conditions imposed by the Planning Tribunal. When news got out that drilling rigs were heading their way, one-way bridges were blocked by protesters. The public could pass but the drilling rigs were barred … until the police arrived. Large numbers of protesters tramped into remote locations and passively stood in the way of rig operators to delay their work. Sometimes they'd stall the work for days until being moved on by the police.[179] But this kind of effort wasn't sustainable and it was taking its toll. What they really needed was a law change. Trouble was, by then, Bolger's National Government was in power and was unlikely to support any change.[180]

Denis Tegg, from Coromandel Watchdog, drafted a Private Member's Bill that prohibited any prospecting and mining on all conservation land on the Coromandel Peninsula north of Te Aroha. The Bill was introduced to Parliament in June 1995 and referred to a select committee after a huge effort by Watchdog supporters. Around 1000 individually written letters were sent to key MPs and ministers, with one minister saying it was the largest letter-writing campaign he'd ever seen. Hearings were held in Wellington, Auckland, and Thames, with several hundred people speaking to their submissions. The Thames-Coromandel District Council strongly supported the Bill.

To block the Bill, the National Government decided to introduce a Bill of its own, called the Amendment to the Crown Minerals Act. It included a clause that would severely restrict prospecting or mining north of the road between Kopu and Hikuai, which was a good start, but not ideal — south of the Kopu-Hikuai Road lie landscapes of great natural beauty as well, with special conservation values that equally deserved protection. But by then the Watchdog supporters were so exhausted they had to accept it was the best they'd achieve at that time, if bitterly disappointing.[181] The amendment passed into law in 1997.

Martha Mine compared to the size of Eden Park, Auckland.

However, in 1998 locals were pleased when the Thames-Coromandel District Council banned mining in coastal and conservation zones, as well as all recreation areas and open spaces. The mining industry and the government's own Ministry of Economic Development worked against them, advising ministers that mining should be classified as a "discretionary" (optional) activity on all state-owned coastal and conservation land. This would mean companies were able to apply for resource consent to mine there, which would be devastating news for the community. In May 2004, the District Council decided to fight this in the Environment Court. Various anti-mining groups supported the council and thought there was little chance they'd lose. Right at the very last minute the council changed its mind and told the hearing it wanted to reclassify only "underground" mining as "discretionary" in all parts of the district. This meant underground mining could begin again with a resource consent, though any new opencast pit mining would remain prohibited.

Environmentalists fired back, saying the only difference between underground and surface mining was its outward appearance. All the other effects of mining remained – the dust, vibration, noise and acid mine drainage. They said that resuming mining would "introduce a new era of toxic pollution".[182] To add to their woes, the District Council's 1998 decision to ban mining in protected areas was overturned by the High Court in 2005. The situation looked grim ... but they didn't give up.

In 2007, Coromandel Watchdog won an important legal battle to protect conservation and coastal land in the Thames-Coromandel District. The Court of Appeal upheld their appeal against both the Environment and High Court decisions, which allowed the District Council to legally prohibit mining on conservation land (which is up to 70% of the Coromandel Peninsula) and around the district's coastal areas. Mining companies could no longer apply for consent to mine those zones.[183]

While the Coromandel district was having some success at limiting mining, in 2010 the National Government announced plans to open 7058 hectares of protected conservation land and marine reserve for mining, while protecting a further 12,400 hectares. It said the value of resources underground could be $140 billion.[184] In response, on 1 May, an estimated 50,000 marchers joined one of the biggest protests in Auckland for decades. They told the government to stay away from mining on conservation land. Greenpeace claimed more than 50% of the country didn't want to see it mined. This many protesters have real power to sway politicians – and the government eventually backed down.[185]

By December 2012, the land under Waihī was again under threat. Plans to extend the gold mine were given the green light, with new tunnelling proposed right under the town. It was said this move could keep the mine operating for another 10 years, which would be good for local jobs. Plans included stabilising the wall of the open pit to allow access to the bottom of the mine and extending the mine by burrowing under more private homes.[186] Over 100 protesters gathered outside Newmont Waihī Gold's office to voice their distress.

September 2014 dealt yet another blow, when the Department of Conservation (DOC) granted consent to New Talisman Gold Mines to carry out underground drilling and blasting trials in an area that lay roughly halfway between Waihī and Paeroa. Their permit allowed them to extract up to 600 tonnes of ore per month. New Talisman's Chief Executive denied the sampling would cause any harm to the Karangahake Gorge, a scenic treasure within this area. He said existing tunnels meant little work was required compared to building a new underground mine.

Locals weren't convinced. Around 100 people packed the Paeroa War Memorial Hall to learn more about the operation, preparing to fight. It's little wonder – the Karangahake Gorge is listed as one of our top 14 tourist attractions by Tourism New Zealand. A protest the next day drew 200 residents and campaigners, angry they weren't publicly consulted before the permit was issued. Local group Protect Karangahake was formed and is still fighting to stop mining activity there today.[187]

In May 2019, OceanaGold (who now run the mines at Waihī) applied to purchase 178

hectares of farmland just outside the town to create a new tailings reservoir to store the mine's waste. Land Information Minister Eugenie Sage blocked the application, saying that converting good farmland into a dam and reservoir to store hazardous mining waste long term had "no noticeable benefit" for Aotearoa or a sustainable economy.[188] That October, OceanaGold made a new application to buy the same land, and Ministers Grant Robertson and David Parker announced that the application had been approved, though Sage stood by her ruling.[189] Coromandel Watchdog sought a judicial review of Ministers Robertson and Parker's actions but the High Court refused their application. This fight, too, goes on.

SAVE HAPPY VALLEY COALITION – FIGHTING AN "UNFORTUNATE EXPERIMENT"

Happy Valley, in the Upper Waimangaroa, near Westport, was once a striking natural landscape, home to 30 roroa (great spotted kiwi), a rare species of snail, and 11 other endangered birds and animals. It was originally a colourful patchwork of stunning red tussock wetlands and lush mountain beech forests, with mossy mats of undergrowth sprawling over dramatic sandstone rocks and bluffs.[190]

Though tiny and elusive, Aotearoa's Powelliphanta augusta snail became the symbol for an energetic campaign to stop this beautiful area and the mountain near it, Mount Augustus, from being mined for coal. Named after its original habitat on the mountain (a cloudy spine of rock above the sea), this snail species is ancient. Yet it has only been known of since 1996, when botanists from Nelson were roaming the Stockton plateau and stumbled across six large shells, each swirled in a distinctive koru-like pattern. The botanists were surprised to find evidence of snails that high up the mountain. It didn't make sense.

Artist Unknown

While most snails prefer damp soil and mild weather, with lots of foliage to eat, the Stockton plateau is the opposite: a kilometre above sea level, in the clouds, with little sun and swept by raking winds. Recording about six metres of rainfall per year, it's one of the wettest places in Aotearoa and the sparse topsoil is extremely acidic.[191]

At first, these six improbable shells were wrongly identified as another species of our giant, carnivorous snail family, Powelliphanta patrickensis, a species with a relatively large habitat, including Happy Valley and other areas. The shells were put away and forgotten until the protests over Happy Valley began.

THE DISRUPTION STARTS

In 2004, state-owned company Solid Energy applied for resource consent to develop a new opencast coal mine on the eastern border of Stockton Mine, to be called the Cypress Mine. The land they intended to use included the site where the shells had been found. When both the Buller District Council and the West Coast Regional Council granted Solid Energy the consent, environmental groups rallied, ready to fight.

Solid Energy also ran Stockton Mine, the country's largest opencast mine, hollowing out mountains and extracting 1.041 million tonnes of coal in 2019.[192] They export 95% of Stockton coal produced, though its carbon emissions still affect us all. By the early-2000s, the local river was so polluted with fine coal waste and dust that its water ran black and poor acid drainage poisoned the river and stained the native bush a sickly yellow.[193] Although Solid Energy was made to clean up its mess at great expense, activists feared the company had little genuine interest in the environment.

The Buller Conservation Group, Forest and Bird, Te Rūnanga O Ngāti Waewae, and even the government's own Conservation Department appealed the Cypress Mine decision in the Environment Court. Their efforts failed and the mine was approved in 2005. Forest and Bird then appealed the decision in the High Court … but the court dismissed it. Solid Energy promised to preserve the environment as much as they could, later suggesting they "roll up" the snails' wetland habitat, storing it for several years, and then rolling it back out. In the areas where they eventually attempted this, the habitat did not thrive.[194]

A NEW SPECIES ENTIRELY

During the process of working through permits and appeals, DOC's snail expert Kath Walker realised the shells she'd seen in 1996 were not the species she'd first thought. They belonged to a new species entirely, an exciting discovery. She tracked down the botanists who'd handed them in and was told the precise location. But when she hiked up to the site on Mount Augustus in early 2005, all she found was a gaping hole in the ground. The only known habitat of this new species had been chewed up and spat out by the mining company. She realised, however, there was one tiny glimmer of hope: the long ridge marked the border between the mine and conservation land beyond. And the border, as drawn on the mine licence, meant a small peak that was part of the ridgeline technically sat within conservation land. To her delight,

Walker found a population of these unique snails there and correctly guessed there must be others within the mine site. She estimated these were the last 2–5% of their original population and found that the snails were contained within roughly five hectares, nearly all inside the mine's boundaries, in an area due to be dug up.[195]

THE CAMPAIGN TAKES SHAPE

A group of keen students who'd formed the Save Happy Valley Coalition (SHVC) to stop the coal being dug from the ground were joined by more seasoned campaigners like Jeanette Fitzsimons, Jo McVeagh and Simon Oosterman.

Together they took a speaking tour on the road to gather support. They organised public meetings to raise awareness and spoke about acid mine drainage, the loss of roroa/kiwi and tussock habitat, and stressed how digging up Happy Valley's coal would add millions of tonnes of CO to the atmosphere and why that was completely unacceptable, especially from a company essentially owned by taxpayers.[196] At this stage, the snails weren't part of their campaign, this would come later.

They organised postcard and letter writing, lobbied the people wielding power, and even occupied the head office of Solid Energy after scaling a four-storey building. They blockaded Solid Energy's coal trains, with one group tying themselves to the track to stop a shipment of coal to Lyttelton.[197] Others dug up the lawn at Solid Energy's Christchurch headquarters. All these antics were designed to amplify their message and capture the public's attention. At the mine company's annual conference, protesters dressed as Santa Claus invaded the stage with bags of coal. One of them lobbed a pie at the chief executive, nearly hitting him. Protesters set up camp in the valley and then took turns to keep the occupation going for three whole years.[198] They also briefly occupied Mount Augustus, staying in the "blast exclusion zone" to stop Solid Energy blowing up the mountain, which worked but not for long.

STATE-SPONSORED SPECIES EXTINCTION

By this time, the fate of the Powelliphanta augusta species was making news

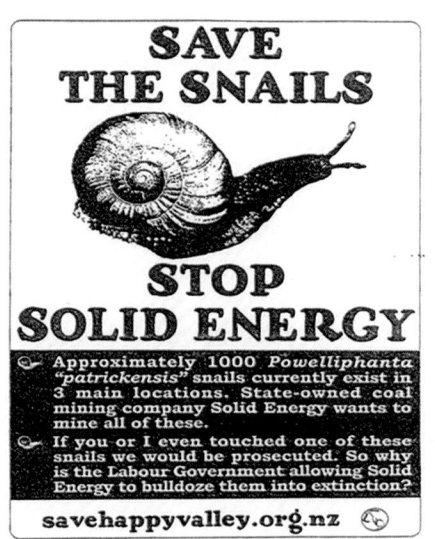

and the SHVC decided to take this issue on as well as trying to keep the coal in the ground. Solid Energy offered to relocate 100 snails (all the while arguing it didn't have to) but insisted the mine would go ahead. In April 2006, Forest and Bird obtained a legal ruling that required that Solid Energy seek permission from the Ministers of Energy and Conservation to move all the snails before they could begin mining. This they were granted in April 2006, although the court's judgment was scathing.[199] It said Solid Energy's decision to mine the snails' habitat was "noxious", and "there is little doubt that from the scientific and environmental point of view, the snails should not be moved."[200] Yet they were.

The Save Happy Valley Coalition were appalled and claimed it was Aotearoa's 'first state-sponsored species extinction'. They accused the minister of bowing to pressure from Solid Energy and ignoring advice from his own Conservation Department.[201] The SHVC took Solid Energy to court again and sought a judicial review of the minister's decision. In March 2007, the High Court refused their request and ordered them to pay Solid Energy $5760 toward their costs, a stinging blow.[202]

In the meantime, back on Mount Augustus, work was underway to uplift the snails. For months, people inched across the rugged ground on hands and knees, expecting to find around 250 snails, maybe 1000 at most. In the end, over 6000 snails were found and 8000 eggs, yet this success was bittersweet, as searchers knew the snails' only natural habitat was about to disappear. Some snails were shifted to other sites on the plateau, though it wasn't certain they'd survive. Others were packed in chilly bins and sent to Nelson, until they had found so many a special cool store was built in Hokitika, lined with shelves where the snails were stored in plastic containers, kept at a steady temperature, with a constant light cycle and access to food. Over the next 10 years, Solid Energy would spend an estimated $7 million to store them.[203]

CATCHING SPIES

In 2008, a Sunday newspaper reported that private investigators Thompson and Clark had offered a Christchurch man $500 a week to spy on the SHVC for Solid Energy[204] – and this wasn't the first time, or even the second. In the period from April 2006 to April 2008, Thompson and Clark were caught spying on SHVC campaigners four times, as well as spying on members of Peace Action Wellington and the Wellington Animal Rights Network.

A SHVC spokesperson said that no reasonable person could describe Solid Energy's activities as legal, moral or ethical: "They have pushed a species to extinction, a process described as noxious in the Environment Court. They are responsible annually for carbon emissions equivalent to the entire domestic transport fleet in New Zealand. Now, we know that they planted an unregistered spy in our group – a clear breach of the law."[205]

Why would Solid Energy do it? It's quite simple: they were planning a dramatic increase in how much coal they would dig up, ready to export to China and elsewhere, right at the time climate change was sparking global concern. By spying on the SHVC they'd get warning of any protest plans in advance so they could turn it to their advantage.

At the time, PM Helen Clark said the spying was "unacceptable behaviour from a state-owned enterprise" and insisted it stop. The State-Owned Enterprises Minister stated that it went "over the limit of what we expect" in Aotearoa and ordered Solid Energy to cease the practice. But *did* this practice stop? No.[206] Later this same agency was involved in investigating some of the Christchurch homeowners making earthquake claims and an inquiry found that this breached some of the State Services rules around "external security consultants".[207] In April 2021, it was also revealed that Thompson and Clark were spying on student climate protesters on behalf of the fossil fuel lobby, and in particular oil-exploration company OMV.[208]

PLAYING 'PASS THE SNAIL'

By the decade's end, Solid Energy was in such financial strife it claimed it could no longer afford the upkeep of the snails and they sold the cool store, handing care of the snails to DOC. For activists who'd fought their removal, this was heartbreaking. "This is exactly what we predicted," said Frances Mountier, of the SHVC. "A whole species is languishing, it has nowhere to go […] by pushing through with the mining of Augustus, Solid Energy effectively locked them into this fate."[209]

Meanwhile, in Happy Valley mining hadn't actually started. In October 2012 Solid Energy announced that work on Cypress Mine would be delayed.[210] The following year, the Biodiversity Defence Society (BDS) took a new case back to the Environment Court, arguing that Solid Energy's resource consent had expired.[211] The case looked strong, but BDS lost in both the Environment Court (July 2013) and a further attempt in the High Court later that year. They felt they'd run out of options and reluctantly dropped the case. But the damage had already been done. Today mining has devastated the land, exposing any snails still on the site to collapses from undercut hillsides and erosion, or at risk of being smothered. What little habitat there is left is littered with coal fines, gravels and falling rocks from the land disturbed by the mining above.[212]

The Save Happy Valley Campaign released 150 inflatable Kiwi in a popular inner-city park and acted out street theatre, 2006. (Save Happy Valley Campaign/Timothy Bailey)

This story has no happy ending, but the activists behind the Save Happy Valley Campaign made an impact that's visible today. They were among the first to focus attention so acutely on climate change in that way, building a strong base for current climate activists. And many continue to work on climate justice and similar issues today; they are still deeply committed to protecting our planet.

BUT WHAT ABOUT THE SNAILS?

It's not great news. Powelliphanta augusta are now "functionally extinct"; in other words, they no longer have any of their original natural habitat left and their population is locked away in plastic bins or struggling in habitats they're not adapted to. In early December 2006, 20 were released back to the wild, one later found dead. Another 20 were released about 800 metres from where they were found, into an area that won't be mined. In 2007, DOC announced plans to release another 200 snails back into the wild at Stockton Mine.

In 2010, a DOC officer reported that 1552 snails were still held in refrigerators in Hokitika. That same year, even though Forest and Bird said of the Mount Augustus site that "the once complex mosaic of dense, low sub-alpine scrub and deep undisturbed litter has gone", 1600 snails were still relocated there. Another 2300 were moved to two sites at Mount Rochfort. At each, 50 snails were tagged and 30% died within 18 months. It's not at all clear yet whether these transplanted populations will survive long term. These are no ordinary snails. They take eight years to start breeding and can live for up to twenty years but they have evolved to survive in a very specific and unique habitat. Some in captivity are nearing 30 years old and have grown so large they'd fill the palm of a child's hand. Storing the snails costs the taxpayer roughly $50,000 per year.[213]

In November 2011, 800 snails died when a fault in a DOC fridge froze them solid, by which time DOC claimed that roughly 4000 snails had already been relocated to new habitats:[214] "Fortunately we've already managed to relocate more than 60% of the original population into new habitats and we still have more than 800 unaffected snails in the other cool rooms and environmental chambers. The remaining snails are breeding well, producing good numbers of eggs, and we expect the captive population to recover the loss within a few years."

Forest and Bird, however, told a different story: "Landcare Research says the snails moved from the fridges to new sites last year are breeding too slowly for the populations to survive. New homes for the Powelliphanta augusta snails are limited because the snails can't adapt to different habitats or because other snail species are already there. This has been an unfortunate experiment in keeping threatened native animals."[215]

Government documents showed there'd been a proposal to release all the captive snails into the wild by the end of 2018 and to "mothball" the facility in case the snails needed rescuing again. But the release didn't go ahead after expert advice warned it would be too risky, particularly for the southern species. The tiny area of potentially suitable habitat was vulnerable to natural disasters like fire, flood or drought. One report said: "Extinction of the southern sub-species would be likely and a reduction in genetic diversity probable."[216] How did we let it come to this?

MINING FOR OIL AND GAS

For the millions concerned about climate change, the continued drilling for oil and gas seems unacceptable. We need to embrace more sustainable energy solutions and we're lucky Aotearoa is blessed with excellent renewable options such as hydro, thermal, solar and wind. If we're serious about reducing our carbon footprint, we have the means to make that shift.

But exploiting our natural resources has been a feature of Pākehā culture since Europeans first arrived. Generations have worked in these industries and whole populations have relied on the jobs – which makes letting go of that mindset painful. Transitions are always hard, but time is against us. It's important we act now.

The first oil drilled for in Aotearoa flowed from the Alpha well near Mikotahi, New Plymouth, in 1865.[217] It was the first in the Commonwealth and one of the first in the world. As a result, the petroleum industry expanded from Moturoa (a coastal suburb of New Plymouth), digging more

Oil wells in New Plymouth, around 1913. (Auckland Library Collection)

An oil gusher at Kotuku near Greymouth.

wells and building refineries to turn the unrefined crude oil into products like petrol, paraffin and diesel. The last refinery in the area was closed in 1972, though the field still produces a little oil.[218]

The Kapuni gas field in South Taranaki was discovered in 1959 and started production in 1970. The North Island natural gas network has operated since 1970, first supplying Auckland, Hamilton, New Plymouth, Wanganui, Palmerston North and Wellington. The offshore Māui gas field was discovered in 1969 and started production in 1978. This led to several other large energy projects, including gas-fired power stations at New Plymouth and Huntly, an ammonia-urea plant at Kapuni, a gas-to-methanol plant at Waitara and the synthetic petrol plant at Motunui.[219]

Kiwis who want to stop all further mining for oil and gas aren't solely worried about climate change. There's also the danger of an environmental disaster if oil leaks into the sea, which we learnt first-hand in October 2011 after a foreign-owned container ship, the *Rena*, became grounded on Astrolabe Reef in the Bay of Plenty while approaching Tauranga Harbour. The ship was carrying 1368 containers – eight containing hazardous materials – as well as 1700 tonnes of heavy fuel oil and 200 tonnes of marine diesel oil. Bad weather the night of the grounding pushed the ship further onto the reef and the crew was evacuated. Left abandoned, the pounding of the keel on the reef ripped the ship's own oil tanks open and 130–350 tonnes of oil spewed out. The thick, black tar-like substance covered several beaches and coastlines ... and dead fish and birds started washing ashore at Mount Maunganui beach five days later.[220] Within a week, 88 of the containers had fallen into the sea and more containers were lost as the ship broke up. Many containers cracked open, their contents washing onto beaches as far away as Whangapoua Harbour and the far side of Great Barrier Island. The oil slick spread five kilometres of oozing black death through these fish-rich waters.

Containers falling off the *Rena*. (Maritime NZ)

Dozens of locals flocked to rescue wildlife and clean up the oil. Nearby beaches were closed to the public and volunteers were warned that contact with spilled oil could lead to vomiting, nausea and rashes. Local residents were urged to close their windows to reduce fumes.[221] The oil spill killed 2000 seabirds and it's estimated that 20,000 birds (including little blue penguins and the rare spotted dotterel) suffered when their ecosystems and food sources were polluted.[222] The contamination of fish stocks, including shellfish, not only restricted iwi and hapū's ability to collect food, but also risked the health of anyone who ate it.[223] The Environment Minister described the grounding of the *Rena* as Aotearoa's worst maritime environmental disaster.

This disaster added to the call to stop deep-sea mining and dozens of protests have been held against overseas companies drilling in our region, or in special protected places like the Arctic and Antarctica. In 2013, for instance, a group of Greenpeace activists, including actor Lucy Lawless, boarded the drilling ship *Noble Discoverer* at the Port of Taranaki and spent 77 hours up a 58-metre tower to protest against Shell's exploration in the Arctic. Lawless and seven other Greenpeace members were arrested and sentenced to community service. They had to pay the company $651, roughly 0.1% of the $600,000 Shell demanded.[224]

The most common victims of the oil spill: hundreds of diving petrels have died. (A. Tennyson, Te Papa)

Oil Free Wellington is a great example of the many local activist groups creating dynamic campaigns around Aotearoa. Over the years their actions have included:

- Leading a protest march and blockade of the annual Petroleum Summit in Wellington (September 2013).[225]

- Members swimming to an oil surveying ship berthed in Wellington harbour and attaching a banner reading "Oil Free Seas" (January 2014).[226]

- The same surveying boat was stopped from leaving (and other boats were prevented from entering the harbour) when

protesters from Kaikōura swam and bodyboarded into the path of the surveying boat (later in 2014).[227]

- Marching to the offices of oil company Anadarko to deliver a 'trespass notice' signed by Wellington city locals (January 2014).[228]

- Members rigged a banner outside the National Party's conference after they opened protected sea areas to oil exploration and potentially put at risk our critically endangered Māui dolphin. A banner addressed to the Minister, Simon Bridges, read, "Hey Simon, extinction is forever!" (June 2014).[229]

- Members scaled a building in Wellington to fly a "Stop Deep Sea Oil" banner (and other protests held around the country) after Norwegian company Statoil was granted permits to explore in our waters (October 2014).[230]

- The group hosted protests at Wellington's waterfront on the day the climate change talks in Paris ended. There were dozens of kayaks, waka and yachts, and hundreds of protesters on shore (December 2015).[231]

SEABED MINING – ONE AIM, ONE SHARED VOICE

Almost immediately after the Foreshore and Seabed Act (2004) was passed, mining and oil companies began signing up to make claims to the seabed. The government issued its first permits two months later. But the Resource Management Act required companies to inform tangata whenua of any plans that would affect their ocean rohe (territory). This didn't always happen.

In 2005, Angeline Greensill (Tainui o Tainui) called a public meeting on her hapū land to oppose the prospecting and exploration permits granted to New Zealand Petroleum and Minerals, which covered the North Island's West Coast from south of New Plymouth to north of the Kaipara Harbour. They met at the very place where the Raglan golf course dispute erupted in 1978, but this time Māori and Pākehā in the Whāingaroa Raglan community were united – all highly opposed to the permits. They formed Kiwis Against Seabed Mining (KASM).

In 2013 mining company Trans-Tasman Resources (TTR) put forward a plan to dredge 50 million tonnes of ironsands every year from the seabed off the South Taranaki coast, an area of 65.76 square kilometres, between 12 to 19 nautical miles offshore in Whāingaroa Raglan. Ngāti Ruanui, KASM and many other organisations, fiercely opposed the plans along with the local community. They all attended the hearings to take a stand against dredging. They worried that the stirred-up sediment would wreck fishing and surfing, and put blue whales and other marine life at risk. Submissions poured in opposing the plan, three times more than for any other permit before. In 2014, the Environmental Protection Authority (EPA) ruled against the project and the protesters' united effort was rewarded.

In May 2014, not long after, a similar proposal was lodged to mine for phosphorite nodules (mainly used for fertilisers) within the fishing grounds of the Chatham Rise, east of the South Island.[232] This area had been set aside to conserve and protect the seabed's biodiversity. Moriori ki Rekohu, Ngāti Mutunga, Ngāi Tahu and Ngāti Kahungunu iwi opposed the application, citing existing interests in fishing rights, Te Tiriti matters and other cultural considerations.

KASM, Greenpeace, Deepsea Conservation Coalition and wider communities also opposed the application. Again, their concerns centred around reef system destruction, sediment plumes and impacts on marine mammals. In February 2015, the Environmental Protection Authority (EPA) refused the consent, another victory for the locals.

In 2016, TTR reapplied for consent to dredge in the same area. In August 2017, the EPA granted them marine discharge consent to suck up 50 million tonnes of black ironsand 22–36 kilometres (12–19 nautical miles) offshore from Pātea. KASM and other opponents appealed the consent in the High Court in August 2018, where it was ruled unlawful for consent to be granted on so little information. TTR immediately appealed the decision[233] and lost, so the matter has now gone to the Supreme Court.[234]

PESTERING PETROBAS

Despite these victories, it was only a matter of time until an application was granted. Brazilian state-owned oil company Petrobras was given a five-year exploration permit to drill for oil in the Raukumara Basin, off East Cape. This was part of Te Whānau-ā-Apanui's rohe, and when the government granted this permit without consulting them, the iwi told Petrobras they had no right to be there and would be evicted.

Te Whānau-ā-Apanui sought support for its protest and Greenpeace answered their call. As the protest escalated, they worked together, Greenpeace organising a blockade at sea in April 2011, while Te Whānau-ā-Apunui and others supported them onshore.

For 42 days, seven protest vessels and an Apanui fishing boat buzzed around the seismic surveying ship to disrupt its progress. A navy warship and special tactics police boat were eventually sent to arrest them. Before the fishing boat's captain was arrested, he blocked the survey ship, telling them, "We won't be moving. We'll be doing some fishing." The charges against him were later dropped.

After the *Rena* ran aground, opposition to oil drilling intensified and protests and petitions gathered more support, making their presence felt. By December 2012, Petrobras walked away from its exploration permit. The protesters had won.

- A united response from Māori and Pākehā was needed again in 2013 when the Canadian company TAG Oil sought a permit to frack for natural gas near Gisborne. Taranaki locals had already discovered polluted groundwater after fracking and the people of Gisborne were prepared to fight to avoid this. Fortunately, the company withdrew after claiming it found unsafe pockets of gas.
- Yet another company, the New Zealand Energy Company, also gave up on its East Cape onshore permit in May 2015.[235]

ANADARKO VS THE OCEAN'S GUARDIANS

But 2013 also saw new permits for seismic testing and drilling granted to Texas-based Anadarko, including one off Waikato and another off the South Island's east coast.

Kaikōura's locals were horrified — their economy depended on eco-tourism, with whale watching and an endangered baby seal nursery big business for the town. Residents around Dunedin weren't happy either. Their district was known for its penguins.

Ngāi Tahu Chairman Mark Solomon invited Anadarko and the minister to a hui, asking Greenpeace representatives to sit with tangata whenua to support them. Solomon said, "[Anadarko] tried to restrict who we had on the marae. My response was you do not tell the tangata whenua who they have on their marae [...] They came, incredibly nervous, both the ministry and Anadarko." Solomon explained the concept of kaitiakitanga to Anadarko, stressing the responsibility Māori felt in their role as guardians of the land and sea.[236]

This was a risky time to protest at sea. In response to the Petrobras blockade, the National-led Government had passed the Anadarko Amendment, making it illegal for protesters to go within 500 metres of an oil industry vessel. They also announced plans to end public submissions on mining applications. There was a huge outcry, and many well-known figures spoke out, all saying it breached people's right to protest. And it didn't stop them taking action. In May 2013, a campaign called Hands Across the Sands saw thousands form lines in Kaikōura, Raglan, and along other well-known beaches, demanding an end to fossil fuels. Surfers smeared themselves with oil and others dressed as penguins and Māui dolphins to make their point.

Greenpeace sent six boats to confront Anadarko's exploration ship when it turned up to drill for oil in the Taranaki Basin, roughly 185 kilometres off Raglan. For five days the flotilla dodged arrest, pushing the boundaries, supported by up to 5000 people on land, all part of the Banners on the Beach campaign.[237]

Angeline Greensill once again called Raglan's community together on the former golf course and accused the government of failing to consult with tangata whenua.

When another flotilla confronted Anadarko's other drill ship off Otago the following February, the company ended all drilling. It claimed its tests had not found oil ... but the protesters' celebration didn't last long as attention shifted to the Norwegian state-owned oil company Statoil. They'd been granted exploration blocks in the Reinga Basin off Northland. A hui in November 2013 brought 300 hapū members together in Ahipara,

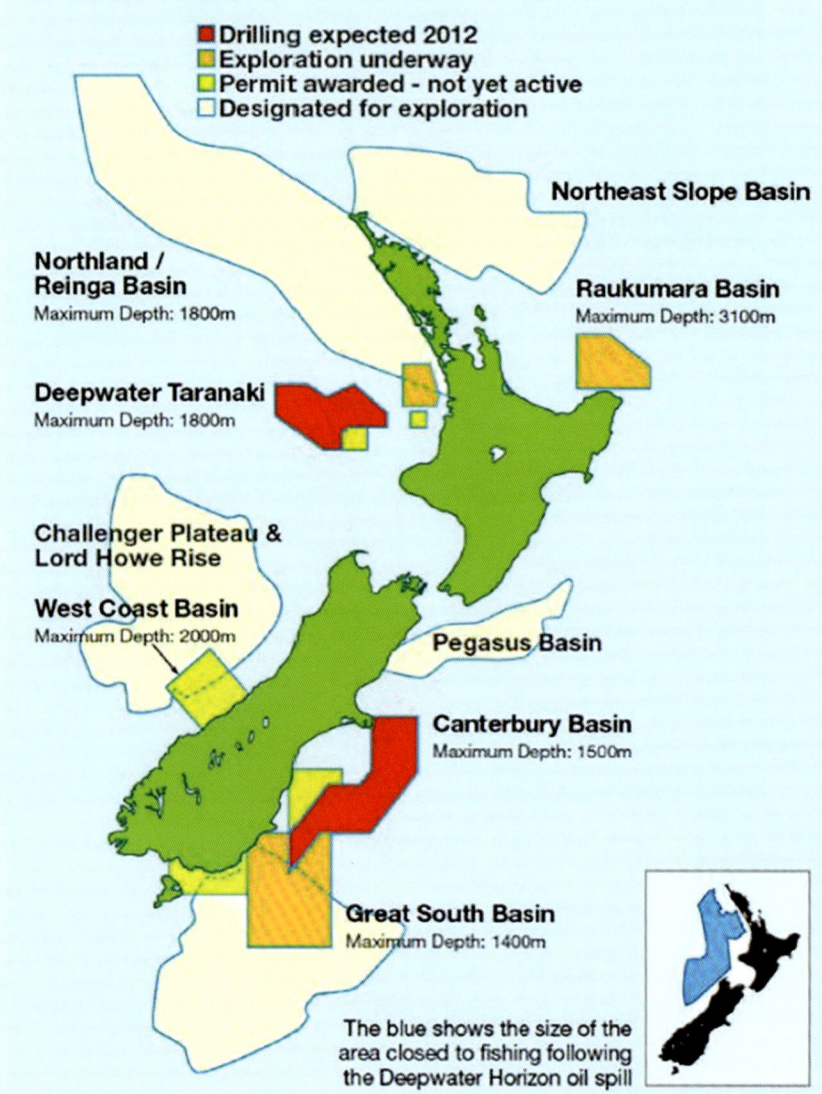

State of oil exploration around NZ, 2012.

where they unanimously opposed Statoil's seismic testing plans. The "seismic testing" exploration method blasts the seafloor with high-powered airguns every 10 seconds and measures the echoes to map offshore oil and gas reserves — it can disturb, injure or kill marine wildlife, including whales and dolphins.[238]

Te Rarawa, Ngāti Kuri, and Ngāti Kahu joined farmers and fishermen, families and activists, to oppose Statoil. Three separate hīkoi set off from Cape Reinga to Auckland in February and September 2014, and again in 2015. After the February hīkoi, anti-mining activist Tim Howard addressed the pōwhiri at Te Tii Waitangi marae, paraphrasing anti-racism activist Mitzi Nairn, saying, "We would like to be the Pākehā you signed the Tiriti with."[239] Meanwhile, Prime Minister John Key was greeted with protests.

Statoil went ahead with seismic testing off Northland in November 2014, and those intense pulses coincided with a series of mysterious whale and dolphin beachings and strandings and an increase in dead seals.[240] The oceangoing waka *Haunui* rowed out to the survey ship to impress on the crew how much their drilling would worsen climate change.

December 2014 saw protesters at a dozen beaches take part in a Heads in the Sand campaign to highlight how the continued granting of oil permits was a form of climate change denial. Protesters also organised a reggae festival to raise awareness and a children's ballet show in Kerikeri, where dancers draped a black tarpaulin over the audience to demonstrate how an oil spill smothers marine life.

Yet another flotilla protested in Hokianga Harbour in January 2015, and local schoolchildren performed the haka as the final hikoī arrived at Waitangi in February. Protesters also flooded into Auckland to protest against another petroleum industry summit (which was promoting oil drilling off Aotearoa), continuously banging drums to disrupt the conference. In May 2015, it was announced a claim would be lodged with the Waitangi Tribunal to stop the drilling.[241]

In August 2017, the EPA granted mining company Trans-Tasman Resources (TTR) marine discharge consents to suck up 50 million tonnes of black ironsand 22–36 kilometres offshore from Pātea. Opponents appealed the consents to the High Court on August 2018, where it was ruled unlawful for consents to be granted on so little information. TTR immediately appealed the decision.[242]

ACTION AT LAST ... WITH A BIG "BUT"

In 2018, the Labour-led Government announced it wouldn't issue any new exploration permits for offshore oil and gas fields – a historic move, fiercely debated. This came only weeks after global oil giant Shell sold its last oil and gas interests in Aotearoa, ending their long activity here. The buyer was Austrian company OMV, who Greenpeace claim is one of the 100 companies responsible for over 70% of the world's climate emissions.[243]

Under a Block Offer system introduced by the previous National-led government in 2012, onshore exploration licences were offered and granted in other parts of the country, though none had gone into production. At the time of the 2018 announcement, Prime Minister Jacinda Ardern said, "There are 31 oil and gas exploration permits currently active; 22 are offshore. These permits cover an area of 100,000 square kilometres [...] and run out as far as 2030 and go an additional 40 years under a mining permit."[244] This was hugely disappointing for those hoping for an immediate ban.

In April 2019, OMV said it was planning to drill three test wells and seven appraisal wells in the Great South Basin, south-east of Dunedin.

Bahamas-flagged *Skandi Atlantic* with a Greenpeace banner declaring "Making Oil History".

Later that year, Greenpeace launched a new campaign to end all deep-sea oil and gas exploration immediately. In October, during a protest outside OMV's headquarters in Austria, Māori climate activist Mike Smith (Ngāpuhi, Ngāti Kahu) announced he was filing a lawsuit at the International Criminal Court against OMV's CEO. In Aotearoa, OMV faced protests in Dunedin, Wellington and New Plymouth.

Overnight blockade of the OMV building, New Plymouth.

On 24 November 2019, 30 people from Extinction Rebellion, Oil Free Otago, 350 Aotearoa and others were joined by a team of Greenpeace climbers. At dawn they stormed aboard the support vessel for OMV's oil rig, some locking themselves to the ship to stop it leaving port and occupied the vessel for three days. After that, they moved to OMV's headquarters in New Plymouth,[245] where around 100 climate protesters formed a human barricade around the office, shutting it down for a further three days. A spokesperson said: "If we stand any hope of averting a climate catastrophe, we need to rid ourselves of this final villain looking for new oil and gas we just can't afford to burn."[246]

At the end of this action, the protesters installed an outdoor pop-up museum in OMV's front car park. Two smouldering oil barrels stood each side of the entry to the "Museum of Oil History", beside a wrecked 1970s Mercedes sprayed bright pink, a four-metre oil platform, and a 1980s petrol pump. Exhibits included the "pilot drill from the Deepwater Horizon oil disaster in the Gulf of Mexico", a petrel seabird which "narrowly escaped the *Rena* oil spill off Tauranga" and an ancient fax machine "used to send the first exploration permit" in Aotearoa.[247]

Greenpeace's Niamh O'Flynn said they were bringing the resistance to OMV's front doorstep, supported by activists from School Strike 4 Climate, Extinction Rebellion, 350 Aotearoa, Climate Justice Taranaki and Oil Free groups around the country. "As we face the climate crisis, it's great to see all these brave Kiwis prepared to come together just when the world needs them," O'Flynn said. "We want to send a clear message to OMV: we're over it. They must acknowledge their role in heating the planet and give up their oil and gas exploration permits." [248]

In April 2020, OMV announced that it was indefinitely postponing its last remaining exploration plans in the Taranaki Basin and had no further plans to bring a new rig to Aotearoa. Greenpeace claimed it was a win of generational significance. Their climate and energy campaigner, Amanda Larsson, said: "Following the departure of Petrobras, Anadarko, Equinor/Statoil, Chevron and others, OMV was the last major oil company searching for new oil and gas in New Zealand waters. It's one of the only companies that still had the right to search for oil here after securing drill permits prior to the 2018 ban on new offshore oil exploration."[249]

OTHER OCEAN-RELATED CAMPAIGNS

As well as concerns around deep-sea mining and oil-related environmental disasters, there have been many other ocean-related protests in Aotearoa. From Māori fighting to protect their rohe, to government-backed anti-whaling campaigns and concerns about overfishing, many Kiwis have spoken up against the pollution and pillaging of our seas and for protection of unique marine creatures. Here are just a few issues that have sparked protests, each offering a very brief overview. Use them as a starting point to go and find out more — they all have fascinating protest stories.

ANTI-WHALING

Among the first Europeans to arrive in Aotearoa were whalers and sealers. Whales were hunted for blubber that was rendered down into oil used for lamps and machinery, as well as baleen to make corsets and whips, and ambergris (an excretion of sperm whales), used as a fixative in expensive perfumes. The first whaling stations were established in southern Aotearoa in the late 1820s, and Māori were employed as crew though they had no tradition of hunting whales. At its peak in 1839, around 200 ships were whaling in our waters. Kororāreka, in the Bay of Islands, was the largest whaling port in the southern hemisphere, with 740 vessels visiting in 1840. But so many of the right whales they hunted were killed, the population was almost wiped out and whaling declined.[250]

Humpback whale being processed at J. A. Perano's factory in Tory Channel. (Alexander Turnbull Library)

In 1911, Italian immigrant family the Peranos set up a whaling station in Tory Channel (one entrance to the Marlborough Sounds), where they used steam-driven vessels and new explosive harpoons to hunt humpback whales. In 1960, a record 361 humpback whales were killed in our waters — 135 by Gulf Whaling Industries on Great Barrier Island and 226 by the Peranos in Tory Channel. This whaling stopped in 1963 when stocks collapsed.

In 1946 Aotearoa became one of the founding members of the International

An adult and baby Minke whale are dragged aboard the Nisshin Maru, a Japanese whaling vessel that is the world's only factory whaling ship, 2008. (Australian Customs and Border Protection Service)

Whaling Commission (IWC) to manage the world's remaining whale resources. We left the organisation in 1969, when the whaling industry here stopped, but in the early 1970s anti-whaling campaigns by Friends of the Earth and Project Jonah put pressure on our government to join the IWC again and change its pro-whaling stance to pro-whale.[251] Aotearoa signed up again in 1976, and now our government is considered one of the strongest voices in support of whale conservation.[252]

But this didn't happen by chance. In 1975 Greenpeace's Save the Whales campaign was launched in Vancouver and it soon spread here. Since then, many environmental groups have spoken out against whaling, and organisations like Sea Shepherd and Greenpeace have taken to the water, risking their lives to disrupt whaling, sometimes attacked by the crews they pursue.[253]

In 1982 a moratorium on commercial whaling was voted in by a majority of the IWC members. It came into effect in 1986 and remains in place today, although the few countries that continue whaling, such as Japan and Norway, have fought to abolish it. In 1994 the Southern Ocean Whale Sanctuary was established and when combined with the Indian Ocean Sanctuary created by the IWC in 1979, almost a third of the planet's oceans are now sanctuaries for the world's remaining whales. As well, all marine mammals within Aotearoa's 200 nautical mile Exclusive Economic Zone are protected under the 1978 Marine Mammals Protection Act.[254]

While this is great, outside of these sanctuaries whales are now at greater risk from pollution, especially plastics, and clogged shipping lanes. These days, ex-whalers work in Aotearoa with DOC to record yearly counts of humpback whales as they migrate through Cook Strait and Whale Watch Kaikōura takes out 80,000 visitors a year to observe sperm whales in their natural setting.

TRAWLING THE SEABED

Around Aotearoa's coastline there are many potential risks for marine mammals, including being hit by boats, mining exploration, seismic testing, coastal development, pollution, marine tourism, marine farming and climate change. But the single biggest known threat is unsafe fishing practices.

One of the current fishing practices that causes great harm to dolphins as well as the seabed and fish stocks is called "bottom trawling", a method that involves dragging heavy weighted nets across the sea floor. It's popular with commercial fishing companies as it catches large quantities of fish in one go. In Aotearoa, commercial fishing companies bottom trawl both within our territorial waters and beyond. In fact, we're one of only seven countries still using this practice in international waters.[255]

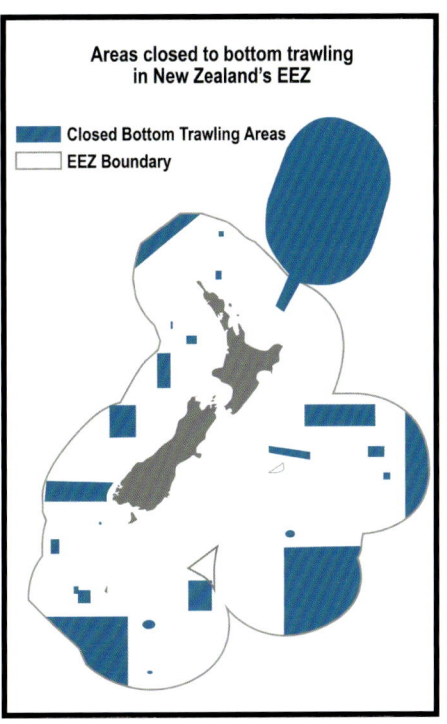

According to the Sport Fishing Council's LegaSea website, there are three main issues with bottom trawling:

- **Bulk harvesting** – Bottom trawling allows for large quantities of fish to be caught during one sweep. Fish caught early in the trawl end up being crushed as more fish are gathered. Much of the catch is damaged and is of such poor quality it's later sold off cheap.

- **Non-selective harvest** – Many varieties of fish and other organisms are swept up, even if they're not the target species. This bulk harvesting causes ecological problems, unbalancing the natural population levels of each species in the ecosystem, affecting their ability to reproduce. Deep-sea fish have low reproduction rates, meaning they don't easily repopulate once overfished. Non-targeted species are often overfished in the process. Trawlers capture enormous amounts of unwanted catch (by-catch) which later gets dumped.

- **Seabed damage** – The seabed's destruction causes negative impacts on the organisms and fish that are harvested by removing whole ecosystems used as food and shelter for many species. The destruction often causes permanent damage to these ecosystems. Studies show that a century of ever-expanding bottom trawling has transformed the sea floor from a thriving underwater community of organisms to a desert of fine silt.[256]

In November 2019, Greenpeace's Oceans campaigner Jessica Desmond said that new figures revealed up to 3000 tonnes of coral was destroyed by Aotearoa's bottom trawling vessels in the previous year – and for every tonne of coral brought up in the net, nearly 340 tonnes were destroyed below. Kiwi-owned Talley's and Sealord continue to bottom trawl in both local and international waters. "More than 40,000 New Zealanders have called for the government to ban bottom trawling on seamounts, where these ancient corals grow. But so far, the only action the government has taken is to increase the amount of bottom trawling allowed in the coming fishing season," Desmond said.[257]

The UN advises that all vulnerable areas, with precious ecosystems like seamounts, should

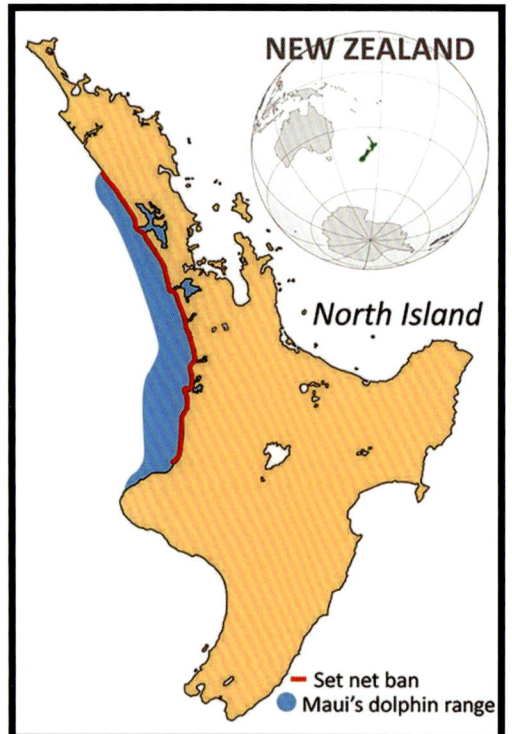

Range of Māui dolphin (blue) in New Zealand's North Island, with the area covered by the net ban marked in red.

be closed to bottom trawling. Aotearoa signed up to these resolutions, but we're failing to live up to international expectations. Greenpeace, along with The Deep Sea Conservation Coalition, WWF, Forest and Bird and ECO, launched a petition calling for an end to all bottom trawling that gained 50,000 signatures by the time they presented it to Parliament on 18 November 2020. At the time, Barry Weeber of ECO said: "Most New Zealanders have no idea that while our fishing industry is continuing to bottom trawl sensitive areas, the rest of the world has mostly banned it. We need to catch up and stop trashing the oceans to fill supermarket freezers."[258]

Calls have also been made for all fishing fleets to have onboard cameras to prove crews are following the rules and to measure the amount of wasteful by-catch and any harm to marine mammals. When cameras were mounted on boats in Australia, the commercial fishing industry admitted to catching eight times as many sea birds, seven times as many marine mammals, and six times as much by-catch as they had previously reported.[259] In Aotearoa we still rely mostly on fishing vessels to volunteer the truth about how much they catch and if they come into contact with protected species. It is estimated that up to 24.7 million tonnes of catch went unreported[260] by Kiwi fisheries between 1950 and 2013, and our Ministry of Primary Industries has admitted to widespread issues with fish dumping.[261]

Forest and Bird Chief Executive Kevin Hague said it was time for the government to act. "We have a new government, with a new ministerial portfolio that marries oceans and fisheries, signalling a big shift in thinking. But the real test of the government's intentions will come with how it deals with this issue, because we cannot have sustainable oceans if we have bottom trawling."

It's only by passionate people bringing these concerns to the public's attention and pushing for action that anything will change.

Greenpeace, Project Jonah, World Wildlife Fund (WWF), Sea Shepherd, Forest and Bird, Our Seas Our Future and many other groups, as well as local iwi, have been protesting to protect the Māui and Hector's dolphins for years. They've lobbied the Department of Conservation to set up "safe" zones, free from all types of fishing that could harm the dolphins. They've launched several petitions and have the support of the WWF-NZ's Executive Director who said, "The fate of the world's smallest and rarest marine dolphin is in our hands. If we don't act now, we will see this amazing creature disappear forever."

UNIQUE DOLPHINS

Both these tiny dolphins are particularly at risk from becoming entangled in set nets, gill nets, or trawling, which prevents a dolphin from returning to the surface to breathe, causing them to drown. While nets have been forbidden in some areas, there are still many places where Māui dolphins continue to be threatened by them.[262] To prevent their extinction, the best available science suggests that human threats like fishing must be reduced by 50–75% within 10 years.

Māui dolphins have a distinctive rounded fin. (Department of Conservation)

MĀUI DOLPHIN

Māui dolphins are only found off the west coast of the North Island and scientists estimate there are just 63 adult Māui dolphins alive today which makes them the world's rarest marine dolphin, critically endangered and at risk of extinction in the very near future.

They're also the world's smallest dolphin, friendly and playful, and have "distinctive black Mickey-Mouse-ear dorsal fins".[263] Female Māui dolphins grow to 1.7 metres in length and weigh up to 50 kilograms, while males are slightly smaller and lighter. They have have been known to live as long as 22 years, are able to reproduce after 6–8 years but produce only one calf every 2–4 years.

HECTOR'S DOLPHIN

Often confused with the Māui dolphin, the Hector's dolphin (also known as tutumairekurai or tūpoupou) also only live in Aotearoa's waters, but prefer the South Island's coast. Adult Hector's dolphins don't often exceed 1.5 metres in length and weigh between 40 and 60 kilograms.[264] In 2013, their population was estimated at around 7000, with the largest group found off the South Island's West Coast. The other main concentration is around Banks Peninsula, with smaller groups off Cloudy Bay in the Marlborough Sounds and Te Waewae Bay in Southland. They're classified as a "vulnerable species" (likely to become endangered) and don't live as long as Māui dolphins.[265]

THE BIGGEST ISSUE OF ALL

CLIMATE CHANGE ACTION

CLIMATE CHANGE – YOUNG PEOPLE VS FOSSIL FUEL DINOSAURS

It's clear from the previous protests here that some people in Aotearoa have been warning about the risks of human-induced climate change for decades, yet action has been painfully slow. Sometimes it takes something out of the ordinary to shift people from thinking a huge threat is too hard to deal with (or too scary to think about) to taking positive action. In 2018, the arrival of Greta Thunberg set smouldering worries alight, encouraging young people everywhere to stand up to protect their future. This was the moment climate change activism finally shifted to the mainstream – thanks to young people the world over shaming older generations to act.

Thunberg's activism began by convincing her parents to change their lifestyle choices to reduce their carbon footprint. In August 2018, at age 15, she started skipping school to sit outside the Swedish parliament, with a sign that read "Skolstrejk för klimatet" (School strike

8

for climate). Soon other students started similar protests in their own communities and together they organised a school climate strike movement called Fridays for Future. In 2018, Thunberg addressed the UN Climate Change Conference and, afterwards, student strikes took place every week somewhere in the world. In 2019, rolling protests were held in cities all over the planet, bringing together hundreds of thousands of students.[266]

Thunberg then sailed to North America to attend the 2019 UN Climate Action Summit, refusing to fly because of aeroplane emissions. In her speech, she rebuked the adults for their lack of action when they'd known of the dangers for decades, famously asking, "How dare you?" The clip went viral, Thunberg voicing what many of her generation were feeling. Her power to inspire others to act has been called "The Greta Effect" and, indeed, her determination to tell the truth so plainly and to push for change is a beacon of hope to many.[267]

After the summit, various politicians acknowledged her speech. Britain's Secretary for the Environment said: "When I listened to you, I felt great admiration, but also responsibility and guilt. I am of your parents' generation, and I recognise that we haven't done nearly enough to address climate change and the broader environmental crisis that we helped to create."

Ed Miliband, who introduced the UK's Climate Change Act (2008), said: "You have woken us up. Thank you. All the young people who have gone on strike have held up a mirror to our society [... and] taught us all a really important lesson. You have stood out from the crowd."[268]

Rousing words, but they're yet to make any real changes or move with the necessary urgency.

SCHOOL STRIKE 4 CLIMATE ARRIVES IN AOTEAROA

Spurred by the powerful role model Thunberg presented, Kiwi students from cities and towns across Aotearoa organised their own student climate movement, united by their concerns about the future. School Strike 4 Climate has taken its place alongside the most visible climate

Green MP Chlöe Swarbrick attended the march. As the youngest MP in our Parliament, she said she was familiar with such patronising (belittling) language:

"I've found that sentiments like 'grow up' are typically synonymous with 'give up' – a passive aggressive, coded articulation that you're making others uncomfortable with your earnest ideas that we could possibly hope to create a better world [...]

"Politicians across the world have their hands on the wheel of a car that they are driving directly into a forest fire. They can see the fire. They have been, and are being, constantly warned about it as they drive. The heat and smoke is starting to make some of the car passengers uncomfortable, sick and coughing.

"Politicians have their hands on the wheel and their feet at the pedals. They can slow the car. They can stop it. They can choose a different path: one that doesn't lead to destruction of the car, its passengers – ultimately of civilisation as a whole." [329]

protest movements, displaying the sense of urgency those in power are lacking. The strikes have no leaders, rather students organise their own protests, though National Coordinators Sophie Handford and Raven Maeder played vital roles. Sophie has since been elected to the Kāpiti Coast District Council – Aotearoa's youngest councillor at 18 years of age. She pressed them to declare a "climate emergency" meaning that climate change must be considered in all decisions, especially any future planning – and they did!

The School Strike 4 Climate's first strike in Aotearoa, on 15 March 2019, drew tens of thousands of students, some excited, some angry, all united – but a terrible tragedy eclipsed this achievement when news broke of a terrorist attack on two mosques in Christchurch, occurring the same day and swamping the nation in horror and grief.

The second School Strike 4 Climate protest held on 24 May 2019 again drew thousands.[269] By their third climate strike, people of all ages marched in support. On 27 September 2019, 170,000 Kiwis took to our streets in more than 40 events across the country, all organised by students from School Strike 4 Climate NZ and Fridays For Future. The protests kicked off a global school strike as protesters stood together, placards held high, chanting in unison for climate justice as they pulled off one of the largest nationwide protests in Aotearoa's history. Crowds poured into Parliament grounds at midday, the biggest gathering in Wellington since the 2004 foreshore and seabed protests,[270] and in Auckland's Queen Street a group of Pasifika students led an estimated 80,000 marchers.[271]

The next day, several politicians dismissed the students' efforts, saying they were wasting their youth and should "grow out" of it. But students argued their actions were vital. "My education doesn't matter if I have no future or if I have no land," one protester said on radio.[272]

School Strike 4 Climate NZ came up with a list of demands they believe the government should address and were planning another nationwide strike in 2020 when the COVID-19 pandemic hit. Although the strike was called off, they continue to lobby and plan more actions.

Fortunately, here in Aotearoa, we also have many others working towards the same goal: Extinction Rebellion (XR), 350 Aotearoa, the New Zealand Climate Action Network, Generation Zero, WWF-NZ, ECO (Environment and Conservation Organisations - a network of 50+ members of environment and conservation organisations in Aotearoa), Lawyers for Climate Action, Forest and Bird, the Green Party, Greenpeace, Coal Action Network, Save Happy Valley and other anti-mining groups, as well as local activist groups like Oil Free Wellington, churches, iwi and other concerned organisations around the country. But, although change has to be made at community levels, ultimately it's the government who has to act.

YEAR	2007	2019
An urgent and immediate problem	08%	43%
A problem now	16%	26%
A problem for the future	37%	13%
Not really a problem	37%	11%
Don't know	02%	08%

It's not only for the safety and security of human lives that protesters are taking action. We're currently experiencing an extinction crisis largely due to the way we've exploited the planet. A UN report in 2019 put it plainly: "Nature is declining globally at rates unprecedented in human history – and the rate of species extinctions is accelerating, with grave impacts on people around the world now likely." It found that around one million animal and plant species are now threatened, and many will be extinct within decades, more than ever before in human history.[273]

This is scary without a doubt, but it's promising to see how increased climate change activism has finally started to shift Kiwis' opinion about the urgent need for action. Surveys on public attitudes to this issue show a dramatic shift in concern between 2007 and 2019. The percentage of the public now seeing action as urgently needed has jumped by 35% – from 8% to 43% – and nearly 70% think climate change is impacting us right now.[274] With so many extreme weather events in 2020 – from flooding and droughts, to wildfires and super-storms – it's probable that percentage is rising.

Nine local authorities have declared climate emergencies recently: Nelson (16 May 2019), Environment Canterbury (23 May 2019), Kāpiti (23 May 2019), Auckland (11 June 2019), Wellington (20 June 2019), Dunedin (25 June 2019), Hutt Valley (26 June 2019), the Hawke's Bay Regional Council (26 June 2019) and Whangārei (26 July 2019) – all after the start of School Strike 4 Climate's protest marches (just saying!).

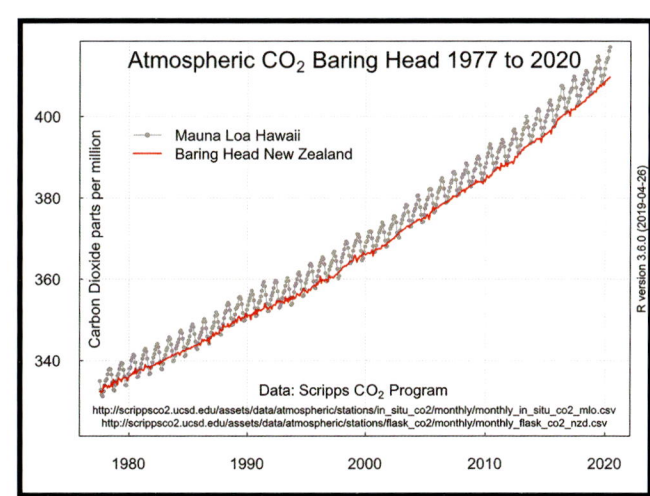

Auckland Mayor Phil Goff said: "Our obligation is to avoid our children and grandchildren inheriting a world devastated by global heating [...] While international and national actions are critical, at a local and personal level we need to play our role in achieving that target."[275]

In May 2019, Chlöe Swarbrick called on Parliament to declare a climate emergency. This motion needed unanimous consent

(every MP had to agree) but it was blocked by the National Party. Prime Minister Jacinda Ardern said: "We're not opposed to the idea of declaring [a climate] emergency in Parliament, because certainly I'd like to think our policies and our approach demonstrates that we do see it as an emergency."

Yet our emissions continue to rise, and a June 2019 poll found that 53% of Kiwis wanted the government to get on with declaring an emergency.[276] Taking the lead, youth MPs symbolically declared a climate change emergency at the Youth Parliament on 18 July 2019, in a move to highlight how critically important this issue is to younger generations.[277]

Earlier that month, more than 50 of the country's top researchers sent an appeal to government: "The scientific consensus is that the world stands on the verge of unprecedented environmental and climate catastrophe for which we are little prepared, and which affords us only a few years for mitigating action. We, the undersigned, urge the New Zealand House of Representatives to declare a climate emergency, now."[278]

On 7 November 2019, the government's Zero Carbon Bill passed with near-unanimous support after the National Party agreed to vote in favour. The law will set up an independent climate change commission to advise government on how to meet targets set within the law – zero net carbon emissions by 2050 and a reduction of between 24% and 47% of methane emissions by 2050. A further methane reduction target of 10% from 2017 levels by 2030 is also included.[279]

The Bill's passing was aided by the hard work of Generation Zero, a group of 38,602 young Kiwis intent on cutting carbon pollution. They championed the Zero Carbon Bill and helped ensure submissions of support flooded into Parliament.

James Shaw, Green Party co-leader said: "Climate change is the defining long-term issue of our generation that successive governments have failed to address. Today we take a significant step forward [...] As the elected representatives [... we] must take the opportunity to act on climate change before the window closes. We've led the world before in nuclear disarmament and in votes for women, now we are leading again."[280]

There's still worry that the dates for these targets are too far off; that more action is needed immediately. And it's a fear that's growing worse as the evidence stacks up. But at the end of 2020, on 2 December, the newly elected Labour-led Government declared a climate emergency in Parliament.[281] Among other actions to help bring down emissions, the government is zeroing in on state-run institutions, planning such actions as phasing out coal boilers at hospitals and schools, and replacing government vehicles with electric cars, all positive efforts to go carbon neutral within the next five years.

"THIS DECLARATION IS AN ACKNOWLEDGEMENT OF THE NEXT GENERATION. AN ACKNOWLEDGEMENT OF THE BURDEN THAT THEY WILL CARRY IF WE DO NOT GET THIS RIGHT AND DO NOT TAKE ACTION NOW." PM JACINDA ARDERN [282]

Movements like Generation Zero, Fridays for Future and School Strike 4 Climate NZ are proof that Aotearoa's younger generations are keenly aware of the challenges they're facing, and, unlike many in older generations, have decided to step up and speak out. That's encouraging news for the rest of us and for the other life that shares our planet

OUR PACIFIC NEIGHBOURS –

This final section is a snapshot of four protests that took place in our neighbouring Pacific nations. There have been hundreds more, of course, all equally worthy of note, and these examples are included as a way to honour them all.

Their struggles to overcome the oppression of colonisation, which changed their lives forever, are similar to those of Māori, with the same battles for fairness, justice, freedoms, fair pay, gender, environment and human rights as we've seen in these pages already. Now our neighbours also face a very modern struggle – climate change as a daily reality. But first we'll start with a story that began a century ago, directly tied to Aotearoa…

SAMOA – THE MAU MOVEMENT

Our government's control of Samoa began after our military occupied German-run Samoa at the beginning of World War One. In 1920, the League of Nations (the forerunner of the UN) handed Aotearoa's government the power to govern Samoa from that time onwards. Their orders were to run it like a British colony, except the coloniser would be Aotearoa.

Samoan locals weren't happy at all. They not only blamed our government for mismanaging the 1918 influenza pandemic (when more than a fifth of their population died), but they were upset their own leaders hadn't been consulted over Samoa's future.

PAST AND FUTURE PROTESTS

A group of men, including Tupua Tamasese Lealofi III (dressed in white), gathered around the office of the Mau, with the slogan "Samoa Mo Samoa" over the door, c 1928.

Several petitions were launched against Aotearoa's colonial-style control. In response, Administrator Major-General George Richardson[283] claimed the Samoans were being stirred up by a handful of local European agitators and ignored their concerns.[284]

But Samoan opposition grew rapidly and was well organised. They held two public meetings in Apia in October and November 1926, where local Europeans and Samoans were invited to air their complaints and organise formal submissions to Aotearoa's government.

In March 1927, a Citizens' Committee agreed to form an organisation called the League of Samoa, known as "O le Mau a Samoa" or the "Mau" ("the firm opinion of Samoa"). Its slogan, "Samoa mo Samoa" ("Samoa for Samoans"), imagined a Samoa without interference from Aotearoa or any other country. The *Samoan Guardian*, established with help from businessman Olaf Nelson (who supported the Mau), had a much more pro-independence stance than *The Samoan Times*, the nation's pro-government newspaper.

Soon the Mau had representatives in all but two of Samoa's districts. The central committee set up its headquarters at Vaimoso, led by Tupua Tamasese Lealofi III, and claimed that 90% of Samoans supported them. The colonial administration estimated the figure at about two-thirds, but it was still significant.

After a visiting MP from Aotearoa caused trouble, Major-General Richardson issued a proclamation ordering the Mau to disband and threatened to deport any non-Samoans who interfered in "native affairs". European Mau supporters ducked for cover and the Samoans were left to steer themselves.

The Mau decided on a campaign of passive resistance to undermine the administration. District councils, village committees and women's welfare committees all stopped meeting, villages ignored visiting officials, children were removed from government schools (forcing some to close), coconuts were left to rot, banana plantations neglected, births and deaths were left unregistered and, rather than paying taxes, fellow Samoans raised money for the Mau.

A Royal Commission set up in 1927 to hear Samoan complaints against the administration sat through evidence from more than 150 witnesses. Three months later it reported back in support of Major-General Richardson's actions and repeated his view that the Mau were an insignificant group of dissatisfied local Europeans and Samoans.

Several key Europeans and "half-castes" were deported to Aotearoa in early 1928, including Olaf Nelson, whose father was Swedish and mother Samoan. Nelson continued his resistance from Auckland, petitioning the government and gaining support from the Opposition Labour Party. In 1928 he published *The Truth about Samoa* and produced his newspaper in Auckland after it was banned in Samoa, now called *The NZ Samoa Guardian*. That same year he presented a petition to the League of Nations in Geneva. It outlined Samoan objections to the administration and was signed by 8000 of Samoa's adult men (of the total population of 9300 adult males).[285] He was denied the right to speak at any of the hearings.

Back in Samoa, the Mau stepped up their campaign. In January 1928, Mau policemen, wearing purple lavalavas with a white stripe as their uniform, imposed a sā (ban) on European shops in Apia. Major-General Richardson responded by requesting back-up from two of our Royal Navy warships. In February 1928, marines from HMS *Dunedin* and HMS *Diomede* helped enforce laws prohibiting Mau activities, arresting hundreds.

With over 400 Mau already crammed into prisons, hundreds more gave themselves up, all at once, together. They knew the prisons couldn't cope with so many of them and they were

right: this huge group overwhelmed the system and it collapsed. All the men had to be released, and Richardson was so humiliated he departed Samoa.

The new Administrator, Colonel Stephen Allen, decided the best way to stamp out the movement was to step up police action. Two violent brawls occurred between police and the Mau, the second ending with the arrest of the Mau's leader, Tupua Tamasese Lealofi III, who was jailed for six months in Aotearoa. Colonel Allen believed the movement would die without their leader, but Mau frustration and fury continued bubbling away beneath the surface. They violently erupted on Saturday 28 December 1929, now known in Samoa as "Black Saturday".

THE HORRORS OF BLACK SATURDAY

The trouble broke out along Apia's waterfront during a Mau parade to welcome two members home from exile in Aotearoa. The Mau secretary was there, though he'd been warned to stay away by police. When they moved in to arrest him, the marchers objected. More police were called in. Tempers flared and the parade transformed to an angry mob. Police responded by firing revolvers towards the crowd. The Mau were enraged and chased the police through town, back to their station … all except one. He was caught and clubbed to death.

Tupua Tamasese Leolofi III lying in state.

As the Mau converged on the police station, a sergeant fired a machine gun from the balcony a barrage of bullets whizzed over their heads to deter them. Three policemen feared the Mau were about to burn the building down and fired their rifles into the crowd. Tragically, Tupua Tamasese Lealofi III was killed, along with seven others, with three dying later and up to 50 injured.[286] As he lay dying, Lealofi's last words were,

> "MY BLOOD HAS BEEN SPILT FOR SAMOA. I AM PROUD TO GIVE IT. DO NOT DREAM OF AVENGING IT, AS IT WAS SPILT IN PEACE. IF I DIE, PEACE MUST BE MAINTAINED AT ANY PRICE."[287]

The administration blamed the deaths on the men who had resisted arrest, and a Kiwi coroner concluded that the shooting was justified "under the circumstances". The Mau swore the police attacked an innocent crowd – and the fact that Tamasese was shot while trying to calm that crowd only made it worse. Their feelings were aggravated even more by the administration's actions in the following weeks.

THE ADMINISTRATION ATTACKS

Believing the Mau were on the verge of defeat, Colonel Allen put in place hard-hitting measures to bring about complete collapse. On 13 January 1930, after the Mau refused to give up its headquarters or surrender any wanted men, Allen declared the organisation treasonous (therefore all members were traitors) and wearing a Mau uniform was now illegal. Up to 1500 men fled into the bush, chased by 150 marines and seamen from HMS *Dunedin* with 50 military police and a seaplane to track them.

Samoa's locals supported the Mau, sharing shelter and food, and passing on news about the troops' positions. The marines tried to stop informers by raiding villages, often at night, brandishing fixed bayonets, stirring up further resentment. The Mau no longer trusted Aotearoa's law enforcers, their fear made worse when an unarmed 16-year-old boy was shot and killed as he ran from a marine, who claimed the boy was about to throw a stone. His excuse was accepted by authorities and no charges were laid.

After weeks of chasing and being chased, both sides were tired. A truce was declared on 12 March 1930, when a second child was killed by the marines, many of whom were weakened by the heat and tropical infections. With the support of local Europeans and missionaries, Mau leaders met Aotearoa's Minister of Defence and agreed to go home, so long as they could retain their right not to cooperate. This was accepted. Back in Auckland, Olaf Nelson and several other exiled leaders continued to lobby the government and report back to the Mau.[288]

Colonel Allen was replaced as administrator by Brigadier-General Herbert Hart in April 1931 and an uneasy stand-off followed. With men still being arrested for supporting the Mau, women stepped in to rally supporters and hold more protests. Olaf Nelson's return from exile in 1933 caused a surge of activity but this was quickly shut down by his re-arrest and deportation the following year. To many it may have seemed the Mau were being subdued, but they were playing a long game.

When Aotearoa's Labour Party was voted into power in 1935 all their lobbying paid off and the new government organised a goodwill mission to Apia the following year to put right some of the injustices. The Mau were recognised as a lawful political organisation and several punishing local laws were repealed. Olaf Nelson was freed from exile and the Mau won majorities in both a newly elected Fono of Faipule (or Fono a Faipule in Samoan) and the legislative assembly. But dissatisfaction rumbled on … they still weren't completely free.

After World War Two, the newly formed United Nations put increased pressure on Aotearoa's government to work towards Samoan independence. Independence finally happened on 1 January 1962, when Tupua Tamasese Mea'ole, son of Tupua Tamasese Lealofi III, became joint head of state with Malietoa Tanumafili II, the son of George Richardson's adviser.

Nearly 90 years after our military first stepped ashore at Apia, Prime Minister Helen Clark went to Samoa on 4 June 2002. At a celebration to mark the 40th anniversary of Samoa's independence, she said: "On behalf of the New Zealand Government, I wish to offer today a formal apology to the people of Samoa for the injustices arising from New Zealand's administration of Samoa in its earlier years, and to express sorrow and regret for those injustices."[289] Her speech was televised from Apia to venues in Auckland, Wellington and Christchurch. In Auckland, hundreds gathered at a local convention centre where they burst into applause as soon as the word "apology" was mentioned. By the end of the speech, many were in tears.[290]

Women's Mau committee

The leaders of the women's Mau: Mrs Tuimaliifano, Mrs Tamasese, Mrs Nelson, Mrs Faumuina,

WHAT ABOUT AMERICAN SAMOA?

In American Samoa, locals were colonised by the United States in 1900. There was also an American Samoa Mau movement, led by Samuelu Ripley, a World War One veteran from Leone village, Tutuila. After travelling to raise support on the US mainland, he was refused re-entry when he tried to return. In the meantime, the US Navy suppressed the Mau movement.

In 1966, the UN gave American Samoa the option of joining the independent nation of Samoa, but locals chose to remain as an unincorporated territory of the United States. Their constitution was ratified in 1966 and came into effect in 1967.[291]

MAASINA RURU – THE SOLOMON ISLANDS' INDEPENDENCE MOVEMENT

After the Spanish explorer Álvaro de Mendaña first reached the Solomon Islands in 1568, rumours spread that he'd discovered where the biblical King Solomon found the gold for his temple in Jerusalem. The islands were given the name *Islas de Salomón* as a result. But they remained uncolonised, even after naval and commercial shipping began to pass through their waters after the English settled Sydney in 1788.

Catholic missionaries arrived in the 1840s but didn't succeed in establishing a settlement in the Solomons until 1898. Anglican missionaries, who'd been taking islanders to Aotearoa for training since the 1850s, settled in the Solomons from the 1870s, with other missions arriving later. By the late 19th century, locals were being shipped as labourers to work on plantations in Queensland, Fiji and other island nations, with around 30,000 taken between 1870 and 1910.

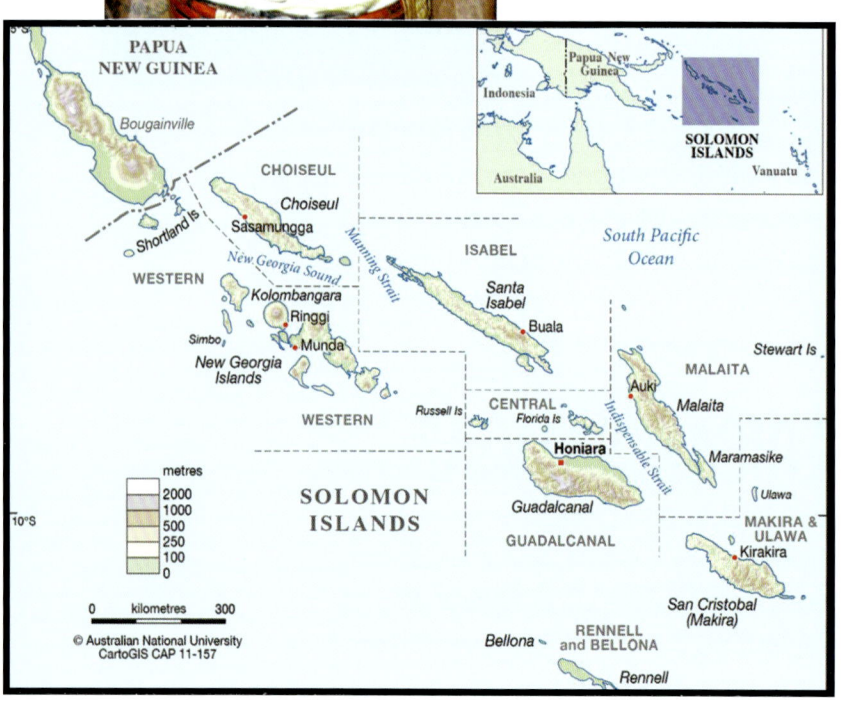

Germany and Britain jointly claimed the Solomons for themselves in 1886, dividing the islands up before Germany transferred all the northern ones (except for Buka and Bougainville) to Britain in 1899. Britain had already claimed the southern islands in exchange for agreeing to recognise Germany's claim over Samoa and parts of Africa. The British Solomon Islands Protectorate was declared in 1893 and colonial rule began there in 1896.[292] The Solomon Islands' people had no say.

In 1927 government tax collectors were murdered by members of the Kwaio people on the island of Malaita, and this triggered a brutal response from British officials. Backed by an Australian warship, they burned and looted villages and killed many of the Kwaio.

When World War Two broke out in the Pacific, the Japanese occupied the Solomon Islands from early 1942. They were stopped from moving further south by US forces, who invaded on 7 August. The fighting in the Solomons over the next 15 months was some of the fiercest in the Pacific and the Battle of Guadalcanal was central to the Pacific War. US forces and their allies were supported by locals who, for many months, were forced to live in the bush without fires at night, fearing the Japanese would find them.[293]

Maasina Ruru (or the Maasina Rule) arose as an independence movement in the British Solomon Islands during World War Two. The name, from the 'Are'are language, means the rule of "relationship of siblings together".

The movement started after several men from Malaita worked together in the Solomon Islands Labour Corps during World War Two. It's said that the African American soldiers stationed there treated the locals much more humanely than the plantation owners, and that this, and tales of revolutions and freedom movements, helped to foster a spirit of independence among the Malaitan soldiers. They began a campaign of passive resistance and civil disobedience that spread to all the Malaitan soldiers.

In June 1947, 6000–7000 Malaitans (most from the north) met with the District Commissioner and his officers in Auki, at that time the largest meeting ever held in the Solomons. Their leaders insisted the government recognise their "kastom" law and courts and allow them to pick the men to head them.[294]

Instead, the British government launched Operation De-Louse to arrest the leaders of the movement, and this name tells us all we need to know about their attitude to the locals. Nine Alaha (chiefs) were also arrested and charged under the Sedition Act for organising secret meetings. Most were sentenced to six-and-a-half years hard labour, including several of Maasina Ruru's key leaders.

As Maasina Ruru evolved, the desire for islanders to have their own government became their main priority.[295] While their leaders were in jail, campaigners encouraged civil disobedience, leading whole villages to refuse to pay their taxes and to barricade themselves against the British. The government launched Operation Jericho and 2000 arrests were made in Malaita alone. Yet resistance continued.

In 1951, with the mood of the world changing, the British government held meetings with the imprisoned leaders and eventually agreed that the islands could govern themselves. The prisoners were released, and Maasina Ruru's demands were met towards the end of that year.[296] After 55 years, these courageous men and women had finally won their freedom.

TONGA MA'A TONGA KAUTAHA – TONGA FOR TONGANS

Sometimes protest comes in the form of a local movement chipping away at a ruling authority's grip on their economy, especially when it affects people's ability to control their own lives. Boycotts are one form of economic protest, as seen in the section on the Springbok Tour. Tonga Ma'a Tonga Kautaha (Tonga for Tongans Cooperative) was another such example.

Although Tonga was declared a British Protectorate in 1900, its colonial status was unique in the Pacific. It already had its own strong monarchy and an organised central government, which enabled the kingdom to resist more formal colonial domination. But after European settlers and rival Tongan chiefs tried to cast out the king, he entered into an agreement (the Treaty of Friendship), which allowed the British government to control Tonga's foreign relations and exercise authority over British and foreign residents. In return, Britain would have no authority to interfere in Tonga's domestic concerns.[297]

However, in 1905, the agreement soured when King Tupou II was threatened with invasion and deportation if he didn't sign a new agreement that declared Britain's Agent in Tonga must "be consulted and his advice taken".[298] The British made it clear they viewed Tongan systems as inefficient and often corrupt. After granting Britain this power, its officials began forcing "advice" onto the Tongans. King Tupou II, who ruled Tonga from 1893–1918, fought unsuccessfully against it, arguing that it violated not only the 1900 treaty, but also his kingdom's own 1875 constitution.[299]

When William Telfer Campbell was appointed as British Agent in Tonga in September 1909, British interference grew even worse. He saw no value in the Tongan way of life or in their local system of government and thought it was his duty to "save" them. His hostile attitude spurred a new movement.

The Tonga Ma'a Tonga Kautaha was established in May 1909 by a local European resident, Alexander D. Cameron. Within months, it transformed into an important organisation, both commercially and symbolically

Initially, the Kautaha (as it became known) simply worked as another agency to export its members' copra and give them a fair price (less duty, freight and a small commission to the president). It also directly imported bulk goods, so members could buy supplies at a cheaper price. This way, the Kautaha ensured real savings for its members, as British traders often charged Tongans twice as much for goods as Europeans.

But it wasn't only the money that attracted members. The Kautaha also fostered Tongan ambitions to regain political and economic independence, and by February 1910, they had 3280 members (1280 in Tongatapu, 1200 in Vava'u and 800 in Ha'apai), amounting to 60% of all taxpayers.[300] Members included many of Tonga's most influential chiefs and nobles.

Richard Seddon (Aotearoa's 15th Premier) visits Tonga in 1900.

Campbell made attempts to discredit Alexander Cameron, claiming he was a rogue who was shamefully exploiting "ignorant and trustful natives".[301] Most other British officials in Tonga shared his view.

In August 1910, Campbell seized the Kautaha's financial books (which Cameron claimed was illegal) and gave them to the Tongan government, saying other Tongans were being exploited "in a scandalous manner". Although an investigation found that there was no evidence to back this statement, it was used as the excuse to close down the Kautaha. Campbell directed the Minister of Police to guard the Kautaha premises and seize their assets. The Minister of Police later reported to the High Commissioner that "The Premier [Mateialona] told me he had instructions from the Consul and that these instructions were more powerful than the Privy Council [... He] told me to close it or I might get into trouble.'[302]

Cameron was charged with fraud but let off when no evidence was produced. Various other court proceedings went back and forth, and relations between the Tongans and the British remained tense. A law change made it illegal for "any Tongan to give, subscribe, collect, or to aid, assist or abet in the subscription or collection of any money or produce for the purpose of helping any non-native who in the past may have been associated with natives of Tonga for the purpose of trading or in any Kautaha".[303] But these efforts to undermine the Kautaha simply made local heroes of its members and supporters.

Alexander Cameron later attempted to rebuild the Kautaha under the new name Tonga Ma'a Tonga Company Limited but it was unsuccessful and ceased business about 1916. Yet, because of all the trouble caused by William Campbell's heavy-handed dealings with King Tupou II, and the king's insistence on following through the entire legal process, it actually strengthened the king's position and power – which, in turn, shored up the nation's independence from the British.[304]

The King wrote of this time:

"I am weary beyond measure of the existing condition of things. I have tried to preserve to my people their national existence, but there is a limit to my endurance. What does Great Britain want? Does she desire to further extend her dominions by adding to her wide empire the little kingdom of Tonga? No resistance can be offered. We can make no appeal to arms – our only appeal can be made to the justice which is supposed to characterise Great Britain's treatment of weaker nations [...] Does Great Britain desire to render the foreign traders richer, or does she truly desire to leave my people happy and contended? [...] If we do not adopt the wisest course in managing our own concerns, that will be our affair. No nation has always seen clearly the right course to follow. If we are to make mistakes, then let us learn wisdom by experience, but as long as the interests of the few foreigners living in our midst are not endangered, no just cause can be found for robbing us of our independence, under the guise of giving us the 'advice' of the British Agent."[305]

King Tupou II threatened to prosecute the Premier, but eventually agreed to withdraw the charges if the Premier resigned. He did. Charges were then brought against others who'd tried to damage the king's power. That's the great twist here – even though the Kautaha first set out to break the British control on their trade, it was the unjust way they were closed down that resulted in a much more significant outcome, a successful protest against British domination. From that time on, the British Agent's power to intervene in Tonga's domestic affairs was carefully managed and much more limited.

"WE ARE NOT DROWNING, WE ARE FIGHTING!" – KIRIBATI

We finish with a current and desperately urgent example of Pacific people fighting to protect their families, homes and futures. The Republic of Kiribati (pronounced *Kiri-baas*) is an independent nation in the central Pacific Ocean, right now at the very forefront of the climate crisis. It has a permanent population of just over 110,000 inhabitants,[306] more than half living on Tarawa atoll. The republic covers 32 atolls and one raised coral island, Banaba, with a total land area of 811 square kilometres, scattered over 3.5 million square kilometres of ocean.[307] Twenty-one of these atolls are inhabited, each surrounded by a ring-shaped coral reef only a few metres above sea level, making them extremely vulnerable to the effects of climate change.

Kiribati gained independence from the United Kingdom in 1979. Its capital, South Tarawa, has the highest population and features a string of islets connected by causeways. In 1999, the two small uninhabited Kiribati islets of Tebua Tarawa and Abanuea disappeared underwater, in what is now considered one of the first signs of the effects of global climate change.[308] With sea levels predicted to rise at least 50cm by 2100 and further rises expected, it's likely within a century the nation's productive growing land will be tainted by saltwater and end up largely submerged.[309]

Three or four times a year, king tides can also result in seawater flooding low-lying areas, and soil and vegetation on the islands risk being stripped away if a cyclone strikes. In March 2015, Kiribati experienced flooding and destruction of seawalls and coastal infrastructure when Cyclone Pam (a Category 5 storm) swept through.[310] All these stresses affect the health and well-being of Kiribati's residents, fear and insecurity now a part of daily life.

The Kiribati Adaptation Program (KAP) started in 2003 with a US$5.5 million programme first put in place by Kiribati's government with the support of global institutions (like the UN and World Bank) and the Japanese government. Later, Australia donated another US$1.5 million. This money funds projects such as improving Tarawa's water supply, coastal protection like replanting mangroves and shoring up roads, seawalls, sewage and power, strengthening laws to reduce coastal erosion and emergency planning for the evacuation of the entire population to safer sites if needed.[311]

In February 2014, Fiji's president announced Fiji would assist the people of Kiribati in any way it could and would provide a home if their country is submerged. Kiribati has purchased 6000 acres of land on Fiji's second biggest island, Vanua Levu, to ensure it can feed its people if sea rise swamps its crop-growing land. "The spirit of the people of Kiribati will not be extinguished," Fiji's president said. "It will live on somewhere else because a nation isn't only a physical place. A nation – and the sense of belonging that comes with it – exists in the hearts and the minds of its citizens wherever they may be."[312]

Meanwhile, people all over Kiribati are taking climate change action, desperate for others to recognise the seriousness of the situation. Young people, supported by the youth climate movement 350 Pacific and others, are actively protesting and working to raise awareness, demanding governments free their countries from fossil fuel dependence. A coalition of many youth and women's groups in Kiribati also actively works to combat climate change. With other Pacific nations such as Tuvalu also facing an uncertain climate future, it's up to all of us to support those fighting at the front line of this unfolding emergency. Together we can turn the tide and make a safer future for every person on the planet.

ACKNOWLEDGEMENTS

My thanks to OneTree House publishers, Christine Dale and Jenny Nagle, for making this book possible, and to Creative New Zealand for funding support. Thank you too, to the many kind people who have contributed their time and resources: Paul Bensemann, for allowing me to quote from his beautiful book *Fight for the Forests* (Potton & Burton 2018) and for fact-checking; Dean Baigent Mercer, for an excerpt from his description of the Timberlands protests; John Hanlon, for his kind permission to quote the lyrics of his song Damn the Dam in full; Denis Tegg, of Coromandel Watchdog; Tim Jones, of the Save Aramoana campaign; Cindy Baxter, Tara Forde and Frances Mountier for fact-checking and images from the Save Happy Valley campaign; Tania Roxborogh, for checking the section on Bastion Point; Paulina Sadowska and Mailbu Hamilton, from Kiwis Against Seabed Mining; photographer John McCombe, for kindly searching through his files to find the photos of the treetop protests and granting me permission to use them; Te Miringa Hohaia, who, in 2005, acquainted me with the story of Parihaka; Amnesty UK, Kit Wilson, Generation Zero, Greenpeace, Ira Bailey, Phil Braithwaite, Coal Action Network, Scoop, Indymedia, Tom Scott, Eric Heath, Wellington Rape Crisis, Bill Logan, Dylan Owen, NZ Labour Party, Amnesty Aroha and Mark Hurwitt (cartoonist) for their kind permissions to use images. To my brother Nicky Hager, thank you for all your fact-checking and support, and for all the incredible work you have done to uphold human rights and protect the environment, so proud of you!

I'd also like to acknowledge the great wealth of information available at NZ History, https://nzhistory.govt.nz/, produced by the History Group of the New Zealand Ministry for Culture and Heritage, and Te Ara: The Encyclopedia of New Zealand, https://teara.govt.nz/en. These resources have formed the backbone of much of this book.

Finally, I'd like to thank every Kiwi who has engaged in our democratic process by speaking out and taking action when they saw something they believed was wrong. You are the real heroes of this book and your contribution to improving the lives of fellow Kiwis and the land we live in will not be forgotten.

GLOSSARY

Accessible – a place able to be reached, entered or used.

Activism – the use of direct and noticeable action to achieve a result, usually a political or social one.

Activist – someone involved in activism.

Adjacent – nearby; not distant; having a common endpoint or border.

Apartheid – the former South African policy that legalised racial segregation and political and economic discrimination against 'non-whites'.

Arbitration – the use of an arbitrator/mediator (who acts like a referee) to settle a dispute.

Bargain – an agreement between two or more people or groups as to what each will do for the other, or to discuss the terms and conditions of a deal.

Bicultural – having or combining the cultural attitudes and customs of two nations, peoples or ethnic groups.

Boycott – to withdraw from commercial or social relations with a country, organisation or person as a punishment or protest.

Breach – an act of breaking or failing to observe a law, agreement or code of conduct.

Campaign – to work in an organised and active way towards a particular goal, typically a political or social one.

Civil disobedience – the refusal to comply with certain unjust laws as a peaceful form of political protest.

Coalition – the joining together of different political parties or groups for a particular purpose, usually for a limited time; a government that is formed in this way.

Cold War (the) – the state of hostility that existed between Soviet-led countries and Western powers from 1945 to 1990.

Collective – when something is owned or done by people acting as a group.

Communal – of, belonging to, or shared by the people of a community; shared ownership and control of goods and property.

Communist/communism – a social political movement aiming to set up a society based on common ownership of the means of production; would not rely on social classes or money.

Compensation – something (typically money) awarded to someone in recognition of loss, suffering, or injury.

Compulsory – something that *must* be done; made necessary by a rule or law.

Conqueror – one who conquers; one who wins a country in war, subdues or overpowers a people, or overcomes an opponent.

Confiscate – the action of taking or seizing someone's property by a government or other public authority.

Cultural revival – where aspects of culture that a group identifies with have been recovered after losses due to colonisation, forced or voluntary relocation, oppression or modernisation.

Customary law/right – a set of customs, practices and beliefs that are accepted as binding rules of conduct by indigenous peoples and local communities. Customary law forms an underlying part of their social and economic systems and way of life.

Disillusioned – disappointed and unhappy after discovering the truth about something or someone that you liked or respected.

Displace – to force someone to leave their home, typically because of war, oppression or natural disaster.

Disruption – disturbance or problems which interrupt an event, activity or process.

Divisive – something tending to cause disagreement or hostility between people.

Domination – the exercise of power or influence over someone or something, or the state of being so controlled.

Ecological – relating to or concerned with the relation of living organisms to one another and to their physical surroundings. (Also 'ecosystems' – where the living organisms live.)

EU – European Union

Eviction – the act or process of officially forcing someone to leave a house or piece of land.

Flagstaff – the pole that flies the flag.

Fono of Faipule (Fono a Faipule) – an advisory body of Samoan leaders established by the German administration and retained during Aotearoa's military occupation.

Frack/fracking – the process of injecting liquid at high pressure into underground rocks, boreholes, etc. to force open existing fissures and extract oil or gas.

General election – an election held to choose members of Parliament to run the country.

Haka – performance of the haka, posture dance – vigorous dances with actions and rhythmically shouted words. A general term for several types of such dances.

Hapū – kinship group, clan, tribe, subtribe; section of a large kinship group and the primary political unit in traditional Māori society. It consisted of a number of whānau sharing descent from a common ancestor, usually being named after the ancestor, but sometimes from an important event in the group's history. A number of related hapū usually shared adjacent territories forming a looser tribal federation (iwi).

Hīkoi – collective march (usually to Parliament) to send a political message.

Hui – gathering, meeting, assembly, seminar, conference.

Iwi – extended kinship group, tribe, nation, people, nationality, race – often refers to a large group of people descended from a common ancestor and associated with a distinct territory.

Kaitiakitanga – guardianship or management.

Kaumātua – adult, elder, elderly man, elderly woman, old man – a person of status within the *whānau*.

Kīngitanga movement – arising in the 1850s, some tribes from the central North Island joined together and set up a Māori King to champion their interests and challenge the overall power of the British monarchy. The current Māori monarch, Tūheitia Paki, was elected in 2006.

Korowai cloak – The Korowai is a traditional woven Maori cloak, worn by those who are looked upon as holding prestige and honour. The name Korowai is symbolic of leadership, and includes the obligation to care for the people and environment.

Kōhanga Reo – Māori language nests

Kuia – elderly woman, grandmother, female elder.

Kura Kaupapa – Māori immersion schools

Lavalava – (also known as an *'ie*, short for *'ie lavalava*) an article of daily clothing traditionally worn by Polynesians and other Oceanic peoples. It consists of a single rectangular cloth worn similarly to a wraparound skirt or kilt.

Legacy – something that is a part of your history or that remains from an earlier time.

Lobby/lobbied/lobbying – seek to influence (a government official) on an issue.

Local election – an election to select members for a town, regional or city council.

Marae – courtyard – the open area in front of the *wharenui*, where formal greetings and discussions take place. Often also used to include the complex of buildings around the *marae*.

Migrant – a person who moves from one place to another, especially in order to find work or better living conditions.

Monocultural – relating to a culture that is the same across a vast area, not allowing for individual differences in culture.

OECD – Organisation for Economic Co-operation and Development.

Occupy/occupied/occupation – an army or group of people move into and take control or possession of a place.

Pā – fortified village, fort, stockade, screen, blockade, city (especially a fortified one).

Pākehā – English, foreign, European, exotic – introduced from or originating in a foreign country; New Zealander of European descent – probably originally applied to English-speaking Europeans living in Aotearoa.

Passive resistance – non-violent opposition to authority, especially a refusal to cooperate with legal requirements.

Pass laws – one of the dominant features of the apartheid system, this was a form of internal passport designed to racially segregate the population, manage growth of towns and cities and control migrant labour.

Patu – beating, hitting, assault, killing, weapon, club.

Petition – a formal written request, typically one signed by many people, appealing to authority in respect of a particular cause.

Persecute – to subject (someone) to hostility and ill-treatment, especially because of their race, or political or religious beliefs.

Pitted – set opposing groups against each other.

Pōwhiri – invitation, rituals of encounter, welcome ceremony on a marae, welcome.

Proclaiming – to announce something publicly or officially.

Radical – believing or expressing the belief that there should be great or extreme social or political change.

Radome – a structural, weatherproof enclosure that protects a radar antenna and looks like a giant puffball.

Rangatira – noble

Recession (economic) – a period of economic decline.

Rohe/ocean rohe – Māori term for boundary, district, region, territory, area, border (of land or ocean).

Self-determination – the ability or power to make decisions for yourself, especially the power of a nation or people to decide how it/they will be governed.

Sovereign – a king or queen.

Sovereignty – the authority of a state to govern itself or another state.

Stealth/stealthy – slow, deliberate and secret in action or character.

Submission – the action of presenting a proposal, application, or other document for consideration or judgment, particularly used when sending feedback on proposed bills in parliament.

Suffrage – the right to vote in political elections.

Surveyor – a person who inspects something officially for the purpose of ascertaining land boundaries, condition, value, etc.

Sustainability – the avoidance of the over-use of natural resources in order to protect the ecological balance.

Symbol/symbolic – expressing or representing an idea or quality without using words.

Tangata whenua – local people, hosts, indigenous people – people born of the whenua, i.e. of the placenta and of the land where the people's ancestors have lived and where their placenta are buried.

Te Reo Māori – Māori language

Te Kotahitanga – An independent Māori Parliament convened annually in New Zealand from 1892 until 1902.

Te Tiriti o Waitangi – The Māori language version of the Treaty of Waitangi, first signed on 6 February 1840 by representatives of the British Crown and Māori chiefs from the North Island of Aotearoa.

The Crown – the New Zealand Government.

Think Big policy/programme – an economic strategy of the third National government, promoted by Prime Minister Robert Muldoon in the early 1980s. It focused on large-scale industrial projects, particularly in the petrochemical and energy sectors. The Think Big scheme saw the government borrow heavily from overseas.

Tino rangatiratanga – self-determination, sovereignty, autonomy, self-government, domination, rule, control, power.

Trade Union – an organised association of workers in a trade, group of trades, or profession, formed to protect and further their rights and interests.

Trait – a distinguishing quality or characteristic, typically one belonging to a person; a genetically determined characteristic.

Undermine/undermining – to attack by indirect, secret, or underhand means; attempt to subvert (overthrow or damage) by stealth.

Waka – traditional Māori canoe.

Whānau – extended family, family group, a familiar term of address to a number of people; the primary economic unit of traditional Māori society. In the modern context the term is sometimes used to include friends who may not have any kinship ties to other members.

Whistle-blower – a person who exposes information or activity within a private, public, or government organisation that is deemed illegal, illicit, unsafe, a waste, fraud, or abuse of taxpayer funds.

ENDNOTES

1. Land Protests – Home is Where the Heart is

1. The UN Declaration on the Right and Responsibility of Individuals, Groups and Organs of Society to Promote and Protect Universally Recognised Human Rights and Fundamental Freedoms.
2. Quote from Margaret Mead, American anthropologist.
3. Place holder for 185
4. 'Hōne Heke cuts down the British flagstaff – again', Ministry for Culture and Heritage, https://nzhistory.govt.nz/hone-heke-cuts-down-british-flagstaff-for-a-third-time (updated 21 January 2020)
5. As above.
6. Freda Rankin Kawharu, 'Heke Pōkai, Hōne Wiremu', Dictionary of New Zealand Biography, first published in 1990. Te Ara – The Encyclopedia of New Zealand https://teara.govt.nz/en/biographies/1h16/heke-pokai-hone-wiremu (accessed 16 June 2020).
7. Dick Scott, Ask that Mountain – The Story of Parihaka, Raupo Publishing (NZ) Ltd, 2008.
8. DENIAL OF THE EFFECTS OF COLONISATION? Peace Movement Aotearoa newsletter (31 August 2000).
9. 'Tears as Crown apologises for Parihaka atrocities', RNZ, https://www.rnz.co.nz/news/te-manu-korihi/332613/tears-as-crown-apologises-for-parihaka-atrocities (9 June 2017).
10. Explanation from: https://www.tupu.nz/en/tuhono/about-maori-land-in-new-zealand/history-of-maori-land
11. From Why We March, Archives NZ https://www.flickr.com/photos/archivesnz/20633566803
12. J. Metge, Rautahi: The Maori of New Zealand. Routledge, 2004. p. 177
13. 'Mocked haka proved a turning point', One News, http://tvnz.co.nz/content/2694643/2591764.xhtml (1 May 2009).
14. https://en.wikipedia.org/wiki/Ng%C4%81_Tamatoa
15. Mark Hickford, 'Law of the foreshore and seabed', Te Ara – the Encyclopedia of New Zealand, http://www.TeAra.govt.nz/en/law-of-the-foreshore-and-seabed (accessed 26 June 2020).
16. Waitangi Tribunal finds Marine and Coastal Area Act breaches Treaty of Waitangi', NZ Herald, https://www.nzherald.co.nz/nz/news/article.cfm?c_id=1&objectid=12344202 (30 June 2020).

2. Employment Issues – Striking For a Better Life

17. Most of this section was sourced from Mark Derby, 'Strikes and labour disputes – The 1912 and 1913 strikes', Te Ara – the Encyclopedia of New Zealand, http://www.TeAra.govt.nz/en/strikes-and-labour-disputes/page-5 (accessed 2 July 2020).
18. 'The 1951 waterfront dispute', Ministry for Culture and Heritage, https://nzhistory.govt.nz/politics/the-1951-waterfront-dispute (updated 17 May 2017).
19. 'Behind the 1951 waterfront lockout – Philip Ferguson', https://libcom.org/history/behind-1951-waterfront-lockout-philip-ferguson
20. As above.
21. The 1951 waterfront dispute', Ministry for Culture and Heritage, https://nzhistory.govt.nz/politics/the-1951-waterfront-dispute (updated 17 May 2017).

3. Shaking Up the System – Gender and Disability Rights

22. Megan Cook, 'Opposition and support from the 1960s', Te Ara – The Encyclopedia of New Zealand, https://teara.govt.nz/en/abortion/page-3 (8 November 2018)
23. https://en.wikipedia.org/wiki/Sisters_Overseas_Service
24. Alison McCulloch, Fighting to Choose: The Abortion Rights Struggle in New Zealand. Victoria University Press, Wellington NZ, 2013.
25. Megan Cook, 'Controversy: 1974 to 1980s', Te Ara – The Encyclopedia of New Zealand, https://teara.govt.nz/en/abortion/page-4 (8 November 2018)
26. From an article by J. Davidson, M. Ingram, L. Benson, in Broadsheet, December 1979, No. 75.
27. 'Homosexual law reform in New Zealand', Ministry for Culture and Heritage, https://nzhistory.govt.nz/culture/homosexual-law-reform/homosexual-law-reform (updated 14 June 2016).
28. 'Reforming the law', Ministry for Culture and Heritage, https://nzhistory.govt.nz/culture/homosexual-law-reform/reforming-the-law (updated 1 July 2014).
29. As above.

4. The Peacemakers

30. 'Recruiting and conscription', Ministry for Culture and Heritage, https://nzhistory.govt.nz/war/recruiting-and-conscription (updated 17 Nov 2016).
31. 2018 statistics https://en.wikipedia.org/wiki/List_of_New_Zealand_urban_areas_by_population
32. 'Conscientious objection and dissent', Ministry for Culture and Heritage, https://nzhistory.govt.nz/war/first-world-war/conscientious-objection and 'Conscription', Te Ara – The Encyclopedia of New Zealand,https://teara.govt.nz/en/conscription-conscientious-objection -and-pacifism/page-1 and WW100, https://ww100.govt.nz/history-guide
33. 'World War I', Britannica, https://www.britannica.com/event/World-War-I and Ministry for Culture and Heritage, www.nzhistory.govt.nz
34. Information from 'Conscientious objection and dissent in the First World War', Ministry for Culture and Heritage, https://nzhistory.govt.nz/war/first-world-war/conscientious-objection (updated 14 Jan 2020).
35. Archibald Baxter, We Will Not Cease, The Caxton Press, Christchurch, 1968. http://nzetc.victoria.ac.nz/tm/scholarly/tei-BaxWeWi.html
36. https://www.archibaldbaxtertrust.com/

37 'Te Puea Hērangi', Ministry for Culture and Heritage, https://nzhistory.govt.nz/media/photo/te-puea-h%C4%93rangi (updated 29 Apr 2020).

38 'Māori objection to conscription', Ministry for Culture and Heritage, https://nzhistory.govt.nz/war/first-world-war/conscientious-objection/maori-objection (updated 1 May 2020)

39 As above.

40 Commander of the Most Excellent Order of the British Empire.

41 Mark Derby, 'Conscription, conscientious objection and pacifism - Conscientious objection', Te Ara – The Encyclopedia of New Zealand, http://www.TeAra.govt.nz/en/conscription-conscientious-objection-and-pacifism/page-2 (accessed 3 June 2020).

42 'The Families of Conscientious Objectors', Lest We Forget, https://lestweforget.org.nz/profiles/the-families-of-conscientious-objectors/

43 Quoted from 'Protesters and police clash Vietnam War – 15 Years of News', Dominion Post, https://www.stuff.co.nz/dominion-post/capital-life/72757317/protesters-and-police-clash-vietnam-war---150-years-of-news (8 October 2015).

44 'Anti-Vietnam War protests in Auckland', Ministry for Culture and Heritage, https://nzhistory.govt.nz/anti-vietnam-war-protests-on-queen-street (updated 15 Dec 2016).

45 'Vietnam War', Ministry for Culture and Heritage, https://nzhistory.govt.nz/war/vietnam-war

46 'Fact Sheet 8: The use of defoliants – Agent Orange', Ministry for Culture and Heritage, https://nzhistory.govt.nz/files/documents/vietnam-fact-sheet8.pdf

47 'What is Agent Orange?' Ministry for Culture and Heritage, https://www.aspeninstitute.org/programs/agent-orange-in-vietnam-program/what-is-agent-orange/

48 'Fact Sheet 8: The use of defoliants – Agent Orange', Ministry for Culture and Heritage, https://nzhistory.govt.nz/files/documents/vietnam-fact-sheet8.pdf

49 'Kiwi Vietnam veterans urged to re-apply for government support', One News, https://www.tvnz.co.nz/one-news/new-zealand/kiwi-vietnam-veterans-urged-re-apply-government-support (19 October 2019).

50 'The War's Effect on the Vietnamese Land and People', Encyclopedia.com, https://www.encyclopedia.com/history/encyclopedias-almanacs-transcripts-and-maps/wars-effect-vietnamese-land-and-people (updated 22 March 2021).

51 Susan Brownmiller, Against Our Will: Men, Women and Rape. Simon & Schuster, 1975. p. 103–05, and 'Murder in the name of war: My Lai', BBC News, http://news.bbc.co.uk/2/hi/asia-pacific/64344.stm (20 July 1998).

52 Netx C. Crawford, 'War-related Death, Injury and Displacement in Afghanistan and Pakistan 2001–2014', Watson Institute, https://watson.brown.edu/costsofwar/files/cow/imce/papers/2015/War%20Related%20Casualties%20Afghanistan%20and%20Pakistan%202001-2014%20FIN.pdf

53 'Thousands March in Auckland Against USA War', Scoop, https://www.scoop.co.nz/stories/HL0302/S00104/thousands-march-in-auckland-against-usa-war.htm (15 February 2003).

54 Nicky Hager, Other People's Wars, Craig Potton Publishing, NZ, 2011. p. 99–100

55 As above.

56 Nicky Hager, Secret Power: New Zealand's Role in the International Spy Network, Craig Potton Publishing, NZ, 1996.

57 'Ploughshares Penetrate Waihopai Base Deflate Dome', Ploughshares press release, https://www.scoop.co.nz/stories/PO0804/S00443.htm (30 April 2008).

58 'Veteran activist one of Waihopai three', Otago Daily Times, https://www.odt.co.nz/news/national/veteran-activist-one-waihopai-three (1 May 2008).

59 'Waihopai three walk free', Stuff.co.nz, http://www.stuff.co.nz/national/crime/3468003/Waihopai-three-walk-free (20 March 2010).

60 'U.S. Cold War Nuclear Target Lists Declassified for First Time', National Security Archive, https://nsarchive2.gwu.edu/nukevault/ebb538-Cold-War-Nuclear-Target-List-Declassified-First-Ever/ (22 December 2015).

61 'The Big Nuking of 1959: How the US Would Have Nuked East Asia', The Diplomat, https://thediplomat.com/2016/05/the-big-nuking-of-1959-how-the-us-would-have-nuked-east-asia/ (6 May 2016).

62 'Operational & Long-Term Shutdown', IAEA, https://pris.iaea.org/PRIS/WorldStatistics/OperationalReactorsByCountry.aspx

63 'A Brief History of Nuclear Weapons States', Asia Society, https://asiasociety.org/education/brief-history-nuclear-weapons-states

64 'Mururoa fallout worse than first thought', Stuff.co.nz, http://www.stuff.co.nz/world/south-pacific/8872214/Mururoa-fallout-worse-than-first-thought (3 July 2013).

65 'Nuclear Weapon Stockpiles: Past and Present', The Diplomat, https://thediplomat.com/2013/09/nuclear-weapon-stockpiles-past-and-present/ (2 September 2013).

66 'Number of nuclear warheads worldwide 2020', Statista, https://www.statista.com/statistics/264435/number-of-nuclear-warheads-worldwide/ (1 December 2020).

67 Max Roser and Mohamed Nagdy, 'Nuclear Weapons', Our World in Data, https://ourworldindata.org/nuclear-weapons#citation

68 'Nuclear Weapons – The Facts', New Internationalist, https://newint.org/features/2008/06/01/nuclear-weapons-facts (2 June 2008).

69 As above.

70 'Nuclear Power in the World Today', World Nuclear Association, https://www.world-nuclear.org/information-library/current-and-future-generation/nuclear-power-in-the-world-today.aspx (updated November 2020).

71 Reported thus far are 237 cases of acute radiation sickness and 31 deaths. William H. Hallenbeck, Radiation Protection, CRC Press, '94. p. 15

72 htts://en.wikipedia.org/wiki/Chernobyl_disaster#cite_note-Hallenbeck_1994_15-163

73 Julian Ryall, 'Nearly 36pc of Fukushima children diagnosed with

thyroid growths', The Daily Telegraph, https://www.telegraph.co.uk/news/worldnews/asia/japan/9410702/Nearly-36pc-of-Fukushima-children-diagnosed-with-thyroid-growths.html (19 July 2012).

74 'Fukushima: How the ocean became a dumping ground for radioactive waste', Deutsche Welle, https://www.dw.com/en/fukushima-how-the-ocean-became-a-dumping-ground-for-radioactive-waste/a-52710277

75 'Fukushima fishermen concerned for future over release of radioactive water', The Guardian, https://www.theguardian.com/environment/2019/sep/16/fukushima-fisherman-fear-for-future-over-release-of-radioactive-water (16 September 2019).

5. Calling Out Racism – At Home and Abroad

76 '1981 Springbok tour', Ministry for Culture and Heritage, https://nzhistory.govt.nz/culture/1981-springbok-tour/politics-and-sport

77 Robert Consedine, 'Anti-racism and the Treaty of Waitangi', Te Ara – The Encyclopedia of New Zealand, https://teara.govt.nz/en/anti-racism-and-treaty-of-waitangi-activism

78 https://www.noted.co.nz/archive/listener-nz-2011/inside-the-1981-springbok-tour/ DEAD LINK

79 Geoff Chapple, 1981: The Tour. A H & A W Reed, Wellington, 1984.

80 'A battle for the soul of New Zealand', Stuff.co.nz, http://www.stuff.co.nz/blogs/opinion/2663799/A-battle-for-the-soul-of-New-Zealand (12 August 2009).

81 James Mitchell, Immigration and National Identity in 1970s New Zealand, University of Otago, 2003.

82 http://archive.stats.govt.nz/browse_for_stats/people_and_communities/pacific_peoples/pacific-progress-demography/population-growth.aspx DEAD LINK

83 James Mitchell, Immigration and National Identity in 1970s New Zealand, University of Otago, 2003.

84 From Truth newspaper editorial, 12 February 1974.

85 Paul Spoonley, 'The Multi-Cultural Workforce: The Role of Employers as Gatekeepers', New Zealand Journal of Industrial Relations, v. 3, 1978, p. 65

86 James Mitchell, Immigration and National Identity in 1970s New Zealand, University of Otago, 2003. See Table 2, p. 134

87 James Mitchell, Immigration and National Identity in 1970s New Zealand, University of Otago, 2003.

88 https://en.wikipedia.org/wiki/Police_raid

89 W G Coppell, Problems of Polynesia's Biggest City, PIM, v. 45, no. 11, Nov. 74, p. 35–6

90 '1976 – Key Events', Ministry for Culture and Heritage, https://nzhistory.govt.nz/culture/the-1970s/1976 (updated 10 May 2018)

91 https://polynesianpanthersparty.weebly.com/polynesian-panthers.html

92 As above.

93 Graham Reid, 'Polynesia's radical spirit', NZ Herald, https://www.nzherald.co.nz/nz/news/article.cfm?c_id=1&objectid=196354 (22 Jun 2001).

94 Catherine Masters, 'Brown Power', NZ Herald, https://www.nzherald.co.nz/nz/brown-power/LCQZYFQKHSUT7F2YFWBLOZEPPA/ (14 Jul 2006).

95 As above.

96 Transcribed from the documentary Dawn Raids (directed by Damon Fepulea'I), Isola Productions, 2005. https://www.nzonscreen.com/title/dawn-raids-2005

97 https://www.bwb.co.nz/books/platform

98 https://polynesianpanthersparty.weebly.com/polynesian-panthers.html and Dawn Raids (directed by Damon Fepulea'I), Isola Productions, 2005. https://www.nzonscreen.com/title/dawn-raids-2005

99 As above.

100 As above.

101 http://salient.org.nz/2010/05/how-the-polynesian-panthers-changed-our-world/ DEAD LINK

102 'When Pacific Islanders were raided in their beds', NZ Herald, http://www.nzherald.co.nz/nz/news/article.cfm?c_id=1&objectid=11413079 (7 March 2015).

103 From the documentary Dawn Raids (directed by Damon Fepulea'I), Isola Productions, 2005. https://www.nzonscreen.com/title/dawn-raids-2005

104 'How the Polynesian Panthers gave rise to Pasifika activism', RNZ, https://www.rnz.co.nz/international/pacific-news/306630/how-the-polynesian-panthers-gave-rise-to-pasifika-activism (18 June 2016)

105 'Racism was all around us', E-Tangata, https://e-tangata.co.nz/history/melani-anae-racism-was-all-around-us/ (18 June 2016).

6. People Not Profit – We are the 99%

106 The Occupied Dominion Post, Issue 1 https://img.scoop.co.nz/media/pdfs/1110/Occupied_Dominion_Post_Issue_1.pdf (24 October 2011).

107 You can find the wording at https://en.wikipedia.org/wiki/Occupy_protests_in_New_Zealand

108 Kalle Lasn quoted in 'Measuring Occupy Wall Street's impact, 5 years later', Chicago Tribune, https://www.chicagotribune.com/nation-world/ct-occupy-wall-street-s-impact-20160917-story.html (17 September 2016).

109 https://www.tpp.mfat.govt.nz/

110 https://www.itsourfuture.org.nz

111 https://www.mfat.govt.nz/en/trade/free-trade-agreements/free-trade-agreements-in-force/cptpp/explaining-cptpp-2/

112 'The CPTPP: What does it mean for New Zealand?' Stuff.co.nz, https://www.stuff.co.nz/business/109673930/the-cptpp-what-does-it-mean-for-new-zealand (31 December 2018).

113 'Thousands protest TPPA in downtown Auckland', NZ Herald, https://www.nzherald.co.nz/nz/news/article.cfm?c_id=1&objectid=11228782 (29 March 2014).

114 'Thousands protest in NZ against Pacific-wide free trade', Pacific Media Centre, https://www.bilaterals.org/?thousands-protest-in-nz-against&lang=fr (7 March 2015).

115 'Protest march over Trans-Pacific Partnership', Otago Daily Times, https://www.odt.co.nz/news/dunedin/protest-march-over-trans-pacific-partnership (22 May 2015).

116 'TPP protests "send a clear message"', RNZ, https://www.rnz.co.nz/news/political/281491/tpp-protests-%27send-a-clear-message%27 (16 August 2015).

117 'Thousands rally against TPP across New Zealand', NZ Herald, https://www.nzherald.co.nz/business/news/article.cfm?c_id=3&objectid=11497553 (15 August 2015).

118 'TPP: It's Not Over! 14 November – Nationwide Day of Action! It's Our Future press release, https://www.scoop.co.nz/stories/PO1511/S00177/tpp-its-not-over-14-november-nationwide-day-of-action.htm (11 November 2015).

119 'TPPA protests shut down Auckland intersections to "send a message"', Stuff.co.nz, https://www.stuff.co.nz/auckland/76567783/tppa-protests-shut-down-auckland-intersections-to-send-a-message (4 February 216).

7. Protecting the Environment – Part One: Lakes, Forests, Wetlands and Rivers

120 https://www.noted.co.nz/planet/planet-planet/manapouri-the-campaign-that-changed-a-nation DEAD LINK

121 As above.

122 Kennedy Warne, 'Manapouri Damning the Dam', New Zealand Geographic, https://www.nzgeo.com/stories/manapouri-damning-the-dam/

123 As above.

124 Paul Bensemann, Fight for the Forests: The Pivotal Campaigns that Saved New Zealand's Native Forests, Potton and Burton, NZ, 2018. p. 50

125 https://www.noted.co.nz/planet/planet-planet/manapouri-the-campaign-that-changed-a-nation DEAD LINK

126 '1969 – Key Events', Ministry for Culture and Heritage, https://nzhistory.govt.nz/culture/the-1960s/1969 (updated 9 May 2018).

127 https://www.noted.co.nz/planet/planet-planet/manapouri-the-campaign-that-changed-a-nation DEAD LINK

128 John Hanlon, 'Damn the Dam', The New Zealand Music Channel, https://www.youtube.com/watch?v=7nkPI6BDZsE

129 https://www.rnz.co.nz/news/national/434490/tiwai-point-aluminium-smelter-to-keep-operating-until-end-of-2024

130 'Decision on power for smelter', Otago Daily Times, https://www.odt.co.nz/business/decision-power-smelter (29 June 2015).

131 'Rio Tinto's smelter closure unnerves Mataura locals on waste removal', RNZ, https://www.rnz.co.nz/news/national/420964/rio-tinto-s-smelter-closure-unnerves-mataura-locals-on-waste-removal (10 July 2020).

132 Native Forest Action Information Series, http://www.apc.org.nz/nfa/Info.html

133 As described by John Dawson in Forest Vines to Snow Tussocks: The Story of New Zealand Plants http://nzetc.victoria.ac.nz/tm/scholarly/tei-DawFore-t1-body-d5-d3.html

134 Paul Bensemann, *Fight for the Forests: The Pivotal Campaigns that Saved New Zealand's Native Forests*, Potton and Burton, NZ, 2018. p. 60

135 Blog posts from the New Zealand Wilding Conifer Group, https://www.wildingconifers.org.nz/

136 Simon Nathan, 'Conservation – A history – Environmental activism, 1966–1987', *Te Ara – The Encyclopedia of New Zealand*, http://www.TeAra.govt.nz/en/conservation-a-history/page-8 (accessed 8 September 2020).

137 Paul Bensemann, *Fight for the Forests: The Pivotal Campaigns that Saved New Zealand's Native Forests*, Potton and Burton, NZ, 2018. p. 77

138 Simon Nathan, 'Conservation – A history - Environmental activism, 1966–1987', *Te Ara – The Encyclopedia of New Zealand*, http://www.TeAra.govt.nz/en/conservation-a-history/page-8 (accessed 8 September 2020)

139 Paul Bensemann, *Fight for the Forests: The Pivotal Campaigns that Saved New Zealand's Native Forests*, Potton and Burton, NZ, 2018. p. 84

140 As above, pp. 93 and 94

141 As above, pp. 93 and 94

142 As above, p. 108

143 As above, p. 109

144 As above, p. 114

145 As above, p. 115

146 'Occupy the Forest', New Zealand Geographic, https://www.nzgeo.com/stories/occupy-the-forest/

147 Paul Bensemann, *Fight for the Forests: The Pivotal Campaigns that Saved New Zealand's Native Forests*, Potton and Burton, NZ, 2018. p. 123

148 https://web.archive.org/web/20100125004104/http://www.nznfrt.org.nz/index.php?page_id=111

149 'Secrets and Lies: How Shandwick PR Tried to Destroy the Rainforests of New Zealand', *PR Watch*, volume 7, number 1, First Quarter 2000, https://www.sourcewatch.org/index.php/Secrets_and_Lies:_How_Shandwick_PR_Tried_to_Destroy_the_Rainforests_of_New_Zealand

150 Under its provisions, forest owners agreed not to clear native forests to establish plantations and to protect remnants of indigenous vegetation within their plantations. For their part, conservationists acknowledged the environmental benefits of sustainably managed plantation forests.

151 Details from Paul Bensemann, *Fight for the Forests: The Pivotal Campaigns that Saved New Zealand's Native Forests*, Potton and Burton, NZ, 2018.

152 Otago Daily Times, Dunedin, 6/4/90. In *Aramoana: clippings from Dunedin newspapers. Volume 4*, p. 27

153 https://www.orc.govt.nz/managing-our-environment/water/wetlands-and-estuaries/dunedin-district/aramoana-saltmarsh

154 https://dunedin.recollect.co.nz/nodes/view/200961

155 Angela Findlay, *Vive Aramoana – The Save Aramoana Campaign, 1974–1983*, Masters Thesis, University of Otago, 2004.

156 As above, pp. 19–20

157 As above, p. 20

158 https://en.wikipedia.org/wiki/Save_Aramoana_Campaign

159 'Super Sites for Conservation Education – Aramoana', Department of Conservation, https://www.doc.govt.nz/globalassets/documents/getting-involved/students-and-teachers/field-trips-by-region/004-aramoana.pdf

8. Protecting the Environment – Part Two: GE, Mining and Oceans

160 Wendy McGuinness, Miriam White and Steph Versteeg, *The History of Genetic Modification in New Zealand*, Sustainable Future Limited, April 2008. http://www.mcguinnessinstitute.org/wp-content/uploads/2016/08/Project-2058-The-History-of-Genetic-Modification-in-New-Zealand.pdf

161 As above

162 'Green Gloves Direct Action Pledge', Green Gloves press release, https://www.scoop.co.nz/stories/PO0110/S00186/green-gloves-direct-action-pledge.htm (31 October 2001).

163 'Seeds of Unease', New Zealand Geographic, https://www.nzgeo.com/stories/seeds-of-unease/

164 *Nicky Hager, Seeds of Distrust, Craig Potton NZ, 2002.* https://www.nickyhager.info/seeds-of-distrust-foreword-and-chapter-1/

165 'Corngate probe fails to agree over contamination', NZ Herald, https://www.nzherald.co.nz/genetic-engineering/news/article.cfm?c_id=220&objectid=3602035 (19 October 2004) and https://en.wikipedia.org/wiki/Corngate

166 'Hager's Facts Fine – Environment Ministry CEO', Scoop, https://www.scoop.co.nz/stories/HL0207/S00083.htm (11 July 2002).

167 'Seeds of Change: Saturday's Big Anti-GE March', Scoop, https://www.scoop.co.nz/stories/HL0310/S00097/seeds-of-change-saturdays-big-anti-ge-march.htm (12 October 2003).

168 'Thousands unite to send anti-GE message to Government', NZ Herald, https://www.nzherald.co.nz/nz/news/article.cfm?c_id=1&objectid=3528347 (12 October 2003).

169 'Ronald McDonald quits McDonald's over GE chicken', *Greenpeace press release,* https://www.greenpeace.org/new-zealand/press-release/ronald-mcdonald-quits-mcdonalds-over-ge-chicken/ *(12 April 2004).*

170 *'Greenpeace claims victory in GE battle with McDonald's', NZ Herald,* https://www.nzherald.co.nz/nz/news/article.cfm?c_id=1&objectid=3567592 *(20 May 2004).*

171 *'The Basics of Genetic Engineering', Penn State,* https://sites.psu.edu/english202geneticengineering/genetic-engineering/what-is-genetic-engineering/

172 *'Potential benefits and risks of genetic engineering', BBC,* https://www.bbc.co.uk/bitesize/guides/zsg6v9q/revision/7

173 *Norther University's student-run science magazine article: 'Genetic Engineering Gone Wrong?' Nu Sci,* https://nuscimag.com/genetic-engineering-gone-wrong-ad3d508eb17d *(15 December 2014).*

174 'A tale of mining in New Zealand – and the tragic tailings of Tui Mine', https://envirohistorynz.com/2010/05/02/a-tale-of-mining-in-new-zealand-and-the-tragic-tailings-of-tui-mine/#more-2472 (2 May 2010).

175 Carl Walrond, 'Gold and gold mining – Recent mining', *Te Ara – the Encyclopedia of New Zealand*, http://www.TeAra.govt.nz/en/gold-and-gold-mining/page-11 (accessed 5 October 2020).

176 'The Original Martha Mine', Waihi Gold, http://www.waihigold.co.nz/history/the-original-martha/

177 Alison McCulloch, 'Mining Below The Floorboards', Werewolf, http://werewolf.co.nz/2013/06/mining-below-the-floorboards/ (retrieved 30 August 2018) and 'Waihi – OceanaGold', OceanaGold, https://www.oceanagold.com/our-business/new-zealand/waihi/ (retrieved 27 September 2016) and https://www.waihigold.co.nz/mining/ and https://apps.indigotools.com/IR/iac/?ticker=OGC&exchange=TSX for annual returns

178 'Sinkhole found alongside mine in Waihi', Stuff.co.nz, https://www.stuff.co.nz/environment/96301642/sinkhole-found-alongside-mine-in-waihi?rm=m (30 August 2017).

179 As described by Denis Tegg in correspondence to me.

180 Coromandel Watchdog, https://watchdog.org.nz/about-us/history/

181 As above.

182 'Coromandel Peninsula braced for new gold war', NZ Herald, https://www.nzherald.co.nz/nz/news/article.cfm?c_id=1&objectid=3577398 (9 July 2004).

183 'Coromandel Watchdog Wins Prohibition on Minding on Coromandel Peninsula', ECO, http://www.eco.org.nz/news/90/15/Coromandel-Watchdog-Wins-Prohibition-on-Mining-on-Coromandel-Peninsula.html (31 October 2007).

184 'Huge protest says no to mining on conservation land', NZ Herald, https://www.nzherald.co.nz/nz/huge-protest-says-no-to-mining-on-conservation-land/4IW7LEDGSMHOAAEXDEPQ6SA7ZI/ (1 May 2010).

185 As above.

186 'Pretty sad situation: Waihi gold mine extension slammed by watchdog', Newshub, https://www.newshub.co.nz/home/new-zealand/2018/12/pretty-sad-situation-waihi-gold-mine-extension-slammed-by-watchdog.html (19 December 2018).

187 'Gold seekers say sampling won't hurt gorge', Stuff.co.nz, http://www.stuff.co.nz/business/industries/10506833/Gold-seekers-say-sampling-won-t-hurt-gorge (17 September 2014).

188 'Mayor says jobs will suffer after Minister Eugenie Sage cans mining company's land buy', Stuff.co.nz, https://www.stuff.co.nz/national/112518119/mayor-says-jobs-will-suffer-after-minister-eugenie-sage-cans-mining-companys-land-buy (7 May 2019).

189 'Waihi land purchase approved overturning Eugenie Sage's previous veto', NZ Herald, https://www.nzherald.co.nz/nz/news/article.cfm?c_id=1&objectid=12274571 (8 October 2019).

190 https://en.wikipedia.org/wiki/Save_Happy_Valley_Coalition

191 'What Happened Here', Stuff.co.nz, https://interactives.stuff.co.nz/2018/10/what-happened-here/#section-XeDm1Qt8WH

192 'Operating coal mine production figures', NZ Petroleum & Minerals, https://www.nzpam.govt.nz/nz-industry/nz-minerals/minerals-statistics/coal/operating-mines/

193 'What Happened Here', Stuff.co.nz, https://interactives.stuff.co.nz/2018/10/what-happened-here/#section-XeDm1Qt8WH

194 From personal discussion with Frances Mountier.
195 As above.
196 As above.
197 https://en.wikipedia.org/wiki/Save_Happy_Valley_Coalition
198 As above and 'What Happened Here', Stuff.co.nz, https://interactives.stuff.co.nz/2018/10/what-happened-here/#section-XeDm1Qt8WH
199 'Permits approved to move Mt Augustus snails', New Zealand Government press release, http://www.scoop.co.nz/stories/PA0604/S00233.htm (12 April 2006).
200 https://interactives.stuff.co.nz/2018/10/what-happened-here/#section-XeDm1Qt8WH
201 'Carter signs off on species extinction', Save Happy Valley Coalition press release, http://www.savehappyvalley.org.nz/pressreleases/pr_12-04-06_shvc.htm (12 April 2006).
202 'Snail campaigners to pay costs', Newstalk ZB, http://tvnz.co.nz/content/1021332/423466.html (13 March 2007). Archived from the original on 13 June 2011.
203 'What Happened Here', Stuff.co.nz, https://interactives.stuff.co.nz/2018/10/what-happened-here/#section-XeDm1Qt8WH
204 'Private investigators still digging on West Coast', The Sunday Star-Times, http://www.stuff.co.nz/sunday-star-times/features/feature-archive/374156 (20 April 2008).
205 'Solid Energy neither legal, moral or ethical', Save Happy Valley Coalition press release, https://www.scoop.co.nz/stories/PO0705/S00514/solid-energy-neither-legal-moral-or-ethical.htm (28 May 2007).
206 'Private investigators still digging on West Coast', The Sunday Star-Times, http://www.stuff.co.nz/sunday-star-times/features/feature-archive/374156 (20 April 2008).
207 'Thompson and Clark spied on earthquake victims, inquiry finds', RNZ, https://www.rnz.co.nz/news/national/378521/thompson-and-clark-spied-on-earthquake-victims-inquiry-finds (18 December 2018).
208 https://www.stuff.co.nz/national/300283529/school-children-targeted-by-private-investigators-thompson-and-clark
209 'Solid Energy neither legal, moral or ethical', Save Happy Valley Coalition press release, https://www.scoop.co.nz/stories/PO0705/S00514/solid-energy-neither-legal-moral-or-ethical.htm (28 May 2007).
210 Keira Stephenson, 'More job losses at Stockton', NZ Herald, Westport News, http://www.nzherald.co.nz/business/news/article.cfm?c_id=3&objectid=10837929 (2 October 2012).
211 'Mining consent expired for Happy Valley', Biodiversity Defence Group press release, https://www.scoop.co.nz/stories/AK1306/S00204/mining-consent-expired-for-happy-valley.htm (12 June 2013).
212 From govt papers included in article 'What Happened Here', Stuff.co.nz, https://interactives.stuff.co.nz/2018/10/what-happened-here/#section-XeDm1Qt8WH
213 'What Happened Here', Stuff.co.nz, https://interactives.stuff.co.nz/2018/10/what-happened-here/#section-XeDm1Qt8WH
214 'DoC staff upset mishap killed rare snails', NZ Herald, https://www.nzherald.co.nz/nz/doc-staff-upset-mishap-killed-rare-snails/KMVUPMZNRVIOFFWHPMPLZDAVWE/ (10 November 2011).
215 'Snail fridge deaths an avoidable tragedy', Forest and Bird press release, https://www.scoop.co.nz/stories/SC1111/S00022/snail-fridge-deaths-an-avoidable-tragedy.htm (10 November 2011).
216 'What Happened Here', Stuff.co.nz, https://interactives.stuff.co.nz/2018/10/what-happened-here/#section-XeDm1Qt8WH
217 Ron Lambert, *In Crude State – A History of the Moturoa Oilfield New Plymouth*, Methanex New Zealand, 1995.
218 Sorrell Hoskin, 'Moturoa Black Gold – "The Good Oil"', Puke Ariki, http://www.pukeariki.com/en/stories/businessAndIndustry/moturoaoil.htm (19 November 2004). Archived from the original on 8 April 2009.
219 'History of New Zealand's gas sector', MBIE, http://www.mbie.govt.nz/info-services/sectors-industries/energy/gas-market/nz-gas-sector-history (8 January 2016).
220 'Rena crew "terrified" by tipping', New Zealand Herald, http://www.nzherald.co.nz/nz/news/article.cfm?c_id=1&objectid=10758195 (11 October 2011).
221 Shane Cowlishaw, 'Cleanup crew warned of health risks', Dominion Post, http://www.stuff.co.nz/environment/rena-crisis/5776794/Cleanup-crew-warned-of-health-risks (13 October 2011).
222 'Rena: Oil clean-up chemical worries Greenpeace', New Zealand Herald, http://www.nzherald.co.nz/rena-oil-spill/news/article.cfm?c_id=1503203&objectid=10768517 (25 November 2011).
223 https://www.mfe.govt.nz/sites/default/files/rena-long-term-environmental-plan.pdf
224 'Lucy Lawless gets fined for protest', NZ Herald, https://www.nzherald.co.nz/nz/lucy-lawless-gets-fined-for-protest/4BZK35VAQ55SV2UK75DF4PSQLM/ (7 February 2013).
225 'Protesters waddle on petroleum industry's summit,' New Zealand Herald, http://www.nzherald.co.nz/nz/news/article.cfm?c_id=1&objectid=11126427 (18 September 2013).
226 Katie Chapman, 'Oil protest targets survey ship', Stuff.co.nz, http://www.stuff.co.nz/dominion-post/news/wellington/9642430/Oil-protest-targets-survey-ship (23 January 2014).
227 Emma Dangerfield, 'Swimmers attempt to stop ship', Stuff.co.nz, http://www.stuff.co.nz/marlborough-express/news/9718449/Swimmers-attempt-to-stop-ship (13 February 2014).
228 Andrea O'Neil, 'Second day of Anadarko oil protest', Stuff.co.nz, http://www.stuff.co.nz/dominion-post/news/wellington/9647052/Second-day-of-Anadarko-oil-protest (24 January 2014).
229 "Banners against drilling in Maui's habitat target National conference", 1 News, https://www.tvnz.co.nz/one-news/new-zealand/banners-against-drilling-in-maui-s-habitat-target-national-conference-6014067
230 Bradley, John Weekes, Grant (1 October 2014). "Oil protesters disrupt event, scale building". via New Zealand Herald.
231 'We will fight every step of the way', RNZ, http://www.radionz.co.nz/news/

232 Defined as: to a depth of 450m in an area 10,192 km2 within a Fisheries Benthic (seabed) Protection Area

233 'Date Set for South Taranaki Bight iron sand mining battle to head to Court of Appeal', Whanganui Chronicle, https://www.nzherald.co.nz/whanganui-chronicle/news/date-set-for-south-taranaki-bight-iron-sand-mining-battle-to-head-to-court-of-appeal/C4ZJCA7R556L66YSBYDB7NBDFI/ (13 July 2019).

234 Thanks to Malibu Hamilton from KASM for additional information

235 'New Zealand Energy Relinquishes East Coast Permit', Press release, New Zealand Energy Corp., http://www.newzealand-energy.com/News-and-Events/News-Releases/News-Releases-Details/2015/New-Zealand-Energy-Relinquishes-East-Coast-Permit/default.aspx (21 May 2015).

236 Kaituhi Mark Revington, 'The risk and reward of offshore mining,' Te Rūnanga o Ngāi Tahu, http://ngaitahu.iwi.nz/author/te-runanga-o-ngai-tahu/ (22 January 2014).

237 Bronwen Beechey, 'New Zealand: Protests target deep sea drilling', *Green Left Weekly*, https://www.greenleft.org.au/node/55466 (25 November 2013).

238 https://www.biologicaldiversity.org/campaigns/seismic_blasting/

239 Also stated in this essay: https://nwwhangarei.files.wordpress.com/2012/11/sotn2015.pdf

240 Mike Dinsdale, 'Answers being sought for whale strandings', *Northern Advocate*, http://www.nzherald.co.nz/northern-advocate/news/article.cfm?c_id=1503450&objectid=11326989 (18 September 2014).

241 Tepara Koti, 'Te Ahipara Kōmiti Takutaimoana attempt to stop Statoil', Māori Television, https://www.teaomaori.news/te-ahipara-komiti-takutaimoana-attempt-stop-statoil (22 May 2015). This whole section sourced from *Māori Opposition to Fossil Fuel Development in Aotearoa New Zealand*, by Zoltán Grossman, The Evergreen State College, Olympia, Washington (2015).

242 'Date Set for South Taranaki Bight iron sand mining battle to head to Court of Appeal', Whanganui Chronicle, https://www.nzherald.co.nz/whanganui-chronicle/news/date-set-for-south-taranaki-bight-iron-sand-mining-battle-to-head-to-court-of-appeal/C4ZJCA7R556L66YSBYDB7NBDFI/ (13 July 2019).

243 '30 people occupying OMV support vessel to halt oil operations', Greenpeace, https://www.greenpeace.org/new-zealand/press-release/30-people-occupying-omv-support-vessel-to-halt-oil-operations/ (24 November 2019).

244 'NZ govt ends new offshore oil and gas exploration', NZ Herald, https://www.nzherald.co.nz/business/nz-govt-ends-new-offshore-oil-and-gas-exploration/TJ5KDR5BRBICTIVGB3UABI45UU/ (12 April 2018).

245 '30 people occupying OMV support vessel to halt oil operations', Greenpeace, https://www.greenpeace.org/new-zealand/press-release/30-people-occupying-omv-support-vessel-to-halt-oil-operations/ (24 November 2019).

246 'Climate protesters shut down New Plymouth oil giant', Greenpeace, https://www.greenpeace.org/new-zealand/press-release/climate-protesters-shut-down-new-plymouth-oil-giant/ (2 December 2019).

247 'Greenpeace installs oil museum at OMV', Greenpeace, https://www.greenpeace.org/new-zealand/press-release/greenpeace-installs-oil-museum-at-omv/ (5 December 2019).

248 'Climate protesters shut down New Plymouth oil giant', Greenpeace, https://www.greenpeace.org/new-zealand/press-release/climate-protesters-shut-down-new-plymouth-oil-giant/ (2 December 2019).

249 'OMV exit signals end of offshore oil exploration in NZ', Greenpeace, https://www.greenpeace.org/new-zealand/press-release/omv-exit-signals-end-of-offshore-oil-exploration-in-nz/ (10 April 2020).

9. The Biggest Issue of All – Climate Change Action

250 https://www.doc.govt.nz/nature/native-animals/marine-mammals/whales/whaling/

251 https://www.nzgeo.com/stories/thar-she-blows-a-grisly-trade-in-bone-and-oil/

252 https://www.doc.govt.nz/nature/native-animals/marine-mammals/whales/whaling/

253 'NZ likely to send Navy to watch over anti-whaling protesters', Earth Times, http://www.earthtimes.org/conservation/nz-navy-anti-whaling-protestors/36/ (18 November 2010).

254 https://www.doc.govt.nz/nature/native-animals/marine-mammals/whales/whaling/

255 *'What is bottom trawling and why is it bad for the environment?' Greenpeace*, https://www.greenpeace.org/new-zealand/story/what-is-bottom-trawling-and-why-is-it-bad-for-the-environment/ *(11 April 2020).*

256 *'What is bottom trawling?' LegaSea*, https://legasea.co.nz/2019/10/31/all-about-trawling/ *(31 October 2019).*

257 'Bottom trawled coral dumped at Parliament', Greenpeace, https://www.scoop.co.nz/stories/PO1911/S00230/bottom-trawled-coral-dumped-at-parliament.htm *(19 November 2019).*

258 *'50,000 strong petition calls for an end to bottom trawling on seamounts', Greenpeace*, https://www.greenpeace.org/new-zealand/press-release/50000-strong-petition-calls-for-an-end-to-bottom-trawling-on-seamounts/ *(18 November 2020).*

259 *'Case for cameras on boats stronger than ever,' Greenpeace*, https://www.greenpeace.org/new-zealand/story/case-for-cameras-on-boats-stronger-than-ever/ *(13 May 2020).*

260 *'Greenpeace and Labour call for MPI to be investigated over fisheries failure', Stuff.co.nz*, https://www.stuff.co.nz/national/politics/80000939/greenpeace-and-labour-call-for-mpi-to-be-investigated-over-fisheries-failure#comments *(16 May 2016).*

261 *'MPI official admits fish dumping widespread', RNZ*, https://www.rnz.co.nz/news/national/313631/mpi-official-admits-fish-dumping-widespread *(19 September 2016).*

262 https://www.projectjonah.org.nz/Take+Action/MauiDolphins.html

263 https://www.wwf.org.nz/what_we_do/species/hectors_maui/maui_dolphin/index.cfm

264 https://www.doc.govt.nz/nature/native-animals/marine-mammals/dolphins/hectors-dolphin/

265 https://teara.govt.nz/en/dolphins/page-3

266 Suyin Haynes, 'Students From 1,600 Cities Just Walked Out of School to Protest Climate Change. It Could Be Greta Thunberg's Biggest Strike Yet', Time, https://time.com/5595365/global-climate-strikes-greta-thunberg/ (24 May 2019).

267 Gaby Hinsliff, 'How Greta Thunberg became the new front in the Brexit culture war', The Guardian, https://www.theguardian.com/commentisfree/2019/aug/17/greta-thunberg-brexit-culture-war-nigel-farage (17 August 2019). Archived from the original on 20 August 2019.

268 Jonathan Watts, 'The Greta Thunberg effect: at last, MPs focus on climate change', The Guardian, https://www.theguardian.com/environment/2019/apr/23/greta-thunberg (23 April 2019). Archived from the original on 28 August 2019.

269 'New Zealand's climate change power list', Stuff.co.nz, https://www.stuff.co.nz/environment/climate-news/115727267/new-zealands-climate-change-power-list (16 September 2019).

270 'Climate change march: Thousands of schoolkids' action inspired by Greta Thunberg', NZ Herald, https://www.nzherald.co.nz/nz/climate-change-march-thousands-of-schoolkids-action-inspired-by-greta-thunberg/VVKHXTTIPBOTPJETQLF74664SI/ (27 September 2019)

271 Chlöe Swarbrick, 'Time for a new tribe of anybody-MPs to smash the marble walls', The Spinoff, https://thespinoff.co.nz/politics/01-10-2019/chloe-swarbrick-time-for-a-new-tribe-of-anybody-mps-to-smash-the-marble-walls/ (1 October 2019).

272 'Tens of thousands of New Zealand children kick off new climate strikes', Reuters, https://www.reuters.com/article/us-climate-change-strike-idUSKBN1WC0A5 (27 September 2019).

273 'UN Report: Nature's Dangerous Decline "Unprecedented"; Species Extinction Rates "Accelerating"', United Nations, https://www.un.org/sustainabledevelopment/blog/2019/05/nature-decline-unprecedented-report/ (6 May 2019).

274 Public concern over climate change hits new high', HorizonPoll, https://www.horizonpoll.co.nz/page/541/public-conc (9 May 2019).

275 'Auckland Council declares climate emergency', Our Auckland, https://ourauckland.aucklandcouncil.govt.nz/articles/news/2019/06/auckland-council-declares-climate-emergency/?link_id=9&can_id=cfae6f7234d0e22ca60cab502b-d0978e&source=email-newsletter-23-ransom-rattled-radiohead-rears-into-righteous-rebellion&email_referrer=email_563011&email_subject=newsletter-23-ransom-rattled-radiohead-rears-into-righteous-rebellion (13 June 2019).

276 It's time for NZ to declare a climate emergency, majority of Kiwis say in new poll', 1 News, https://www.tvnz.co.nz/one-news/new-zealand/its-time-nz-declare-climate-emergency-majority-kiwis-say-in-new-poll (13 June 2019).

277 'Youth Parliament 2019 declares climate emergency', RNZ, https://www.rnz.co.nz/national/programmes/the-house/audio/2018704687/youth-parliament-2019-declares-climate-emergency (18 July 2019).

278 'We must face climate emergency head-on', Stuff.co.nz, https://www.stuff.co.nz/environment/climate-news/113984415/we-must-face-climate-emergency-headon (4 July 2019).

279 'Zero Carbon Bill passes with near-unanimous support, setting climate change targets into law', Stuff.co.nz, https://www.stuff.co.nz/national/politics/117244331/national-will-support-climate-change-zero-carbon-bill (7 November 2019).

280 'Historic day for landmark climate change legislation in New Zealand', NZ Government, https://www.beehive.govt.nz/release/historic-day-landmark-climate-change-legislation-new-zealand (7 November 2019).

281 'Jacinda Ardern declares climate emergency in New Zealand after decades of rising greenhouse gas emissions', Newshub, https://www.newshub.co.nz/home/politics/2020/12/jacinda-ardern-declares-climate-emergency-in-new-zealand-after-decades-of-rising-greenhouse-gas-emissions.html (2 December 2020).

282 'New Zealand declares a climate change emergency', The Guardian, https://www.theguardian.com/world/2020/dec/02/new-zealand-declares-a-climate-change-emergency (2 December 2020).

10. Our Pacific Neighbours – Past and Future Protests

283 https://teara.govt.nz/en/biographies/3116/richardson-george-spafford

284 'New Zealand in Samoa', Ministry for Culture and Heritage, https://nzhistory.govt.nz/politics/samoa (updated 30 April 2020).

285 Ministry for Culture and Heritage, https://nzhistory.govt.nz/politics/samoa/stepping-up-mau-campaign

286 https://en.wikipedia.org/wiki/Mau_movement

287 https://nvdatabase.swarthmore.edu/content/mau-opposition-new-zealand-rule-samoa-1927-1933

288 https://en.wikipedia.org/wiki/Mau_movement

289 'Towards independence' and other sections, Ministry for Culture and Heritage, https://nzhistory.govt.nz/politics/samoa/towards-independence (updated 2 September 2014).

290 'Apology to Samoa surprises New Zealand', BBC News, http://news.bbc.co.uk/2/hi/asia-pacific/2025041.stm (4 June 2002).

291 https://en.wikipedia.org/wiki/American_Samoa

292 https://www.britannica.com/place/Solomon-Islands/History#ref513786

293 https://scholarspace.manoa.hawaii.edu/bitstream/handle/10125/15551/OP36-27-35.pdf?sequence=1

294 https://www.solomonencyclopaedia.net/biogs/E000181b.htm

295 https://nvdatabase.swarthmore.edu/content/solomon-islanders-withdraw-colonialism-maasina-rule-1944-52

296 https://en.wikipedia.org/wiki/Maasina_Ruru

297 *Treaty of Friendship Between Great Britain and Tonga, 18 May 1900, Laws of Tonga (revised 1948), Government Printer, Wellington, 1951.*

298 *Article II, "Supplementary Agreement" Between Great Britain and Tonga, or "Note of Points Accepted by the King", (18 January 1905).*

299 *The bulk of this section is taken from Penny Lavaka's 'The Tonga Ma'a Tonga Kautaha: A Watershed in British-Tongan Relations', Pacific Studies, Institute for Polynesian Studies, 4 (2, Spring 1981).* https://web.archive.org/web/20160304201416/https:/ojs.lib.byu.edu/spc/index.php/PacificStudies/article/viewFile/9209/8858 *Archived from the original but also sourced from* https://anyflip.com/lvfi/qpnj/basic

300 *Document "M" Appendix to Tonga Government Gazette Extraordinary, No. 8 1911.*

301 *Campbell to Major, 26 August 1910.*

302 *Interview with Minister of Police, 9 September 1911, encl 7 in May to S/S, conf, 23 September 1911, CO 225/97.*

303 *Ordinance No. 4, 1911.*

304 https://en.wikipedia.org/wiki/Tonga_Ma%27a_Tonga_Kautaha

305 *Tupou II to May, 7 September 1911, encl 4 in May to S/S, conf, 23 September 1911, CO 225/97.*

306 as of 2015

307 'Kiribati: 2011 Article IV Consultation-Staff Report, Informational Annexes, Debt Sustainability Analysis, Public Information Notice on the Executive Board Discussion, and Statement by the Executive Director for Kiribati', International Monetary Fund Country Report No. 11/113, https://www.imf.org/external/pubs/cat/longres.aspx?sk=24871.0 (24 May 2011).

308 'Islands disappear under rising seas', BBC News, http://news.bbc.co.uk/2/hi/science/nature/368892.stm (14 June 1999).

309 Juliet Eilperin, 'Debate on Climate Shifts to Issue of Irreparable Change', The Washington Post, https://www.washingtonpost.com/wp-dyn/content/article/2006/01/28/AR2006012801021.html (29 January 2006).

310 'Flooding in Vanuatu, Kiribati and Tuvalu as Cyclone Pam strengthens', SBS Australia, http://www.sbs.com.au/news/article/2015/03/13/flooding-vanuatu-kiribati-and-tuvalu-cyclone-pam-strengthens (13 March 2015).

311 'Climate change in Kiribati: Adapting to climate change', Office of the President of Kiribati, https://web.archive.org/web/20120202020502/http:/www.climate.gov.ki/Kiribati_climate_change_strategies.html Archived from the original on 2 February 2012.

312 'Fiji will support Kiribati as sea level rises', PR Newswire, http://www.digitaljournal.com/pr/1732761#ixzz2toRgdI9D (11 February 2014).

Quotes

313 Hōne Heke to Henry Williams (5 February 1845, at Kaikohe) https://www.karuwha.org.nz/quotes/

314 https://www.karuwha.org.nz/quotes/

315 https://e-tangata.co.nz/history/bastion-point-a-desperate-struggle-and-a-dream-fulfilled/ With thanks to E-Tangata for permission to quote.

316 https://teara.govt.nz/en/law-of-the-foreshore-and-seabed/print#1

317 Mark Derby, 'On the Waterfront: Wellington at war – the 1913 Strike', NZ Geographic, https://www.nzgeo.com/stories/on-the-waterfront/

318 Andrea Gillian Hotere, The 1951 Waterfront Lockout in Port Chalmers, University of Otago BA honours dissertation, 1989. p. 14–15

319 Quote from Connie Birchfield, as reported in 'War on the wharves', Ministry for Culture and Heritage https://nzhistory.govt.nz/politics/the-1951-waterfront-dispute/war-on-the-wharves (updated 27 Feb 2019).

320 Mark Derby, 'Strikes and Labour Disputes – The 1951 Waterfront Dispute', Te Ara – the Encyclopedia of New Zealand, http://www.TeAra.govt.nz/en/strikes-and-labour-disputes/page-7

321 Clifton, J. (2011) "Slutwalk arrives in New Zealand" first published in https://www.noted.co.nz/archive/archive-listener-nz-2011/slutwalk-arrives-in-new-zealand

322 'The Aftermath', Stuff.co.nz, https://interactives.stuff.co.nz/2019/02/metoonz/the-aftermath/

323 https://www.hrc.co.nz/your-rights/your-rights/

324 Brian Laird, in an interview with author 15/8/2020.

325 '49 killed in Featherston POW incident', Ministry for Culture and Heritage, https://nzhistory.govt.nz/49-killed-during-riot-at-featherston-pow-camp (updated 25 Feb 2020).

326 Neville Peat, Manapouri Ssaved! Longacre Press, NZ, (1994

327 https://www.facebook.com/nativeforestaction/ Reproduced with kind permission from Dean Baigent-Mercer.

328 Otago Daily Times, Dunedin, 12/6/98. In *Aramoana: clippings from Dunedin newspapers. Volume 5*, p. 5

329 Chlöe Swarbrick, 'Time for a new tribe of anybody-MPs to smash the marble walls', The Spinoff, https://thespinoff.co.nz/politics/01-10-2019/chloe-swarbrick-time-for-a-new-tribe-of-anybody-mps-to-smash-the-marble-walls/ (1 October 2019).

INDEX

Symbols

350 Aotearoa *126, 135*

A

ACORD *72*
Action for Environment *90*
Ada Wells *48*
Adrian Leason *54*
Afghanistan *52*
    Baghdad *53*
Agent Orange *51*
AIDS *41*
Alexander D. Cameron *147, 148*
Alison Mau *39*
ALRANZ *36, 37*
Alusuisse *98*
Álvaro de Mendaña *144*
Alyn Ware *60*
Alyssa Milano *39*
Amanda Larsson *126*
American Samoa *143, 144*
Anadarko *120, 122, 123, 126*
    Anadarko Amendment *123*
Andrew Robb *19*
Angeline Greensill *121, 123*
Anti-Bases Campaign *54*
anti-tour groups *65*
ANZUS Treaty *55, 59*
Aotearoa *5, 7, 9, 14, 16, 20, 22, 24, 26, 28, 31, 32, 34, 35, 36, 37, 39, 40, 45, 48, 49, 50, 52, 53, 55, 57, 58, 59, 60, 61, 63, 64, 65, 66, 68, 69, 71, 72, 73, 74, 75, 77, 78, 79, 81, 83, 85, 86, 88, 89, 91, 93, 96, 98, 100, 101, 103, 104, 106, 110, 111, 114, 115, 117, 119, 125, 126, 127, 128, 129, 130, 131, 132, 133, 134, 135, 137, 138, 139, 140, 141, 142, 143, 144, 147*
apartheid *see* - South Africa
Aramoana *97*
Arbitration Court *26, 29*
Archibald Baxter *3, 43, 44, 45, 46*
arms race *56, 57*
Arohanui Marae *18*
Asa Budnick *105*
Auckland *10, 15, 16, 17, 18, 19, 20, 21, 24, 27, 28, 29, 32, 47, 52, 54, 58, 59, 65, 66, 67, 69, 71, 74, 75, 76, 78, 79, 83, 88, 101, 103, 104, 108, 109, 117, 118, 124, 125, 134, 135, 136, 140, 142, 143*
Auckland Medical Aid Centre (AMAC) *37*
Australia *36, 37, 49, 53, 54, 55, 61, 69, 71, 77, 78, 98, 104, 130, 150,*
John Howard (Australian Prime Minister) *52, 53*

B

Banners on the Beach *123*
Bastion Point *3, 17, 19, 21, 72, 151*
Battle of Guadalcanal *145*
Battle of Molesworth Street *66*
BFAC *88*
Beech Forest Action Committee (BFAC) *88, 89*
Ben Atiga *73*
Benson Stanley *73*
Bernard Freyberg *28*
Bernard King *92*
Big Business *77*
Bill Birch (National MP) *73*
Blackball *26*
Black Panther *20*
Bloody Friday *30*
Brash, Don *see* - Don Brash
Britain *see* - UK
British Protectorate *146*
Broomfield Act *59*
Buller Conservation Group *95, 112*

C

Campaign for Nuclear Disarmament (CND) *see* - CND
Campaign Power Poll *99*
Canada *54, 61, 77, 78*
Canterbury Women's Institute *48*
Captain Cook *8*
CARE *65, 72*
Chatham Rise *121*
Che Fu *73*
Chernobyl. *see* - USSR
Chevron *126*
China *56, 57, 115*
Chlöe Swarbrick *134, 136, 161, 163*
Citizens' Committee *139*
Clark, Helen. *see* - Helen Clark
Clifton Terrace Primary School *30*
Climate Justice Taranaki *126*
Clive Pearson *60*
CND *57*
Coal Action Network *135, 151*
Cold War *29, 56, 152, 156*
Comalco *81*
Commonwealth Aluminium Corporation *81*
Commonwealth Finance Ministers Conference *66*
communist wreckers *29*
Comprehensive and Progressive Trans-Pacific Partnership *78*
CPTPP *78, 79, 157*
Coromandel *106, 107, 108, 109, 110, 151, 159*
Coromandel Watchdog *108*
Thames-Coromandel District Council *108*
court-marshalled *44*
Crown Minerals Act *108*
CSR Limited *98*
customary laws *9*
customary rights *22, 23*

D

David Lange *59, 60, 72*
David McTaggart *58*
David Parker *110*
Dawn Raids *3, 69*
Dean Baigent-Mercer *94*
Deepsea Conservation Coalition *121*
Denis Tegg *108, 151*
Department of Conservation *110, 130, 131*
DOC *110, 130, 131*
Dick Scott *14*
DNA *51, 104, 105*
Donald Trump *78*
Don Brash *22, 24*
Dunkirk *45*

E

East Berlin *56*
Eastern Europe *56*
Eastern Rugby Union *68*
ECHELON system *54*
ECO *95, 130, 135, 159*
Eddie Williams *71*
Ed Miliband *133*
Edmund Hillary *8, 83*
Educate to liberate *71*
Elsie Locke *57*
Environment Court *109, 112, 114, 115*
EPA *121, 125*
Equinor/Statoil *126*
ERMA *102*
Etta Gillon *72*
EU *70*
Eugenie Sage *110*
Eva Rickard *21*
Exclusive Economic Zone *128*
Extinction Rebellion (XR) *135*

F

Featherston Massacre *49*
Federation of Labour *26, 29*
Fémmina *see* - Mary Ann Müller
Fernando Pereira *59*
Field Punishment No. 1 *45, 46*
Five Eyes *54*
Flagstaff War *10*
Fletcher Challenge *98*
Fono a Faipule *143*
Food Standards Australia New Zealand (FSANZ) *104*
Forest and Bird Protection Society *82, 83*
France *45, 57, 58, 60, 61*
Frances Joychild *39*
Fran Wilde *41*
Fred Evans *27*
Fred Schmidt *71*
French Polynesia *57*
Fridays for Future *133, 137*
Friends of the Earth *88, 128*

G

Gary Knight *67*
GE-free *102, 104*
GE-free Coalition *101*
Generation Zero *135, 137, 151*
genetically modified organisms (GMOs) *100*
genetic engineering (GE) *100 100, 101, 102, 103, 104, 105,*
genetic modification (GM) *104*
George Armstrong *65*
George W. Bush (President of USA) - *53*
George Gair *73*
George Richardson *139, 143*
George Shultz *59*
Glasgow, Lord David Boyle Lord Glasgow *34*
GM *see* - genetic modification
Government Communications Security Bureau (GCSB) *54*
governor general *28*
Graham Searle *88*
Grant Robertson *110*
Great Britain *see* - UK
Green Gloves *101, 103, 158*
Greenpeace *58, 59, 60, 96, 103, 109, 119, 121, 122, 123, 125, 126, 128, 129, 130, 135, 151*
Greta Thunberg *132, 161*
    The Greta Effect *133*

Guy Salmon (NFAC) 90

H

Hager, Nicky. *see* - Nicky Hager
Halt All Racist Tours (HART) 68
Hamilton 65, 66, 78, 79, 118, 151
Hands Across the Sands 123
Harriet Taylor Mill 32
HART 65, 68, 72
Heads in the Sand 124
Helen Clark 22, 24, 52, 53, 55, 95, 96, 101, 102, 103, 115, 143
Helene Ritchie 59
Henry Patton 45
Herbert Hart 142
Heremia Te Wake 15
He Taua 21
Heterosexuals Unafraid of Gays 41
High Commissioner 147
High Court 21, 109, 110, 112, 114, 115, 121, 125
Hīkoi 14, 153
Hiroshima 57, 60
Hiroshima Day 57
HMAS Supply 58
HMS
    Diomede 140, 142
    Dunedin 140, 142
Homosexual Equality 41
Hone Harawira 21
Hōne Heke 3, 8, 9, 10
Hōri Ngātai 23
HortResearch 102
Howard, John *see* - John Howard
Hugh Watt 82
Human Rights Act 42
Human Rights Commission 39, 41
Huntly 27, 30, 118
Huntly mine 27

I

Ihumātao 3, 24
Independent State of Aramoana 98
Indian Ocean Sanctuary 128
Interim Assessment Group 100
International Court of Justice 60
International Criminal Court 126
International Whaling Commission 127
Iraq 3, 52, 53, 55
    Saddam Hussein 53
Iriaka Matiu Rātana 32
Islas de Salomón 144

J

Jacinda Ardern 125, 136, 137, 162
Jacques Chirac 60
James K. Baxter 3, 43, 44, 45, 46
James Shaw 137
Jane Kelsey 78
Japan 49, 61, 62, 77, 78, 128
    Fukushima 61, 62
Jean Chrétien (Canadian Prime Minister) 52, 53
Jeanette Fitzsimons (Green Party Leader) 78, 95, 100, 113
Jenny Shipley (National Prime Minister) 95
Jessica Desmond (Greenpeace) 129
Joannee Hawke 18
Joe Biden (President of USA) 79
Joe Hawke 18
John Ballance 34
John Hall 34
John Howard (Australian Prime Minister) 52
John Jerram 90
John Key 24, 84, 124
John Stuart Mill 32

K

kaitiakitanga 14, 123
Kapuni gas field 118
kastom law 145
Kate Sheppard 32, 33, 34
Kath Walker 112
Kaumatua Pakira Tutaki 93
Kautaha 147
Keith Holyoake 50
Ken Mair 21
Kevin Jackson 86
King George III 9
Kīngitanga 24, 47, 153
King Tāwhiao 47
King Tupou II 146, 148
Kiribati 3, 149, 150, 162
    The Kiribati Climate Action Network (KiriCAN) 150
Kiwis Against Seabed Mining (KASM) 121, 151, 160
Kōhanga Reo 20, 153
Korean War 49
Kororāreka 9, 10, 127
Kura Kaupapa (Māori immersion schools) 20

L

Labour Party 23, 59, 83, 95, 140, 143, 151
Ladi6 73
Lake Manapōuri 80, 81, 82, 83
Lancaster Park 67
Landcare Research 117
Land March 20
Lawrence Kirwan 45
Lawyers for Climate Action 135
League of Nations 138, 140
League of Samoa (O le Mau a Samoa) *see* - Mau
Lesbian Coalition 41
Logan Petley 101
Lord Glasgow 34
Lucy Lawless 119

M

Maasina Ruru 3, 144, 145, 146
    Maasina Rule 145
Mabel Howard 30
Malietoa Tanumafili II 143
Mana Party 74
Māori Land 3, 14, 15
    Māori Land Hīkoi 14
Māori Party 23
Marine and Coastal Area (Takutai Moana) Act (2011) 23
Marine Mammals Protection Act 1978 128
Mark Briggs 45
Mark Solomon (Ngāi Tahu Chairman) 123
Maruia Declaration 89
Mary Ann Müller 32
    Fémmina 32
Mary Colclough 32
    see also - Polly Plum 32
Mary Müller 32
Mary Wollstonecraft 32
Mary Woodward 57
Massey's Cossacks 27, 28
Mateialona (Premier of Tonga) 147
Matiu Rātana 32
Matiu Watiu Rata (Labour MP) 32
Mau 3, 39, 138, 139, 140, 141, 142, 143, 162
Mau, Alison. *see* - Alison Mau (media)
Māui gas field 118
Mau, The. *see* - Mau
Melani Anae 72
Meridian Energy 84
Meri Te Tai Mangakāhia 32, 32–168
Michael J. Savage (Labour Prime Minister) 28

Mike Smith (Ngāphui, Ngāti Kahu) 126
Mill, Harriet Taylor *see* - Harriet Taylor Mill
Millicent Baxter 46
Mill, John Stuart *see* - John Stuart Mill
mines 26, 27, 107, 110
    Cypress 112, 115
    Stockton 111, 112, 116
Minister of Immigration 70
Minister of Police (Tonga) 147
Miriama Rauhihi 72
Mitzi Nairn 124
MMP (Mixed Member Proportional) 34, 35
Moana Maniapoto 79
Moriori ki Rekohu *see* - Chatham Rise
Mother of the Nation *see* - Dame Whina Cooper
Mothers Against Genetic Engineering (MAdGE) 103
Mount Eden prison 47
Mt Victoria 37
Muldoon, Robert *see* - Robert Muldoon
Müller, Mary *see* - Mary Müller
Mururoa atoll 57

N

Nagasaki 57, 60
Narrow Neck 47
National Development Act 99
National Government 58, 84, 94, 108, 109
National Peace Council (NPC) 48
Native Forest Action Council (NFAC) 89, 90
Native Forest Restoration Trust 93
Nelson Mandela (South African President) 11, 66, 68
Newmont Waihī Gold 110
New Talisman Gold Mines 110
New Zealand Climate Action Network 135
New Zealand Day 20
New Zealand Energy Company 122
New Zealand Federation of Labour (NZFOL) *see* - NZFOL
New Zealand House of Representatives 136
New Zealand Nuclear Free Zone, Disarmament and Arms Control Act (1987) 59

New Zealand Petroleum *121*
New Zealand Rugby Football Union (NZRFU) *64, 66*
New Zealand Scenery Preservation Society *82*
Ngāi Tahu. *see* - Chatham Rise
Ngāpuhi *9, 10, 126*
Ngāti Kahungunu *see* - Chatham Rise
Ngāti Mutunga *see* - Chatham Rise
Nicky Hager *54, 95, 151*
Niggs *see* - Will 'Ilolahia
Niniwa Heremaia *32*
Noble Discoverer *119*
Nooroa Teavae *71*
Norman Jones (National MP) *40, 80, 82*
Norman Kirk (Labour Prime Minister) *20, 59, 83*
North Island natural gas network *118*
Nuclear Non-Proliferation Treaty Review Conference *60*
Nuclear Umbrella *55*
NZ AIDS Foundation *see* - AIDS
NZFOL *26*
NZ Homosexual Law Reform Society *41*

O

Occupy Movement *3, 74*
OceanaGold *110, 159*
OECD *74, 153*
Official Information Act *85*
Oil Free Wellington *119, 135*
Otago *126*
Olaf Nelson *139, 140, 142, 143*
OMV *115, 125, 126*
Operation Rugby *63*
Orakei *17*
Oswald Jackson (Mayor of Greymouth) *90*

P

Pākaitore (Moutoa Gardens) *21*
Parengarenga Harbour *21*
Parihaka *11*
Parliamentary Network for Nuclear Disarmament *60*
Parnell, Samuel *see* - Samuel Parnell
passive resistance *6, 12, 14, 15, 25, 139, 145*
Paul Dapp *71*

Peace Action Wellington *114*
Peranos *127*
Pete Hodgson *96*
Peter Dunne (Associate Minister for the Environment) *97*
Peter Fraser (Labour Prime Minister) *28*
Peter Murnane *55*
Petrobras *122, 123, 126*
PHARMAC *77*
Phil Goff (Auckland Mayor) *136*
phosphorite nodules *121*
Pita Sharples, Dr (Maori Party MP) *23*
Pitt Island *see* - Rangihaute
Planning Tribunal *99, 108*
Ploughshares *55*
    Waihopai ANZAC Ploughshares *55*
Police Investigation Group (PIG) *72*
Polly Plum *see* - Mary Colclough
Polynesian Panthers *20, 71, 72, 73 see also* - Educate to liberate
Ponsonby People's Union *72*
Powelliphanta augusta *111, 113, 116, 117*
Power For Our Future *84*
Privy Council (Tongan) *147*
Project Jonah *128, 130*
Protect Karangahake *110*
Pro-tour groups *65*

Q

Quakers *44*
Queen Charlotte Sound *8*
Queen Elizabeth II *24*

R

Radio Hauraki *73*
radomes *54*
Raglan golf course *121*
Rainbow Warrior *59, 60*
Rangihaute *43*
Rangiora *44*
Rata, Matiu Watiu. *see* - Matiu Watiu Rata
Raven Maeder *134*
Reclaim the Night *3, 37*
Rēkohu (Chatham Island) *43*
Rena *118, 119, 122, 126*
REPEAL *37*
Resource Management Act *85, 120*
Richard Seddon (Premier) *34, 147*

Rickard, Eva. *see* - Eva Rickard
Rio Tinto *8*. *see also* - Comalco
Robb, Andrew *see* - Andrew Robb
Robert Muldoon (National Prime Minister) *19, 66, 92*
Ron McLean *80, 83*
roroa *111*
    great spotted kiwi *111*
Rowling, Bill *see* - Bill Rowling
royal commission of inquiry *100*
Rugby Park *66, 67*
Rugby Tour *3, 63*

S

Saddam Hussein. *see* - Iraq
Salvation Army *41*
Sam King *92*
Sam Land *55*
Samoa for Samoans (Samoa mo Samoa) *139*
Samuel Parnell *25, 166*
Sarah Page *48*
Savage, Michael J.. *see* - Michael J. Savage
Save Aramoana Campaign *3, 97, 98, 158*
Save Manapōuri *80, 82, 83, 84, 85, 88*
Save Our Unique Landscape (SOUL) *24*
Save the Whales *128*
School Strike 4 Climate *3, 126, 133, 134, 135, 137*
Scribe *73*
Sealord *129*
Sea Shepherd *128, 130*
Seddon, Richard. *see* - Richard Seddon
Sharples, Dr Pita. *see* - Pita Sharples, Dr
Sheppard, Kate. *see* - Kate Sheppard
Sheppard, Walter. *see* - Kate Sheppard
Shirley Guildford *93, 166*
Shultz, George *see* - George Shultz
Sidney Holland (National Prime Minister) *29*
Simon Bridges (National MP) *120*
Sisters Overseas Service (SOS) *37*
Society for the Protection of the Unborn Children (SPUC) *37*
Solid Energy *112, 113, 114, 115*
Solomon Islands (Islas de Solomón) *3, 144, 145*
Sophie Handford *134*

South Africa *64, 66, 68, 69, 71*
Southern Ocean Whale Sanctuary *128*
South West New Zealand World Heritage Area *93*
Soviet Union *see* - USSR
Springbok *see* - South Africa
Statoil *120, 123, 124, 126*,
Stephen Allen (Colonel) *141*
Stephen King (Young Conservator of the Year) *92, 95*
Steven Joyce (National MP) *24*
Sue Kedgley (Green Party MP) *38*

T

TAG Oil *122*
Tainui-Waikato *47*
Ta Iuli *71*
Takaparawhā *17, 19 see* - Bastion Point
Takutai Moana *23 see also* - Marine and Coastal Area Act 2011
Talley's *129*
Tāmaki Makaurau. *see* - Auckland
Tāmati Wāka Nene *10*
Tariana Turia (Maori Party MP) *22*
Te Arawa *64*
Te Hāpua *15*
Te Haratua *9*
Te Kirihaehae Te Puea Hērangi (Tainui) Kīngitanga leader *47*
Te Kotahitanga (the Māori Parliament) *32*
Te Paina pā *47*
Te Puea Marae *15*
Te Rarawa *124*
Te Reo Māori *20*
    Kōhanga Reo *20*
    Kura Kaupapa *20*
Te Rūnanga O Ngāti Waewae *112*
Te Tii Waitangi marae *124*
Te Tiriti o Waitangi *9*
    Treaty of Waitangi *9*
Te Wāhipounamu *93*
Te Waimate mission *10*
Te Whiti o Rongomai *11*
Tīwai Point *97*
Tohu Kākahi *11*
Tom Young *28*
Tonga Ma'a Tonga Kautaha (Tonga for Tongans) *146, 147*
    the Kautaha *147*
trade union *25*
    Trade Union Congress *29*

Trans-Pacific Partnership Agreement (TPPA) 77, 79
Trans-Tasman Resources (TTR) 121, 125
Treaty of Friendship 146
Trevor Richards (HART) 65, 68
Tupua Tamasese Lealofi III (Leader of Mau) 139, 141, 143
Tupua Tamasese Mea'ole 143

U

UK 52, 61, 88
    Great Britain 49, 148
UNESCO 93
United Nations (UN) 49
    UN Climate Action Summit 133
    UN General Assembly 60
    UN Secretary-General 60
United States (USA) 49, 50, 55, 61, 77, 78, 102, 143, 144
    US military 51
    US President
        George W. Bush 53
        Joe Biden 79
USS
    Buchanan 59, 61
    Long Beach 58
    Pintado 58
    Truxton 58
USSR 29, 57, 61
    Chernobyl 29
    Russia 29, 57, 61
    Soviet Union 56

V

Vaughan Sanft 71
Venn Young (National MP) 41, 90, 91
Vicki Mae 72
Vietnam War 46, 49, 50
    Mỹ Lai Massacre 51, 52

W

Waihī Miners Union 26
Waihopai Station 54
Waihopai Three 54
Wairarapa 17, 49
Waitangi Day 3, 20, 24, 72
Waitematā Harbour 17
War Resisters' International 43
Wellington 15, 16, 17, 20, 22, 25, 27, 28, 29, 30, 37, 40, 41, 50, 57, 58, 59, 65, 67, 74, 77, 78, 79, 88, 90, 91, 95, 98, 102, 103, 108, 114, 118, 119, 120, 126, 134, 135, 143, 151
Wellington Animal Rights Network 114
West Coast Forest Accord 93
Whina Cooper 14, 15, 16, 20
Wilde, Fran *see* - Fran Wilde
Wildlife Service 92
William Little 45
William Massey 26, 27, 28
William Telfer Campbell (British Agent in Tonga / Administrator) 147
Will 'Ilolahia 71
Wollstonecraft, Mary *see* - Mary Wollstonecraft
Women's Christian Temperance Union (WCTU) 32
Women's National Abortion Action Campaign (WONAAC) 37
World War 145
World Wildlife Fund (WWF)
    WWF 130
    WWF-NZ 130, 135

X

Y

Youth Parliament 136

Z

Zero Carbon Bill 136, 137

ABOUT THE AUTHOR
MANDY HAGER

Photo by David Hamilton

Mandy Hager is a multi-award winning writer of fiction for young adults. She also writes adult fiction, short stories, non-fiction, educational resources, blogs and articles, and tutored the Novel Course for Whitireia's Creative Writing Programme for ten years. She is currently President of the New Zealand Society of Authors, Te Puni Kaituhi o Aotearoa (PEN NZ) Inc.

She is a trained teacher, with an Advanced Diploma in Fine Arts (Whitireia) and an MA in Creative Writing from Victoria University.

From 2005-2008 she worked for The Global Education Centre writing resources on global issues such as the politics of climate change, violence against women, the treatment of refugees, illegal trafficking, global money systems, Parihaka and the gift of non-violent resistance.

AWARDS

2019 - awarded the Storylines Margaret Mahy Medal for life-time achievement and a distinguished contribution to New Zealand's literature for young people.

2015 - The Margaret Mahy Book of the Year award, and the Best Young Adult Fiction Award from the NZ Book Awards for Children and Young Adults ('Singing Home the Whale') It was also awarded the 2016 IBBY Honour Book and subsequently has been translated into Slovenian and Chinese.

The LIANZA Book Award for Young Adult fiction three times ('Smashed' 2008, 'The Nature of Ash' 2013, 'Dear Vincent' 2014).

The NZ Post Children's Book Awards for YA fiction ('The Crossing' 2010).

2003 - Golden Wings Award ('Run For The Trees', 2003) and six Notable Book Awards.

2002 - Golden Wings Excellence Award ('Juno Lucina,').

1996 - Honour Award in the AIM Children's Book Awards ('Tom's Story').

2012 - The Beatson Fellowship.

2014 - Katherine Mansfield Menton Fellowship.

2015 - Waikato University Writer in Residence.

In 2020 Mandy released 'Hindsight: Pivotal Moments in New Zealand's History', published by OneTree House.